BACK TO SCHOOL

The College Guide for Adults

BACK TO SCHOOL

The College Guide for Adults

William C. Haponski, Ph.D.,
and Charles E. McCabe, M.B.A.

Peterson's Guides
Princeton, New Jersey

© 1982 by Peterson's Guides, Inc.

Library of Congress Cataloging in Publication Data

Haponski, William C.
    Back to school.
    Bibliography: p.
    1. Continuing education—United States—Handbooks, manuals, etc. 2. Adult education—United States—Handbooks, manuals, etc. 3. Universities and colleges—United States—Handbooks, manuals, etc. I. McCabe, Charles E. II. Title.
LC5251.H35   1982   374'.973   82-315
ISBN 0-87866-197-2   AACR2

Design by Ronald R. Misiur

Printed in the United States of America

For other Peterson's publications of interest, please see the annotated book list at the back of this volume.

Contents

7 Balancing Work, Family, and College Demands   94

How can I earn a living, be a part of a family, and go to college too?

Time: a priceless commodity—Your employer and you—Your family and you: rights and responsibilities—The single parent—Child care—Marriage partners at college together—Establishing your home study area—Profile of Penny Meek

PART II   SUCCEEDING   105

8 Registering for Courses and Going to Classes   107

How much can I handle? What can I expect in those first few weeks?

Opening of the academic year—Considering types of classes—Assessing how much to take—Choosing courses (and professors)—Sampling courses—Avoiding closeouts—Class locations: avoiding conflicts—That first class!

9 Understanding Professor and Student Relationships   115

How can I get the best grades or most satisfaction (both, I hope) from each course?

Grading systems—Quality or grade points, and honors—So you want to be a straight-A student?—Grades and personal satisfaction—Interaction of students and professors—Peer pressure and classroom politics—Being on time and prepared for class—When to open and shut your mouth—When you think you're in trouble

10 Developing Essential Educational Skills   126

How important are: organization of time? study habits? reading? writing? mathematics? speaking? listening? use of the library? note-taking? taking exams? Can I improve?

Organizing your time and concentrating effectively—Effective study techniques—Reading—Writing—Mathematics—Speaking—Listening—Using the library (and librarian)—Taking notes—Taking tests—Profile of Ann H. Girndt—Annotated Bibliography of Study Aids

11 Utilizing Resources for Coping 153

What are my personal resources for coping, and what college resources may help me?

Adult assets—Adult liabilities—Self-knowledge: your strengths and weaknesses—Interpersonal relationships—Family, friends, other students as helpers—College resources: getting help—Counseling services—Academic advising—Financial aid counseling—Personal and psychological counseling

12 Students' Rights and College Bureaucracy 166

How can I cut through the red tape that hampers my progress? What are my rights and avenues of recourse as a student?

How to deal with bureaucracy—Challenging the @!#—*?! computer—Students' rights: First Amendment, due process—Women's educational equity—Age Discrimination Act—Privacy Act: access to your official records—Adult student power—Profile of Anthony F. Farma

13 Reassessing Goals and Performance 176

After having been in college for some time, I wonder—am I going in the right direction, achieving all I can, and getting the most satisfaction out of college and life?

Reviewing goals, priorities, decisions, activities—Assessing the present—Achievement and satisfaction

14 Life After College 182

Is there really a life after college? What about graduate school, a new career, continued personal growth?

Gazing into the crystal ball—Weighing alternatives for further study—Preparing for graduate school—Graduate admission tests: DAT, GMAT, GRE, LSAT, MAT, MCAT, OCAT, PCAT, VAT—Preparing for that new career: career planning and placement services—Career opportunities for women—Graduation! At last!—Sunset, sunrise? Lifelong learning and you—Profile of Dorothy June Harris

To Nettie Marie Jones
for your lifetime support of lifelong learning

Preface
and
Acknowledgments

As a college professor, one of the authors, William Haponski, tried to guide prospective adult students to written material that would be helpful to them in deciding on college and preparing for it. In his office, in his classes, and at coffee breaks he listened to adult students' aspirations for college success, coupled sometimes with their problems of coping. When, after a determined search, he found no single, comprehensive source of information that would assist these people, the idea for this book was born.

About that time, sitting in one of Professor Haponski's classes at Adelphi University was Charles McCabe. Having himself experienced frustration at finding little information, Chuck was excited by the thought of collaboration. The two prospective authors sketched an outline and soon knew they were committed to the book.

We have attempted to develop a concise, indispensable guide for that heretofore neglected species, you, the prospective or enrolled adult college student. Although the book is intended as a manual, we hope it is also highly readable, even humorous and irreverent on occasion. The approach is sequential, taking you through the various steps and experiences you will most likely encounter somewhere en route to becoming a college graduate. Part I is for those of you who are in the decision and preparation stages. Part II is for those who are already enrolled and want to get the most out of college. The special information and references on financial aid at the end of Chapter 6, the annotated bibliography of study aids at the end of Chapter 10, and the appendixes at the back of the book contain a wealth of additional information for both prospective and enrolled students. You'll find keys to the many sources of financial aid, information on the accrediting process and agencies, and a glossary containing definitions of more than 100 terms that you may encounter as an adult college student. Throughout the book you will find profiles of adult students. Somewhere in this gallery of successful students you will probably recognize elements of yourself, and your trials and aspirations.

From the beginning we wanted to present the broadest possible range of experiences to supplement our own. Consequently, we invited college administrators, professors, and especially students from all over the United States and Canada to contribute. The response was astounding. Over 40 people have contributed directly to the text. Many more have given helpful advice and assisted us in our research. The book truly is a product of the entire spectrum of people involved in adult higher education. Unfortunately, we cannot acknowledge here all of the people who have contributed. But we can extend our thanks especially to those individuals and organizations mentioned in the text, particularly to major contributing authors Philip M. Backlund, Nancy Hawks, Carol Mackintosh, and Glenn Perrone. Also to contributing authors S. Tapper Bragg, Jeanne Crane, Dennis Gerard Ellis, Nancy Lampen, Stephanie Phillips, Janet Wagner, Judith Weber Wertheim, and Robert E. Woods. Our thanks, too, to the following individuals who are not recognized in the text but who provided valuable assistance:

The administration and staff of Utica College of Syracuse University, particularly Director of Continuing Education James J. Carrig, Registrar William W. Endorf, Director of Financial Aid Carol Mackintosh, Director of the Library Harry Tarlin, and Director of Counseling Robert E. Woods, and especially retired registrar Aileen Price who read the entire manuscript and offered valuable advice throughout the project.

The administration and staff of Adelphi University, particularly President Timothy W. Costello, Administrative Assistant to the President Helen H. Probst, Dean Doris Silberstein, Dean Gerald A. Heeger, Dean Joseph Crafa, Dean James F. Bender, Dean Madelene Gardner, Registrar Kitty Weiner, University Counseling Director Charles F. Lyles, Financial Aid Officer Jean Anzalone, and Reference Librarian Carol Schroeder.

Dean Cora Forbush of the University of Wisconsin-Whitewater; Dean Neil P. Cronin and Associate Dean Yvonne Hayes of the School of New Resources, College of New Rochelle; Dean James C. Hall, Dean Peter A. Walsh, and Professor Elayn K. Bernay of Pace University; Katherine Gulliver, Regents External Degree Program of the University of the State of New York; and Lanie Melamed, Director of Programs for Women, Dawson College, Montreal, Quebec, Canada.

The many adult student leaders who also provided advice and assistance, particularly former president Lorraine Phillips and former president Anthony Farma of the United States Association of Evening Students.

The photographs that appear on the cover and with the student profiles were supplied through the courtesy of the following: Bentley College (photographer: Cynthia R. Benjamins), Christopher Reetz Studios, Dawson College (photographer: Dominique Benaich), Pace University (photographer: Bob Goldberg), Suffolk University, Sugar Loaf School (photographer: Steve Killet), University of Denver (photographer: Richard W. Purdie), and University of Wisconsin-Whitewater (photographer: Gregg Theune). Special thanks go to Dale E. Reich, Director of Information Services at the University of Wisconsin-Whitewater, for his cooperation.

We are also indebted to the staff of Peterson's Guides—particularly Sandra Grundfest, acquisitions editor, and Joan Hunter, senior editor—for their professional handling of the book.

Finally we want to thank Sandra Haponski and Marilyn McCabe, our wives, who helped us with our drafts of the manuscript and offered valuable suggestions and constructive criticism. Most importantly, they provided support and understanding throughout the often difficult four-year period of researching, writing, and producing the book.

All of us who have contributed to this book believe it will be a major aid for adults for many years to come. But in order for us to serve these future adult students well, we need your help. We want your comments on the strengths and weaknesses of this book, your suggestions for inclusion or elimination of material in future editions, and your descriptions of the problems you have encountered as an adult student, administrator, or educator of adults—and the ways you have overcome these problems. Please send your comments to ETC Associates, Box 118, Oneida, NY 13421. By doing so, you will serve future adult students better than you have been served. And that's a significant contribution to lifelong learning.

William C. Haponski
Charles E. McCabe

Introduction

College for Adults

Al across this continent adult students are going back to school. They are going to college in the day, in the evening, on the weekend, in the summer. Adults are going to college on college campuses, in their homes, at their places of work. They are even going to college as they commute to work!

As an adult you may become a part of the educational phenomenon of our times. Since the mid-1960s the number of adults attending college has grown significantly as a percentage of total enrollment. Today the traditional bulk of college enrollment—persons under 25—continues to shrink as the adult group expands.

Before World War II, higher education generally was viewed as that four-year period between the end of high school and the beginning of a profession. Then, for awhile after the war, veterans taking advantage of the GI Bill made the sight of older students a familiar one on campus. But the veterans graduated, the campus gradually returned to "normal," and a few years passed before the scene again began to change. Today higher education is regarded less and less as a four-year block in the life of young people; instead, it is a dynamic experience that can continue throughout life and result in invigorating career, social, and personal growth. If you are thinking about attending college or are already enrolled, you are involved in the modern drama of higher education, a drama in which a former bit-part player is rising to become a lead actor—the adult college student.

Statistics show just how important you, the adult, are in the higher-education scene. The percentage of total enrollment in higher education constituted of adults 25 years and older was 25.9 percent (1.9 million) in 1968 and 37.5 percent (4.2 million) in 1978, a 121 percent increase! The percentage is expected to rise even farther to 43.9 percent in 1988.

Great change has been occurring in the educational marketplace, and you, the adult consumer, are the cause of much of this flux. You have awakened to higher education, and it is unlikely that you will ever again consider it to be the privileged territory of the young.

Looking back from our viewpoint in the 1980s, we see the 60s and 70s as a dynamic era. The complexity of going about modern business and living brought large numbers of educated adults back into higher education. They wanted to upgrade their skills and equip themselves for an even more complex future. At the same time, new opportunities for education were opened to the previously disadvantaged, and each year these people were attracted to campuses by the hundreds of thousands. Community colleges bloomed. In the early 60s, about 300 of these public two-year institutions existed. They had no tuition or low tuition. By the late 70s the numbers had tripled. A major reason for this amazing growth was the adult learner, restricted in mobility to his community by job and family considerations, without much money to spare, but with legislators and community college administrators and faculty sympathetic to his needs and dependent upon him for enrollment. Learning centers came into being, and with improved and more accessible counseling, the increasing flow of information on the availability of higher education to prospective adult students brought them onto the campuses. In 1976 the United States Congress passed the Lifelong Learning Act, stating, "American society should have as a goal the availability of appropriate opportunities for lifelong learning for all its citizens." State legislators supported various adult education programs, and corporations, labor unions, and foundations provided grants that immensely benefited the adult learner. Whereas in earlier years only a few colleges and universities had faculty that specialized in teaching adults, and there was no source of training for this specialty, universities began graduating men and women with doctorates in adult education. By the beginning of the 1980s, adult students were widely recognized as higher education's "new learners."

One might think that with so much attention and aid now being given to adult learning, all of its earlier problems have been solved. Such, unfortunately, is not the case. The greatest problem remains. Many adults—perhaps you are one of them—continue to stay away from higher education because of anxiety. Chief among their fears is the belief that they cannot compete with younger students. That is nonsense, shown to be false time after time, yet still a pervasive and destructive myth. Consequently, we are going to put a theme for this book right up front, and, at the risk of redundancy, will stay with it throughout the book.

You Can Compete!

As you read this book, many reasons why you can compete academically will be highlighted, but for now, let's take just four. In the first place, you may not be competing with younger students, which most adults seem to fear. Many colleges and universities have established divisions or schools of continuing education, and their primary if not sole clientele are adult students. The people sitting next to you might not be teen-age students, but, like you, working or retired adults.

Second, even if you should find yourself in classes with younger students, the situation is so normal on campuses by now that you may be the only one who thinks anything about it. And old dogs *can* learn new tricks. Not even advanced age can be taken any longer as an excuse for not continuing to learn. In a pamphlet called "Is My Mind Slipping?" by the Andrus Gerontology Center of the University of Southern California, the first sentence reads: "Let's get the facts straight right now: barring an illness, you can expect your mind to stay strong and healthy well past the age of 80. You'll be able to learn, to think, to remember, to enjoy."

Third, institutions have made special efforts to adjust to the needs of adult students, so your task may not be as difficult as it might have been a few years ago. For instance, a recent publication of the Board of Regents of the University of the State of New York states that "Many higher educational institutions are making adjustments in their programs, schedules, and even locations to serve the special needs of an adult, non-resident, generally part-time student body."

Finally, many professors are aware of your concerns and will do all they can to get you over the hurdle of initial anxiety. As contact with adult learners has increased in these past several years, more and more professors have discovered that they even prefer teaching adults. One educator writes:

> It is fun to teach adults. They are the most responsive, critical, concerned, creative, stubborn, challenging, pleasant two-footed animals on this planet. They will help you with anything from room arrangement to doing their own teaching. They will get along without you. They will tell you what they want to learn if you give them a chance. The adult can be reached by mass media, in large groups, in small groups, or as individuals. An adult will learn in any of a hundred patterns a creative teacher can invent. When they want to learn they will bend to suit your moods. When they are not interested in what you have to offer, you will soon know it. They will not all steal away; some will just up and clamber out. [Burton W. Kreitlow, "Adult Learning Patterns," in *Materials and Methods in Continuing Education*, ed. Chester Klevins (New York: Klevins Publications, Inc., 1976), p. 233]

We have given you only four reasons thus far why *you can compete*. Throughout this book you will discover from adult educators and students dozens more.

Our correspondence with adult students around the United States and in Canada reveals that almost all students show amazement that indeed they can compete. For instance, Evelyn M. Greengross is 60, married, with two children and two grandchildren. Recently she received her B.A. from the School of New Resources, College of New Rochelle, New Rochelle, New York. She says:

> In the beginning, I had two overwhelming concerns about starting a college career at age 55. One, the cost of this education; two, would I be able to "hack it"—to absorb and retain all of this new and unfamiliar

knowledge. (I believed that one loses the ability to learn as one ages.) Both of these concerns were quickly dispelled. From the very first course, a most remarkable one entitled Experience, Learning and Identity, I realized that my potential for learning was as strong as ever. No, stronger, since it was now reinforced by many years of practical living experience which underscored the academic learning experience. This course was designed so that within a short few weeks I was launched on a study that sustained and inspired the next four years of my college career.

Often the competition is not so much against others as against yourself. Among the extraordinary profiles of adult students sent to us from coast to coast was the following story that emphatically proves, "You can compete."

■■■ STUDENT PROFILE ■■■
Lawrence S. Gaskins

"Prison is in the mind. If your mind is free, any amount of bodily imprisonment can be overcome. But if once you let the mind become imprisoned, you are truly in hell."
—written on a cellblock wall

In 1959 I was discharged from the Air Force as "undesirable." From then until 1974 I was constantly in trouble: in jails, prison, and bumming around the country. In 1974 I thought I was dead. I found myself at age 34 sentenced to four years in prison. No education, no skills, no future. End of story. Or so I thought.

Today I am a different man. I have a good job, a loving wife, a new home, and the respect of my fellow workers and my community. Today I feel more alive than at any other time in my life.

I would like to tell you what happened to change my life around and how, if you are confined, you too can take the steps to a better life and a secure future. You can do it now regardless of your age, your prison sentence, or your crime. You can do it now wherever you are: in prison, a hospital, wherever. The most important thing is to *do it*!

When I arrived at Auburn Correctional Facility in upper New York State, I was a high school dropout with no real education. I had taken a couple of courses at Los Angeles City College, but again, it was part of the pattern of the criminal—I went to college so that I wouldn't have to work. In Auburn I made a decision that changed my life around 180 degrees—I decided to get my college degree!

At Auburn, as at any prison, all you have is time on your hands. I decided that I would do something with that time. I contacted the education director and asked him how I could get my high school equivalency diploma. He arranged for me to take the test for the diploma and, lo and behold, I passed. He then suggested that I get a college degree. I nearly laughed in his face. But, later that night, in the quiet of my cell, I reviewed my life and came up with one striking fact. I could get nowhere. I would have no job, no future, no security, no change in the pattern of my life until I became educated—until I had something to balance the heavy debit side of my life. I came to the conclusion that a college degree might just balance that ledger. That decision was and still is the most important one I have ever made—and the best.

The answer for me was the New York State Regents External Degree Program. It is a nontraditional way of earning college credit toward a degree. (There are other ways to get a degree in prison; ask your education director.) The idea was to take tests for college credit after studying for the test. There are all sorts of tests, on all kinds of subjects. There was no rush to take the tests, no class schedules, or homework, or any of the other traditional classroom aspects that turn many of us off. I read in my cell. When I thought I was ready, I took the real test. If I didn't pass, I went back to the books.

The time went by quickly as soon as I decided to get my degree. Thirty-two months passed and I was released. I continued to take tests, and soon I received my associate in science degree from the State University of New York in Albany. My wife and parents were with me at commencement; it was the proudest day of my life.

The attainment of this degree meant great changes. I got a job, a promotion, and permanent appointment to a civil service position of responsibility. I now direct a CETA-funded program in New York and have a staff of twelve persons under me. I am enrolled in a bachelor of science program in the Regents External Degree Program. I just purchased a new home and a new car. I have *not* found it necessary to resort to my past history of criminal behavior. In those 32 months in prison I learned that the key to staying out of trouble is *education*, *responsibility*, and *commitment*. I lacked the first when I went inside the walls. By studying in prison, getting my degree instead of letting the time just "go by," I learned the second two things. The three in total have made me a different man today. I know it can do the same for you.

Part I

Deciding
and
Preparing

1

Considering College

What can I expect from college? Why am I, as an adult, even thinking about college? Are there alternatives to college that might be more suitable?

Adults Returning to College

I f you previously attended college and are considering reentering as an adult, your expectations will probably be based on your memories of college as a young student. You may have dropped out of college originally because you did not appreciate the value of higher education; or perhaps job or family responsibilities or financial constraints forced you to leave college. For whatever reason you left then, you are probably a very different person now. Your outlook on life and your attitude toward learning may have changed entirely. Perhaps the most important difference between then and now is that you will be going to college not because someone else expects you to, but because you yourself want to go. In addition, you now have experience that should enable you to define and structure your goals more clearly, and to temper the theoretical learning of college with your own practical knowledge of reality. Most educators involved with adult education would probably agree that the primary differences between youthful and adult college students are practical experience and motivation. It is these assets (which might also be referred to as maturity) that enable an individual who may have had difficulty in college as a young person to be a successful adult student.

You may find that college has also changed considerably in recent years. Many colleges have become more like businesses, and students are being treated more like clients—and the customers must be satisfied. A variety of new degree programs is now available, with less emphasis on traditional course requirements.

So the chances are good that college is quite different from what you remember. You have changed. College has changed. You can reenter college with confidence that the changes in you and in your campus environment will mesh well enough so that this time around you may complete your program of study.

Adults Entering
College for the First Time

But what if you have never taken a college course? Your anxiety is quite natural; the grandiose image projected by some colleges can be intimidating.

We said that we would come back to the theme, "You Can Compete." Here is what one of the authors, Charles McCabe, feels about his experience:

As an adult entering college for the first time, I remember the feeling quite vividly. I hadn't before seriously considered attending, and I'd never asked anyone what college was like. The few people I knew who had gone to college did not discuss their college experiences with me. Perhaps they sensed my embarrassment about my lack of formal education (I was a high school dropout), and they avoided the subject. College seemed completely out of reach for me, so I chose to disregard it.

My eventual enrollment in college was caused by an abrupt break in my professional career as a manager, an event that initiated a major self-reevaluation. I decided that my lack of academic credentials was a serious shortcoming I would have to correct in order to achieve career advancement and mobility. Fortunately, I learned of a special college degree program for adults. I applied and was accepted as a nonmatriculated student pending my qualifying for the New York State High School Equivalency Diploma by successfully completing 24 college credits.

Here I was, a high school dropout, beginning my first college course, Interpersonal Behavior and Group Dynamics. Most, if not all, of my eighteen classmates had previously attended college or had been in the program for some time. I was concerned about my ability to keep up with the class. Classroom participation was thoroughly enjoyable, but I found the readings extremely difficult; my vocabulary was limited, my reading comprehension was poor, and the psychology texts (there were *three* of them) contained much unfamiliar jargon. By attending all of the free college writing and study skills workshops, I was able to do well on the examinations and assignments. I worked very hard, but my efforts paid off—I earned an A in my first college course. Two years later I graduated summa cum laude with a bachelor of science degree. I ranked number one in my class of 141 evening and adult students.

You can be assured that my success as an adult in college had little to do with my level of intelligence; I am not exceptionally smart. However, success in college, as in life, is not entirely dependent upon an individual's so-called I.Q. More important are certain intangible qualities such as motivation, organizational ability, discipline, and perseverance. The world is full of highly intelligent failures. The most successful people are often those who put everything they have into something they really want to achieve. If you are an adult entering college for the first time, your potential for success is just as good as it is for anyone else.

An Expanded Role for Women

by STEPHANIE PHILLIPS
Associate in Science degree with honors from Dutchess
Community College, Poughkeepsie, New York

Integral to the recent adult movement in education is the new way women view themselves. Throughout the evolution of society, women became the "supporters" of the world. They took care of brothers and fathers; they took care of home and children; and they took care of employer and husband. During a girl's impressionistic growing years, she learned how to succeed in her assigned roles. Love and duty provided the incentives needed to put everyone else first and woman last.

Today college enrollment statistics reflect a change in that priority. The percentage of women enrolled in undergraduate education has increased dramatically, and for the first time since World War II, when so many men were in the military services, it is now over one half of the total. Special courses are designed to meet the needs of these new faces in the college classroom, and all available evidence indicates that this phenomenon will continue. And phenomenon is the word for it. Imagine, after thousands of years of history, women are concentrating on and reacting to their own needs! Whether the reason is employment frustration, the women's movement, or personal growth, the classroom is alive with a new intellect—the adult woman.

As the first days in college begin expanding to weeks, initial anxiety is replaced by confidence. Daily life has provided a valuable research background and has prepared women with knowledge that is unavailable in a textbook. Organization is a necessity when running a home and raising a family; therefore, the ability to organize notes, class schedules, and study time requires only a minor alteration to an already attained skill. Theoretical class discussions about the psychological pressures of a stereotypic role don't have to be researched by the adult woman. She knows very well the boundaries placed on an individual who isn't recognized as capable of achievement beyond the limitations established by society.

For these reasons and others, adult women have flourished in colleges, universities, and professional schools, and they will continue to do so. Feminine expansion has begun, and through continued determination, those role models established in history are crumbling. Women now want to share fully in growth, knowledge, potential, and achievement, and will do so through full participation in higher education.

Reasons for Going to College

To explain adequately the reasons adults are going to college would be impossible, for there are as many reasons as there are adults. *Americans in Transition* by Carol B. Aslanian and Henry M. Brickell (Princeton, N.J.: College Board, 1980) reported that most adults learn for utilitarian reasons, not pleasure. They seek knowledge as a means to a specific end such as promotion, a more satisfying career, or financial security.

Some adults cannot articulate their reasons for attending college beyond a vague, "I always wanted to; now I'm going." Both specific and vague motivations have their own compelling logic.

In our survey of adult students and research on their motivations we discover three broad areas that contain the majority of cases. Adults seem to be going to college for career growth, social and cultural opportunities, and personal growth.

Career Growth

You can find college graduates holding blue-collar or unskilled jobs unrelated to their academic disciplines. On the other hand, you will find relatively few people who lack a college degree or certificate holding high-paying, white-collar jobs. In *The Over-Educated American* (New York: Academic Press, Inc., 1976, p. 187), economist Richard B. Freeman states:

> While the income and occupational attainment of college graduates began falling in the 1970s, college-trained workers continued to have higher earnings and better prospects than their high school peers. The continued, though diminished, value of the degree in the job market and the continued nonpecuniary rewards suggest that for many, college remains a good investment.

In a course called Writing and Social Issues at Adelphi University, the authors (one the professor, the other the student) surveyed their class by questionnaire and asked the members to rate the importance they placed on various possible reasons for the surge of adults to college campuses. Career-related reasons proved strongest, with the following three reasons clearly rated as most important:

1. To qualify for a more challenging position in the same field of work, either with a present employer or a new employer.
2. To qualify for a new or different occupation, including entering or reentering the job market and changing careers.
3. To increase earnings potential either because of financial need or a desire for a higher standard of living, or both.

Since taking that survey of a limited number of adult students the authors have discovered through research that the career concerns and beliefs of that class are quite typical of those in the adult student population as a whole. For example, Helen E. Marshall, a student who has completed her studies at Essex County College in Newark, New Jersey, and is transferring to a four-year college for work toward the baccalaureate, reports:

> It was mandated by the board of nursing in my state that to continue practicing as a licensed practical nurse, all of us would have to return to school. Not being old enough to retire, I had no alternative. So, caught in the middle, 58 years young with this mandate hanging over me, I proceeded posthaste to an institution of higher learning and was accepted at Essex County College.

Adult students from the East Coast to the Hawaiian Islands, from the northern Canadian provinces to the southern states on the Gulf of Mexico are telling the same story: Higher education is important to them for career reasons. Statistics substantiate their beliefs that promotion within a present career, successful career change, improved earnings, and ability to make it alone when suddenly forced to do so are enhanced by degrees. The lack of appropriate academic credentials, even though you may have considerable experience, can effectively block you from getting past the screening process when you apply for a new job.

The less tangible values of a college education should also not be minimized. For many people a college degree or certificate provides needed confidence. Though the credentials you receive may not be directly related to your intended career, the way you feel about them and yourself may help you succeed in that career.

Social and Cultural Opportunities

In today's career-minded society, one might think that adult students would rate social and cultural opportunities as frivolous among reasons for attending college. Not so. There are things to do on college campuses, people to meet, and friends to make. To attain and enjoy higher social status and prestige among friends, relatives, and associates is important to adult students. The message from them seems to be that they go to college to learn, of course, and when the learning brings many other good things with it, that's even better.

From Baldwin-Wallace College in Berea, Ohio, Lynn M. Gallagher tells how important the social atmosphere was in her early college life:

> My first quarter at Baldwin-Wallace was not an easy one. Socially, I was a stranger in a room of approximately 25 students. Strangers as we were, we had shared a lot of common ground, the most obvious being our experience in business. Almost more important to me were the life experiences we all shared. During breaks, as my classmates socialized, and talked about last quarter or the next, I knew that despite the initial uneasiness I felt, I belonged in that classroom.

The social and cultural side of college life seems to be of particular importance to those students who are not taking courses for credit. Dale E. Reich, director of information services at the University of Wisconsin-Whitewater, tells of Zelda Stanke, born in 1905 on a farm near Belleville, Wisconsin. Zelda audited 32 courses during four years at Whitewater. She became so excited about college life that she brought along her 92-year-old mother! Mrs. Stanke said: "I like the fellowship of the students. You don't feel lonely. There's always someone to talk to, to exchange ideas with."

Personal Growth

Strong motivation for higher education has always been personal growth. This motivation sometimes is not well articulated, but it seems to reside deep in the human psyche, urging and prodding, without clearly defining for its "victim" a specific goal or reason for acting. Often, too often we now know, it has been resisted. Only recently have adults in large numbers allowed it to impel them to take the risks, to declare in favor of their own higher education.

Many times a crisis or at least a specific set of painful circumstances is required as a catalyst in order to cause the reaction that sets the feet in motion toward the college admissions office. Oftentimes, though, there is no crisis that causes the decision, just a long-standing dissatisfaction with the way things seem to be going. Helen H. Probst, administrative assistant to the president at Adelphi University, and recently a graduate of the university with a bachelor's degree, reports:

> I graduated from high school 14 months after the 1929 crash, and the depression was very real. It was a question of whether I would be permitted to enter Cornell, where I had been accepted, or would have to settle for a year's secretarial school and then go out into the working world to help put my brother, who was a year behind me, through college. This is what happened, and believe me I was very disappointed and secretly resentful that I had to follow this course and attend New York University downtown in the evening. Why couldn't my brother have followed the same course? He attended Fordham University each day. I didn't think that at all fair. After my first semester at NYU I was forced to drop out due to the overtime requirements of my position at a law firm. Part of my earnings, however, continued to be used to help pay my brother's tuition. Then I married and helped my husband through law school. He passed on right after my daughter started college and my son was still in high school. After I got my children through, I suddenly realized I had been on Adelphi's campus for 22 years and had never sat in one of its classrooms.

In a way, Mrs. Probst and many others whose circumstances kept them from earning a college degree right after high school are fulfilling a dream when they finally go to college.

Personal growth, then, is good enough reason for going to college. Perhaps Maura B. Gregory has the best idea why this is so. Maura is

53, a postal employee, and has received a bachelor's degree in independent studies (B.I.S.) from George Mason University, Fairfax, Virginia. She sums up her feelings for going to college this way: "Chances are I will chug along in my present job until I retire. But when I'm sitting and rocking, too feeble to do anything else, I hope there'll be something in my brain besides recipes and musty nostalgia."

Is College Really Necessary?

To this point we have been dealing with the advantages of a college degree, diploma, or certificate. It increases earning potential, brings the holder into contact with people of higher levels of responsibilities, and can be important to personal growth. But conceivably, the pursuit and attainment of a degree might bring no advantages, and indeed, in some instances, result in harm.

Broken marriages have happened when one partner has gone to college, and an already strained relationship has been taken to the breaking point. In some instances, the partner with the college credentials has later decided that the degree was not worth losing a spouse. Some people, too, have found that a degree has not been the magic ticket to greater career opportunities for them, and they have come to resent the money and time they spent in getting the degree. Other people with credentials in hand may change careers or get promoted, then discover they were happier before all this started. Many professionals with degrees have been forced by bad times to take jobs in crafts and trades and have found that they have never been happier.

A degree, then, is not a panacea; rather, it is a door-opener to options. But perhaps some pursuit other than that for college credentials will also provide options, and in fact will be better suited to your needs. Since the college credit and degree route almost certainly will entail a bumpy ride at least at some point during the journey, you will want to make certain you have explored other alternatives.

Alternatives to College Degrees

Depending on your motives, many alternatives might satisfy you as well as a college degree, or even better. Indeed, numerous though adults have become in degree programs, Dr. K. Patricia Cross, the author of several studies on adult education, reports that "colleges and universities represent only 40 percent of organized learning opportunities" (*Continuing Higher Education,* vol. 27, no. 3, summer 1979, p. 21).

If for some reason you think that college may not be for you, you can choose from a vast smorgasbord of noncollegiate learning experiences. Do you want, for example, a free course in management? Check with your company's education or personnel officer, or the training officer in your union. Hundreds of companies offer such career-enhancing programs. General Electric, for example, not only offers courses in its local plants but also has a 30-acre campus overlooking the Hudson River at Crotonville, New York. The campus has living accommodations for 135 students. Courses are taken there by G. E. employees and students from other organizations around the world. Many of these courses are accepted for college credit. (More on this kind of avenue to credit later.)

Educational programs are available for you through local public schools, religious institutions, museums, and civic and community agencies. Perhaps you should try a noncredit correspondence course or an independent study program. Theater groups, dance companies, and arts councils exist partly to meet your educational needs. The Learning Exchange in Chicago is a service designed to help people get together for educational or recreational activities; to see if there is a similar organization near you, write to P. O. Box 920, Evanston, IL 60204.

Vacations may be the only time you have to take up a new interest or continue one you have been studying for some time. *Learning Vacations* by Gerson G. Eisenberg (Peterson's Guides, Inc., P. O. Box 2123, Princeton, NJ 08540, 1982, paperback, $7.95) describes hundreds of seminars and educational programs in the United States and abroad, and includes a list of Elderhostels as well.

For older adults, the Elderhostel program may provide exciting summers in a variety of locations. Elderhostel is a network of over 400 colleges and universities in 50 states and Canada that offer special low-cost, one-week residential academic experiences that take place primarily during the summer. Elderhostel adults move into college dorms and study college subjects on a noncredit basis. Elderhostel is open to people over 60 or to those whose spouse qualifies. Most of Elderhostel's programs begin Sunday evening and end Saturday morning and are limited to 30–40 persons. Elderhostel expects to be serving 60,000 adults in the near future, and expanding its programs to provide overseas educational opportunities. Tens of thousands of people have already enjoyed this unique experience at such widespread locations as Eckerd College in St. Petersburg, Florida, and the University of Montana in Missoula, Montana. You may find out about this year's program by writing to Elderhostel, 100 Boylston Street, Suite 200, Boston, MA 02116.

In summary, a college certificate, diploma, or degree is but one of many routes to rewarding educational experiences. It is the route, though, that millions of adults are taking.

2

Choosing the Right Program

Which program of study is right for me? Where do I get information about programs?

Which Program?

C hoosing the program that is right for you is crucial to your success. Many more adults drop out of degree programs than complete them. Although statistics on reasons for dropping out are not conclusive, we believe that many adults do not finish because they did not well understand why they embarked upon a particular program in the first place. Obviously you don't want to be one of the dropouts. Therefore you will want to assess your interests against available programs as carefully as possible, preferably before you begin, but certainly before you have committed yourself so far that modifying your approach would be extremely difficult.

Identifying Goals, Determining Necessary Educational Credentials

What are the goals I hope to achieve by going to college? You must first answer this question before you can choose the college program that is right for you. Perhaps you want to advance in your career or enter a new field in order to increase your earnings potential. In this case you should determine as precisely as possible what educational credentials are required for the position you hope to achieve. If, for example, you are interested in business management, your ultimate goal might be to earn a master's degree in business administration (M.B.A.). Before choosing your undergraduate curriculum, you would be wise to look into some M.B.A. programs. You might be surprised to learn that an undergraduate course of study emphasizing business administration is not necessarily the best preparation for an M.B.A. program. Many top graduate schools of business seek individuals with a broad liberal education, including undergraduate course work in English, history, and mathematics.

Similar factors apply to many other professional and technical careers. In the nursing profession, for example, a registered nurse with a two-year associate of arts (A.A.) degree may be faced with stiff competition for desirable positions and little opportunity for advancement because many hospitals have raised their standards and now require a bachelor of science (B.S.) degree in nursing for entry or advancement. Therefore, a person preparing for a career in nursing might have a long-range goal of earning a B.S. degree in nursing. This objective would probably require a different immediate course of action than that involved in earning the A.A. degree.

Imagine your frustration if, after struggling to earn a bachelor's degree, you find you cannot gain entry to the career or graduate program of your choice. Establishing your ultimate objectives will enable you to clearly define your short-term goals, help you to choose a logical curriculum, and improve your chances of avoiding costly and time-consuming mistakes.

Getting Information About Programs

Too many adults never pursue their higher educational interests because they do not know how to go about getting information. Since they may never develop their potential, this certainly is unfortunate for all of us, but it is worse for them. And it is ironic that this should be the case, for the information they need exists all around them.

Where can you begin your search? Your local civic or college library may be a good place. Do you believe that you have to be a registered student in the college in order to use the library? This is probably not the case. Many colleges permit people who are not their students to use at least the reference section of the library, and some even will allow you to check out books.

The sources of program information you may find most helpful will probably be in the reference section, and the reference librarian will get you started. Right now we want to emphasize that *your most important resource in a library is the librarian.* Too many adults fumble around, trying to do things they are not equipped to do. In chapter 10 we will come back to this important point in more detail. *Ask your librarian to assist you!*

Perhaps you want basic information about potential careers. The *Occupational Outlook Handbook,* published by the U.S. Department of Labor, will give you descriptions of various occupations and career prospects. (See chapter 14 for information relating to careers.) Then, to find where educational programs are offered that lead to work in the field that interests you, you may want to look in one or more of the several helpful college guides that the librarian will point out, such as *Peterson's Annual Guide to Undergraduate Study* (Princeton, N.J.: Peterson's Guides, Inc.). Or the library may be equipped with a computer terminal that provides your link to this information.

Once you have identified the colleges that carry your program, you can then ask for the catalog or bulletin of a few of these colleges to learn more about what constitutes the program. College libraries ordinarily will have some current catalogs and bulletins on the shelves, and probably hundreds of others on microfiche (transparent sheets on which material is printed in miniature). In a few minutes of practice with the microfiche machine, you will be reading about programs almost anywhere in the United States or Canada, or indeed in the world.

Let's assume now that your local civic library cannot supply your educational information needs. (Let the board of directors know about it. This kind of service should have high priority.) Further, you have no college library in your immediate area.

Perhaps your local high school can help you. The guidance and counseling office should have books from which you can select a field and then find the appropriate educational institution. Your high school may also have a computer terminal for college placement purposes. (Even the alma mater of one of the authors, Mohawk Central School, in Mohawk, New York—population 2,500—has such a service.) One of the students will conduct a computer search for you, and in a few minutes you will have in your hand a printout containing the location of programs just about anywhere you wish to go.

What are your other local sources of information? The training or personnel office of a large business or of a labor union will probably help you as a public service. Military bases have education offices filled with good career and education information. Most bases have easy access for civilians, and you will probably find the people in the education office quite helpful even though you are not in the military. Veterans Administration offices also may be willing to help the nonveteran. They do a large business in education information. Women's centers are especially good about supplying up-to-date education information and advice. (To men too! Ask and find out.) Newspapers you can buy locally may have an education section. Periodically, some large newspapers also run education supplements.

You can also receive help locally from your state university system and the education departments of your state and federal governments. Some states have a statewide system of education information centers operated either by the state university or the state government. Many states have free telephone networks to satisfy your needs for education information. The United States government has established Educational Opportunity Centers in several large cities. The Canadian government supports similar activities. Some cities and civic organizations have also opened learning exchanges.

How can you find out about such places? Look in your telephone directory under federal, state, or territorial government headings. Make some calls, and don't take "I don't know" or "I'm sorry we can't help you" for an answer. With perseverance you will locate the right agency and get the right answers.

And don't forget your elected representatives. If for some reason you are not getting the information and help you need elsewhere, they have enormous resources and are usually readily responsive to your needs.

One of the best ways of getting detailed information, though, is to locate the closest college seminar held specifically for this purpose. These seminars usually range from a few hours to several weeks in length, and are either free or low in cost. They present facts on adult higher education, build confidence that you, the adult, can compete, discuss sources of information on colleges and programs, and explore cost, financial aid, admission, and other considerations. Individual counseling sessions often are included, as well as courses in basic academic skills and English as a second language for students who need them. (See chapter 10 for further discussion of basic skills.)

You should call or write your closest colleges and universities to determine what is offered that is similar to these seminars. Later in this chapter we will discuss what you can do if the program you want is not available locally, or if you have no college within commuting distance.

Information on higher education is all around you. Reach out for it.

Full-Time or Part-Time Study

Full-time study usually implies a minimum of 12 credit hours per semester or quarter, with the normal load being 15–17 credit hours, depending upon the program. You may believe that you cannot study full-time and maintain your job and family responsibilities. And you may be right. Some schools, though, offer full-time study programs that are particularly compatible with lifestyles of adult students, and the total chronological time you spend in such a program might be no greater than it would be should you choose to quit your job and go to school during the day. You must expect, however, to be an extraordinarily busy person.

Possibilities for part-time study can be investigated in *Who Offers Part-Time Degree Programs?* (Peterson's Guides, Inc., P. O. Box 2123, Princeton, NJ 08540, paperback, $6.95). This publication offers a complete overview of the part-time degree opportunities—daytime, evening, weekend, summer, and external degree programs—available from accredited colleges and universities in the United States.

A problem with adult offerings, generally, is that the range of degree options often is restricted. A college might have a variety of programs in its day division for full-time students, but in the evening and on weekends it simply may not have the teaching resources to accommodate as many programs. The more a college program is tailored specifically to meet adult needs, the more general the degree it is likely to offer compared to programs in the day division of the college. For example, in the day division you might be able to get bachelor's degrees in biology, chemistry, physics, and mathematics, but in the evening division you might find none of these degree offerings and have to settle for a program in general science. (Additional curriculum concerns regarding full-time versus part-time enrollment are addressed in chapter 8.)

Another factor you should weigh is the relative cost of part-time versus full-time enrollment. Tuition rate structures often vary between full- and part-time study in the same college. A pamphlet called "So You Want to Come Back to School" published by Dawson College, Montreal, Quebec, gives information about several colleges in the province. In the section on full- and part-time study, it warns: "Tuition is free to all Canadian citizens or landed immigrants. Less than four courses is considered part-time and tuition is required. The government is presently considering free tuition for all part-time students. Check this before enrolling." Whereas part-time enrollment may be more expensive than full-time at some institutions, at others it is just the opposite. Private colleges and universities, especially, may have lowered part-time evening and weekend rates in recent years in order to compete with the rate structure of nearby public institutions.

Another aspect to check out is the financial aid available to you. Although legislators have begun to address the problem, you may find that you are eligible for far less financial aid if you choose part-time attendance. Conceivably your total college costs could be less if you go full-time because of a better financial aid package available to you. Commuting and baby-sitting costs also could be less if you take more courses in fewer trips to campus. Of course, if you have to give up employment in order to attend full-time, that must be considered. However, don't forget to consider also the potential gain in income that could come with a degree. Full-time attendance could make that happen sooner, and that might offset some disadvantages of such enrollment, particularly if you gain admission to a top school in your field of study.

Credit or Noncredit

Lynn Gallagher describes the problem she faced before enrolling in Baldwin-Wallace College in Berea, Ohio:

> A secretary for three years, I was in a rut. I felt like a mechanical part of the office—you could feed work in one side and, in time, pick up the finished product from the other. It was time to do something for me! My

supervisor and I discussed my career and future assignments. I had the ambition, the intelligence, and the attitude necessary. But I didn't have "that little piece of paper"—a college degree. I hadn't realized how important it was. "That little piece of paper" is the key that can open many doors of opportunity.

Credit may mean everything, as it did to Lynn Gallagher in her quest for "that little piece of paper," or it may mean nothing, as it did to Zelda Stanke who found her noncredit courses the key to "joy, excitement, and self-esteem." Older adults such as Zelda tend to rate credit lower than the learning experience itself. Some, though, are determined to get a degree despite the unlikelihood it will enhance their employment or promotion prospects. An 81-year-old man said, "To hell with everybody if they don't understand why I want my degree."

Some of the best career-enhancing programs in fact are noncredit, and they look great on a résumé. The American Management Association (AMA), for example, offers several noncredit programs leading to a certificate. The certificate is awarded jointly by the AMA and the local college or university with which the AMA is associated. Also, most colleges present valuable educational courses and programs on a continuing education unit (CEU) basis. A CEU is awarded for each ten hours of instruction in one of these noncredit courses or programs, and the student receives a CEU certificate for the total number of CEUs earned. Such noncredit programs may cost nothing or a great deal. Some of them may later be accepted for credit should you wish to apply them toward a degree.

How can you decide, credit or noncredit? To answer this, you have to review your goals. Noncredit courses and programs may selectively strengthen your qualifications for better employment. We believe, though, that if you do not yet have a degree, and career concerns are causing you to consider college, your better course of action would be to get a degree rather than to pursue noncredit certificates and CEUs. The time and cost might not be much more, and the long-term rewards would be greater.

Going Away to School or Staying Where You Are

Most adults would say they have no choice; they have to attend a school near home. What they may really mean is that they choose not to take the risks: perhaps quitting a job, moving a family, leaving friends and relatives, resettling in some distant community where a college offers the program they want, and then after getting the degree, seeking a new job. We have heard all kinds of stories about going away to school—enough to convince us that we ought not try to give advice beyond highlighting a few of the major considerations.

Does that distant school offer one of the best programs of its kind, and are you absolutely sure that program is right for you? Have you talked with a graduate of the school, preferably of the program? Are you willing to make at least a two-day visit to the campus to check out the program and living arrangements?

Unless you are more unattached to your current location than most adults, you should patiently consider such things. You will want to go with confidence if you make that choice, and your satisfaction when you are enrolled at that college will be greater if you have carefully examined the matter. An entirely new environment indeed may be just what is needed for an entirely new you.

If, though, you are like the majority of adults, you will stay where you are and commute to a college near home. What is in our own back-yard tends to get ignored or underrated. You should be aware, however, that whereas the school that is near you may not be of high reputation, a certain program within it might be well respected. Program quality tends to vary a good deal within colleges. Most institutions have at least one or two very good departments, and a degree in one of those programs will carry more career weight than the credential of the college itself.

Weekend and Evening School Programs

"STOP WASTING THOSE WEEKENDS!" reads the glaring headline of the brochure received in response to a *New York Times* advertisement. "Invest them in Marymount's Weekend College in Tarrytown, New York, 45 minutes from midtown Manhattan. In one to four years you can earn a bachelor of arts degree by attending classes every third week-end."

The program at Marymount, a typical example, enables students to complete 30 credits per year by taking 9 credits each trimester plus one independent study or tutorial course in an area of special interest. Classes meet every third weekend from Friday evening at 7:30 to Sunday at 4 P.M. This schedule permits a student to make the same progress as a student enrolled full-time in a conventional college, while attending classes only six weekends each trimester. The program is "designed for highly motivated students, capable of independent work." Marymount's weekend college is one of a large number of such programs offered throughout the United States.

There may have been a time when students attending college at night found few courses to choose from and little hope of studying under the best professors. Today the situation in many places is changed where college administrators, recognizing their dependence upon nontraditional students, have expanded course offerings and improved faculty quality and student services during evenings and weekends.

Most colleges offer evening courses between 6 and 10 P.M. on weeknights with the majority of classes offered from Monday through Thursday. In some locations Saturday classes as an extension of the evening schedule are also popular. Sunday classes are still rare except at colleges offering structured weekend programs.

A major advantage of evening and weekend courses is that they often require just one three-hour class meeting per week. Some courses, though, such as languages, may not be conducive to one meeting a week and may necessitate attendance twice a week. But this is still less demanding than the traditional daytime regimen of two or three or four classes per course each week.

If you are taking two courses during the semester, it may be possible to select courses that meet on the same nights. Evening schedules are often planned to enable students to take a natural sequence of courses on a consecutive time schedule. For many such reasons, evening and weekend programs are popular among adults.

Summer School Programs

Can you arrange job and family commitments to allow you summers free for study? If so, you may be able to have a wonderful time yet take grand strides toward your degree. "Summer by the Sea" says one college advertisement. "Combine a great vacation with an exciting educational experience." If you prefer the mountains, several colleges throughout the country will give you the opportunity of combining summer study and fun in fresh mountain air. Or consider these offerings by the University of California, Santa Cruz, as listed in Learning Vacations by Gerson G. Eisenberg (Peterson's Guides, Inc., P. O. Box 2123, Princeton, NJ, 1982, paperback, $7.95): "International study tours for adults, two to four weeks, usually in the summer. Recent examples include a calligraphy workshop and tour in London (three weeks) and a pottery tour of Japan (17 days)."

Just name your summer sport—sailing, backpacking, horseback riding—and you are sure to find a college to accommodate you and your family while you study. Colleges have become increasingly anxious to make better use of their facilities in summer, so fun and study programs have proliferated. You may happily discover that you can simultaneously get college credit and have a great vacation for less money than you would spend for a similar vacation not attached to college study. You may be able to live in a college dorm room or efficiency apartment, take your meals in the cafeteria, and enjoy cultural and social events for a reasonable price. Gerstin, a widow with two children, works in an elementary school cafeteria from September through the third week of June. Then she and the children pack up and go to a college, or sometimes two colleges, for the summer. Some of her most interesting college work has taken place outside the classroom. She has studied Shakespeare's nature imagery in a cabin in the Adirondack Mountains (while the children swam, played tennis, fished); she has painted the Pacific Ocean for credit and surfed after class just for the fun of it; she has studied the therapeutic aspects of figure skating in a breathtaking setting in the Canadian Rockies. Gerstin has played and learned her way almost to an associate degree, entirely through summer school programs.

You may enroll in virtually any summer course at any school unless you are matriculating in that college. Other than for prerequisite courses in some instances, usually there are no admission requirements for summer school programs. If you are already matriculated, however, and are planning on attending some other college's summer program, be sure beforehand that your college will accept the credits you will earn.

Since summer schools tend to offer credit courses in six- or eight-week sessions, most adults cannot fit such an arrangement into their vacation schedule. For these students, then, summer school is not travel to strange places and a vacation, but simply a continuation of their degree program at their college. If you are contemplating enrolling for the first time, or the first time in a long while, summer school might be a good place to try a course or two. This is particularly true of the day session where the atmosphere may be somewhat more relaxed than you might find during the regular academic year even though the pace of study is faster. In many ways summer may become a new kind of experience for you if you try one of an astonishing variety of summer school programs.

If Your Local College Doesn't Offer Your Program

What can you do if you simply cannot find locally a degree program of the type you are certain you want?

Suppose you want a program in accounting, but your local college only has a business administration program. You might decide to take the business program in its entirety because it's the local program that is closest to meeting your needs. At least it could lead to a job in which you would deal with accounting problems in a general way, and that might prove to be satisfying enough.

Or you might consider using local college courses to advance you well along the path toward a particular degree that you can later complete, either through transfer to another college or through means we will explore in the next sections. In any case you will want to examine carefully the course requirements leading to the degree. And don't rely on your own examination, but check out the matter with the advisers for the program that you will ultimately be completing. Be certain you know which courses you will need, and which ones from your local college they will accept. At that local college you will probably find many of the components of the program you eventually will be completing. For example, if you are determined to be an accountant and your local college offers only the business administration degree, you will certainly find that some basic accounting courses are a part of that business program. You will be able to take them and get them credited later toward your accounting degree. Also at the college near home you might be able to take the economics, mathematics, and core liberal arts and sciences courses that would be required in your eventual accounting program. Thus, even though your local college does not offer a degree in the program you want, a significant portion of that program may be completed there through proper selection of courses.

External Degree Programs

But suppose you cannot leave your local area to complete the program you really want. What is the use, then, of beginning one? Or suppose that a degree program that regularly takes you out of your home presents insurmountable barriers for you as a would-be adult student. Or what if, like Mary Lou Isernhagen, you live in Goodland, Kansas, 150 miles from the nearest college? Can you still get a college degree? The answer is, definitely, yes!

Mary Lou says:

> There were times a degree seemed to be an impossible dream. Even after our daughters were gone from home, my husband's job kept us in Goodland. My outlook on life was at a very low point.
> Then the opportunity to resume my education presented itself through the nontraditional study program of Kansas State University. The program is designed for adult students and especially those with barriers to the more traditional methods of attending classes on the campus. My chosen field of study did make it necessary to do some on-campus work. But I was able to limit it to summer sessions, at which time I took as many hours as could be worked in the time limit.
> I completed 89 hours of college credit by combining several learning options such as independent study, off-campus courses, telenet work (courses taught through telephone hook-up with the instructor), TV and radio courses, and prior experiential learning. These options offered a certain amount of convenience, but didn't make the work easier. They took as much time and energy as regular on-campus courses plus considerable self-discipline. Through this program I received my B.S. in elementary education and am currently working on a master's degree in learning disabilities.

Or suppose that over a period of years you have acquired a good deal of college learning and perhaps even some college credit, but not a degree. You may have taken a smattering of college courses, some on various campuses, some by correspondence. In addition, you may have taken military service school courses and company in-service courses and had a variety of learning experiences that were not the result of any formal instruction. How can you put all this together to earn a college degree?

The Regents External Degree Program of the University of the State of New York may be the answer for you, as it was for Larry Gaskins. This program will allow you to apply all of these educational accomplishments toward an associate or a bachelor's degree in the liberal arts, business, or nursing. Candidates may meet degree requirements through any combination of the following educational experiences:

- Any college course taken for credit through a regionally accredited institution, whether taken in residence or by correspondence
- Scores earned on proficiency exams (those discussed in chapter 4)
- Military service school courses and MOSs
- Experiential learning measured by an RED Special Assessment Examination
- Noncollegiate instruction (as listed in the two guides described in this chapter)
- Certain Federal Aviation Administration (FAA) pilot certificates

Anyone, anywhere in the world, may enroll in the Regents External Degree Program. Its administrative fees are modest, and in return for them you receive evaluation, a master transcript, and advising services, as you request. The RED Program is fully accredited by the Middle States Association Commission on Higher Education.

The Regents Credit Bank is a service of the Regents External Degree Program. The Credit Bank is for people who need to consolidate their educational accomplishments onto a single transcript that is widely acceptable for employment or college enrollment purposes. The same policies on acceptance of credit that govern Regents External Degrees also apply to the Regents Credit Bank.

You may obtain detailed information on either of these services by writing to: The Regents External Degree Program, Cultural Education Center, Albany, NY 12230.

Associate degrees, baccalaureate degrees, and even graduate degrees (including the Ph.D.) can be earned in many disciplines through a variety of external degree programs. Accredited programs are offered in most states. Several programs are open to anyone in the world regardless of age, previous education, or citizenship.

But are these degrees any good?

When Dawn Logan considered earning an associate degree in nursing through the Regents External Degree Program, she asked herself:

> Would it be honored professionally? I spoke to my hospital in-service education director, and although she was enthusiastic, I met with some skepticism in other corners. "Would it be recognized academically?" was their question. "By the Board of Regents, The University of the State of New York!" I replied. I decided I would try. Within a little more than a year and a half I had racked up 146 credits and still had never attended a college class.
>
> Shortly after completing my associate degree I applied to three hospitals for a job as an RN. I was accepted at one almost immediately and was called for interviews by the other two, a good indication that they were seriously considering hiring me. The independent study degree that was somewhat questionable less than two years before was now being accepted as valid without question. The attitude of my fellow staff members had changed from "Do you think it's any good?" to "Oh, you're a brain; you're one of the smart ones who could do it on your own." Whether this is so is a moot point. I have only two performance exams remaining to complete the B.S.N., and I have just applied to a graduate school for admittance into its mental health–psychiatric nursing program.

Some external degree schools, such as Thomas A. Edison College in New Jersey, do not require a student to take any courses through the college in order to receive a degree. In fact, Thomas A. Edison does not offer any courses and it has no faculty in residence; the college is chartered by the state solely for the purpose of guiding and evaluating college-level learning and awarding external degrees. Students have been awarded as many as 90 credits by Thomas A. Edison for life learning (although such large awards are unusual). The remaining 30 credits required for a bachelor's degree could be earned by passing college proficiency exams.

Advantages of external degree programs include freedom from some classroom attendance, open admissions policies, flexible curriculum, low cost, and liberal policies of awarding noncollegiate credit. Disadvantages include lack of classroom contact with other students, limited personal contact with course professors, and the difficulty of maintaining the necessary discipline and motivation needed to pursue a degree independently. Like Dawn Logan you may also be faced with skepticism from potential employers and others, however unwarranted, about the legitimacy of an external degree. Probably this problem will diminish as these degrees become better known. Recently there seems to be some movement in academe toward looking more closely at the quality of external degree programs. Our belief is that most of these programs will be able to survive close examination, and in fact will be strengthened by it.

You should be aware, though, that some so-called external degree programs are run by unscrupulous profiteers. These "degree mills" are not accredited, although clever wording of their advertisements may lead you to believe otherwise. We will come back to this matter in more detail in chapter 3.

Before investing a lot of time and money in an external degree, you should be sure of what you are doing. You might even do well to seek professional advice. William Haponski, the senior author, has established an education/training/career counseling business (ETC Associates), one aspect of which is external degree counseling by mail. Such counseling can assist prospective students in choosing a degree field that is suited to their backgrounds and needs, matching the degree field with an appropriate external degree program, and avoiding the degree mill trap. For information on ETC's external degree publications and personal counseling service, write to Dr. William C. Haponski, ETC Associates, Box 118-BS, Oneida, NY 13421.

Independent Study

Nontraditional degree programs routinely provide for students to pursue research or creative independent-study projects in areas of special interest. "These study projects," one college brochure explains, "may relate to daily work, literary or cultural interests, planned travel abroad, volunteer work, or any avocation of academic value." That college allows up to 18 credits of independent study to be applied toward a degree. (No more than 3 credits may be taken each semester with a single professor.) The student must prepare a detailed independent study proposal including: (1) statement of project, (2) outline of course, (3) work required, (4) schedule of meetings with professor, (5) tentative bibliography. This proposal must be submitted in advance for approval by the student's adviser, a faculty sponsor, the chairman of the sponsor's department, and the dean of the college.

Legitimate independent-study projects are by no means easy courses; the ability of a student to pursue self-directed study demonstrates a significant degree of discipline and maturity. Consider the following views expressed by Paul L. Sressel and Mary M. Thompson in *Independent Study* (San Francisco: Jossey-Bass Inc., 1973, p. 1):

> We strongly believe that no student should receive a baccalaureate degree until he has demonstrated the ability to plan and carry out at least one modest independent study project. This demonstration should be regarded as providing evidence of capability in self-directed learning rather than as the assuming of some body of facts. . . . In fact, *the ability to carry on independent study alone or with peers should be a major goal of education.*

After reading the preceding paragraphs you may think independent study can be a lot of work. You're right, but consider the advantages. First, you have the opportunity to concentrate on a subject that really interests you. Second, you can plan your work to fit into your schedule without being required to follow a classroom schedule. Third, it is usually possible to relate an independent-study project with an objective you had wanted to achieve anyway; therefore, you may be able to kill two birds with one stone. Because of these important advantages, independent study is an excellent option for mature adult students.

Company In-House Programs

An increasing number of major corporations are now providing on-site college degree programs as a fringe benefit for their employees. This practice is spreading rapidly and should continue through the remainder of the 1980s and beyond.

Many progressive companies have learned to appreciate the benefits realized when employees advance their formal educations. These corporations recognize the difficulties encountered by working adults who must attend traditional college courses on campus. According to an August 4, 1980, *Business Week* article ("Earning an Undergraduate Degree at the Plant," pp. 76-77), undergraduate degree programs were being offered at a number of major U.S. corporations including Burroughs Corp., Aetna Life & Casualty Co., and Grumman Data Systems Corp., while graduate programs were available at TRW, Fluor, Digital Equipment, Bechtel, Ford Motor Co., and some divisions of General Motors. According to one educator who was cited, "This is the trend of the future."

If you are thinking about starting a new career, or even changing jobs, the availability of a work-site program may be important to you. Many employers offer tuition assistance, but an in-house college degree program provides the added fringe benefits of eliminating transportation costs while also saving your precious time. Also, such companies should be good places to work since they obviously view their employees as valuable resources worth nurturing and developing.

Of course pursuing a degree at the plant may pose certain limitations. You might not find the program or curriculum you prefer, thus you may have to settle for whatever is available. But if you aspire to a career in the sponsoring company, an in-house college degree may be the most valuable academic credential you could obtain.

Correspondence Programs

If you like to work independently, but feel you need additional structure and direction, you might consider correspondence study. Correspondence courses have come a long way since the days when they were advertised almost exclusively on matchbook covers. Those ads were designed to entice individuals with limited educational opportunities to learn new skills or trades.

Today correspondence education is not limited to the vocational "matchbook schools" that were the early pioneers. Many colleges and universities throughout the country offer home-study, undergraduate-level courses, and a few offer graduate courses for credit. The majority of these colleges are members of the National University Continuing Education Association (NUCEA), whose address is Suite 360, One Dupont Circle, Washington, DC 20036. NUCEA publishes the *Guide to Independent Study Through Correspondence Instruction.* It is available from Peterson's Guides, P. O. Box 2123, Princeton, NJ 08540 (1980, paperback, $4.50). You can take a college course by correspondence in almost any subject, and most residential colleges will allow you to transfer the credits. However, the number of correspondence credits that may be applied toward a degree is usually limited to not more than 30. If you want or need to take a course that is not available at your college, a home-study course might be the answer. Before you proceed, though, make sure the course will be accepted for credit by your college.

A typical correspondence course involves a predesigned series of lessons that must be completed in a prescribed sequence. A text is either provided or purchased locally. As you complete each written assignment (after studying the appropriate section of the text), you mail it to the correspondence school. Your instructor grades your work and returns it within a short time with comments and suggestions. You may either wait for this feedback on your assignment or go right on to the next lesson. Anytime you have questions or problems, you can write to your instructor. Some schools also arrange telephone communication and visits with instructors. Instructors are usually conscientious and thorough when providing feedback to students. The individual attention the correspondence student receives from the instructor is often much greater than would normally be received in the classroom. However, the lack of face-to-face interaction with professor and classmates is a major shortcoming. Also, the correspondence course package does not permit the flexibility that is often possible in conventional classroom courses.

Correspondence study does have certain advantages over the classroom setting. Most noteworthy is the fact that you are entirely free to study at your own pace. It is possible to finish a correspondence course in as little as four to six weeks (if you really push), making it feasible to complete 24–30 credits per year. Or, if this is too fast, you could take a year or more to complete a single course. You are not bound by limited course offerings either; you can start any course at any time you wish. In addition, the cost of correspondence study is generally considerably less than tuition at conventional colleges. And the cost of automobile travel today is another factor that should not be taken lightly.

If you are considering correspondence study, don't rule out private schools that offer college-level courses for profit. Tuition is usually higher at these proprietary schools than at nonprofit colleges and universities offering correspondence programs. These schools, though, may be well worth the extra cost since many of them have more years of experience in home-study education. Because of this experience and substantially higher budgets made possible by higher enrollment, many proprietary schools have been able to develop and maintain excellent course materials, techniques, and student services. If you intend to get college credit for a correspondence course, ensure before you enroll in it that your college will accept this course for credit. A free "Directory of Accredited Home Study Schools," which includes a list of course offerings, can be obtained from the National Home Study Council, 1601 Eighteenth Street, N.W., Washington, DC 20009.

Special Programs for Women

by NANCY LAMPEN
Assistant Professor, Speech Communication
Monroe Community College, Rochester, New York
and JEANNE CRANE
Educational Consultant, Canandaigua, New York

A woman in Pittsburgh hears about the National Congress of Neighborhood Women's college program in her area and is able to pursue the degree she always wanted. In Oregon a woman who received a bachelor's degree in liberal arts 15 years ago discovers she can take a women-in-management program that she views as her ticket to reentering the work force. These are examples of "special programs for women."

The possibilities are exciting yet confusing. There is no one definition of special programs for women and no one single place to look for information. Because federal and state funds were available to start many programs, these programs are often found in places where you might not expect to find them. What exists in your area may or may not meet your goals or fit your circumstances. The offerings can range in length from a two-hour information session for reentry women at one college to a full-scale college degree program at another. Most of these programs have been designed in a painstaking way to address the needs of women from a variety of backgrounds or at least the in-depth needs of one group of women. A few are little more than marketing techniques for increasing the number of enrollees. This section will acquaint you with types of programs and offer suggestions of things to consider before committing yourself to a specific program.

Many colleges recognize that the decision to go to college may be a difficult one, so they have developed programs to provide information and support for making the transition. Such programs include women's orientation programs that cover many of the issues in this chapter as specifically applicable to that college; special counseling for returning women by personnel trained to understand adult development needs, family stresses, and the anxieties faced by someone who has been away from education for a number of years; peer-support groups or women's groups that offer women an opportunity to explore feelings and problems with others who have had or are having similar experiences; and individual and/or group career counseling to explore nontraditional fields, examine marketplace potential for job placement, and facilitate the setting of realistic short- and long-range goals.

Some offerings have been designed to give women opportunities that were not open to them earlier. Past sex stereotyping, particularly in high school, has led to many women not having had the proper preparation (especially in science and math) for beginning the college program of their choice. Both noncredit courses (such as those to reduce math anxiety) and college credit courses (such as introduction to college chemistry or algebra) may be necessary before admission to a specific degree program is granted.

The whole area of women's studies originated to compensate for the lack of serious attention given women. Some institutions have separate departments in women's studies that may offer a major or such elective courses as The History of the Women's Movement and Women in Literature. Some institutions have not created a separate department but rather have integrated women's issues into already existing courses, such as Sociology of the Family, a course that has been redesigned to include a unit on women's roles or on sex equality.

There are many kinds of women's centers to serve you. Ann Diehl, a past president of the United States Association of Evening Students, says:

> An example would be the Women's Educational and Counseling Center at the State University of New York at Farmingdale, which offers a complete range of support services for women. At the Women's Center women find that their "unique" problems are shared by many, and also that there are answers to questions about themselves, their educations, and their careers. A listing of a national network of local resource centers is available at no cost from Catalyst, a nonprofit organization for women, at 14 East 60th Street, New York, New York 10022. Catalyst also offers a list of its publications relating to careers and education for women.

With all the possible options, how do you choose the program of study you want, that's affordable, that's within a reasonable commuting distance, that doesn't stereotype you but has an environment that allows you to be all you're capable of being, and that offers assistance when you need it? Perhaps we can help somewhat by providing a checklist of items you might keep in mind when making your decision. No one college is likely to provide all of these features as applicable particularly to women, but probably only a few of them are of special significance in meeting your specific needs. You might check off those items that are most important to you and then go back and rank them according to your needs.

Checklist

1. Are women present in college programs that traditionally have enrolled only men?
2. Do these women consider their college experience as basically positive?
3. Does the college give credit for what you have learned as a homemaker, a volunteer, or a job-holder?
4. Are adult women depicted in publications of the college?
5. Is there a support group for returning women?
6. What is the percentage of women faculty and administrators? If it seems to be low, is there a satisfactory explanation?
7. Is there a child-care center?
8. Does the financial aid office have information on special sources of financial aid for women?
9. Are there any special programs for women?
10. Are there cooperative education (combined work and study) options for reentering women so that you can gain experience and build a résumé to improve your status in the labor market?
11. Can the placement office tell you about the employment success of other reentry women?

By now you should have a sense of the range of programs for women and some approaches for deciding which program is best for you. If you need further help in making your transition to college, some additional sources are:

Center for Women's Opportunities
American Association of Community and Junior Colleges
One Dupont Circle, N.W., Suite 410
Washington, DC 20036

National Congress of Neighborhood Women
11–29 Catherine Street
Brooklyn, NY 11211

Eckstrom, Ruth B., Abigail M. Harris, and Marlaine E. Lockheed, "How to Get College Credit for What You Have Learned as a Home-maker and Volunteer," designed for adult women entering or reen-tering college. Available from Accrediting Women's Competencies, Educational Testing Service, Princeton, NJ 08541.

Schlachter, Gail Ann. *Directory of Financial Aids for Women.* 1977. Reference Service Press, 9023 Alcott Street, Suite 201, Los Angeles, CA 90035. $16.95.

And one final tip! If the college you choose does not have the special program you want, see what you can negotiate. Be assertive and try to arrange your own special program.

Accreditation

Some of the programs you are considering may be in an accreditation category. What are the sources of accreditation, and how important is it that your program be accredited?

We believe that most educators in traditional colleges and universities would recognize only two ultimate sources of accreditation. These are the United States government and the American Council on Education (ACE), a private agency whose membership includes many colleges and universities and national and regional education associations. They do not directly accredit institutions; rather, agencies within these bodies are held responsible for evaluating the various accrediting authorities. Those institutions that pass their high standards are listed by them and are thereby authorized in turn to accredit educational institutions or individual programs. In most cases, the government and ACE are in agreement on which accrediting authorities they will recognize. In a few cases, only one of the two agencies will list a particular accrediting authority.

Two types of accreditation exist, institutional and specialized. Institutional accreditation has to do with the status of the college or university as an entity. This type of accreditation is discussed in the next chapter. Specialized accreditation relates to certain individual programs within an institution. Most major libraries will carry a recent copy of *Accredited Institutions of Postsecondary Education* (Washington, D.C.: American Council on Education). This is an annual directory of accredited institutions, professionally accredited programs, and candidates for accreditation. For an explanation of the role of accreditation and the addresses of accrediting bodies, see the excerpt from this directory in Appendix A.

In the section in Appendix A on "specialized accrediting," you will note such programs as architecture, dietetics, journalism, and nursing. If you are considering a degree in one of the many fields listed, you then have the problem of determining how important is enrollment in an accredited as opposed to a nonaccredited program.

You should write to the accrediting agency. But then you must put their reply in perspective. Of course they will be inclined to tell you that you should enroll in an accredited program. What you may have to do to get more points of view is to ask a variety of people in the profession. You will find from them that in certain fields accreditation status has critical ramifications. For others you will get mixed reactions: "Who cares?" said one employer. "I just want people who can perform." Some very fine programs are not accredited, often because the directors of these programs do not desire program accreditation. The graduates of these programs often get good jobs and are readily accepted by graduate schools.

If your intended field is one of those represented by an accrediting body, carefully investigate the importance of accreditation as it may apply to the programs in the particular colleges you are considering. Ask the directors of those programs for their opinions. Once you assess those opinions and have this kind of background information, you may elect an accredited program for specific career reasons, or you may choose a nonaccredited program with full confidence that your degree will be well accepted professionally.

Choosing the program that is right for you is of great importance. Don't make a choice without reviewing your goals and determining the credentials necessary to achieve them. Get as precise information about the program as possible; don't base your choice on assumptions, misconceptions, and wish fulfillment. The information you need can be gotten through use of resources that are all around you. You will want to determine the arrangements that best meet your needs: traditional or nontraditional degree programs; full-time or part-time study; credit or noncredit courses; programs near you or far away. Evening, weekend, and summer programs are probably available to you. You will want to check into the accreditation status of your program if it happens to be among those specialized programs for which there are accrediting bodies. Careful preliminary work in choosing your program will significantly enhance your later satisfaction with your choice.

3

Choosing the Right College

What college would best fit my needs?
Where do I get information about colleges?

The Differences Among Colleges

L et's assume you have some choice in the matter of selecting a college, and that you are not restricted by circumstances to the college closest to home. How will you choose?

You are making a big decision. The results of that choice will be with you in a significant way for the rest of your life.

There are over 3,000 licensed or accredited colleges and universities in the United States and Canada that have at least a two-year curriculum. In addition, there are many other postsecondary institutions that do not award degrees but offer programs leading to certificates and diplomas. Like a person, each college or university is unique. Each has an ambiance, a reputation. Colleges and universities take on some of the character of their surroundings as well as the character of the people who come there to administer, teach, and learn. In a curious way, colleges change as the years change, yet they seem to remain constant. When they die, as some have, the pain is felt by many whose lives have been touched by them.

What do you want to be—a mining engineer, a meteorologist, a museum curator? Depending on your program, you might have a choice between a college or university in Washington, D.C. (American University) or one in the state of Washington (Whitworth College); between one in Texas (University of Texas) or one in Missouri (Northeast Missouri State). You might apply to a university of world renown, such as Yale, or to a college that is not so famous, such as Defiance College in Ohio. You can find a college offering a two-year degree, a four-year degree, or a graduate degree. You can mingle with 40,000 students or with fewer than a thousand. Your college might be public or private, located in the country or the city; it might offer a large amount of financial aid or very little, have small classes or large, ramps for wheelchairs or none, a party atmosphere or a serious study environment. What is right for you?

Getting Information About Colleges

In chapter 2 we discussed the matter of getting information about programs. Many of the references you would use in the library to get that information also contain additional information about colleges.

We suggest that you not stop when you have read about a college in one of these guides. Use as many of them as possible. Whereas most guides will cover such basic information as admissions policies, tuition costs, and programs and degrees offered, the format and emphasis will vary from guide to guide. Some guides attempt to categorize schools according to degrees of competitiveness, using SATs, high school class rank and grades, and similar criteria. Others group schools by tuition level or size. Several of these guides contain information on two or three thousand colleges and are a few inches thick.

Where can you get recent, accurate information? For institutions in the United States, see the *Education Directory, Colleges and Universities.* It is an annual publication of the National Center for Education Statistics listing institutions that are legally authorized to offer and are offering at least a one-year program of college-level studies leading to a degree. The information presented for each institution includes its telephone number, address, previous fall enrollment, undergraduate tuition and fees, sex of the student body (men, women, coed), calendar system, control or affiliation, highest level of offering, type of education offered, accreditation, and names and titles of principal officers. The *Education Directory* does not go much beyond those bare facts and, therefore, must be supplemented with other sources. For example, *Peterson's Annual Guide to Undergraduate Study* (Peterson's Guides, Inc., P. O. Box 2123, Princeton, NJ 08540, paperback, $13.00) provides college profiles, detailed college and program descriptions, a directory of basic college data and test score ranges, and a directory of majors and colleges that offer them. The Guide includes information on Canadian colleges and universities, as well as on those in the United States. It is revised annually from input provided directly by the institutions.

College catalogs (bulletins, brochures) on microfilm are other sources of information you will want to examine. Or, using the addresses from sources such as those mentioned above, you can write and get the catalogs of schools that seem interesting to you. Consumer protection laws require certain basic information to be presented in college catalogs. The catalog of an accredited institution probably represents an attempt to deliver reasonably complete and accurate information from which a person can make an informed judgment.

An enormous amount of information about colleges is available to you. When you begin looking through this material you may even feel dismayed because there is so much of it. To help you with your selection, let's further consider certain aspects of academe.

Two-Year Colleges, Four-Year Colleges, Universities

Our degree-granting higher-education system is largely composed of two-year colleges, four-year colleges, and universities. We caution the reader that generalizations about types of institutions can be seriously misleading. You can make a wise choice only by studying the nature of a specific institution as it will affect you in your degree program, not as it may affect someone else in his program. Myths about types of institutions have guided far too many students and parents of students to choose college or university X over Y when Y (or A or B or C) actually would have been the better choice.

What are these myths? Here's just one: "Two-year colleges are small and, therefore, offer close faculty-to-student relationships (which is good), but the faculty is not of high quality (which, of course, is bad)." If this kind of myth were to guide your thinking, you might be shocked to discover that some two-year colleges are huge, many times the size of some universities. Also, the faculty at a two-year college might even be of better quality than that of a nearby university—better at teaching, better at advising, and perhaps even more successful in research and publication. So, having cautioned you about myths, we will proceed, adding further cautions as we go.

Two-year colleges are often called junior colleges or community colleges—the name varies with locality and custom. These colleges grant certificates, associate degrees, or diplomas (in Canada). Junior colleges tend to be small and private whereas community colleges may be small or large, and public.

Junior colleges have been in existence for decades, often affiliated with religious organizations. In the past their policies tended to be conservative and directed mostly toward liberal arts studies and traditional students. Many junior colleges are still oriented that way, but others have adopted career and technical programs and have actively sought to serve adult students. At most junior colleges the student will find small classes and close relationships with professors.

For a time, many community colleges grew so fast that receiving a quality education was questionable at some institutions. Today many fine programs and professors are found on community-college campuses. Usually supported partly by state funds, partly by tuition income primarily from local students, and partly by local public funds, community colleges generally are more responsive than most other colleges to local career needs.

Degree programs at junior and community colleges may be of the terminal or transfer type. Transfer programs are designed to allow the student who is awarded an associate degree to move without loss of credit into an upper-division program; that is, one consisting of the last two years of a baccalaureate degree. However, to be certain of full transfer credit, you should check with the admissions office or registrar both of the two-year college and of the four-year colleges to which you might later transfer.

Terminal programs are those in which no higher-level degree is awarded. Full credit for courses in such programs most likely would not be granted if the student later chose to enter a different type of program at a higher degree level. If you intend to take a terminal degree at a two-year college, be certain you have your long-range goals well defined. You will want to avoid possible loss of credit later if you should decide to continue your education.

Four-year colleges primarily award baccalaureate degrees, but some of them also offer associate degrees and certificates. Some even grant graduate degrees, but the number of their graduate degree programs is likely to be small compared to their undergraduate degree programs. Most four-year colleges afford outstanding student options whereby the degree can be completed in less than four years. Some have three-year degree programs in which waiver of certain credit-hour requirements is granted. You may also find that you can accelerate your program by taking courses during the summer session, or by taking an overload during the academic year. Certain four-year colleges have combination programs that begin with your first three years of work at the college. Then when you are able to gain entry to a professional school, such as one in medicine or dentistry, you can receive your baccalaureate degree from your original college by substituting the first year of professional study for the last year of undergraduate work.

A college with its own campus (that is, not located with other colleges of a university) often states in its catalog that its students can enjoy a close personal relationship with faculty and staff. The emphasis at such a college is more likely to be on teaching students than on conducting research or publishing. Don't depend on it, though. The unofficial motto of the college might be "publish or perish," and the amount of concern shown to students may be minimal despite all the natural advantages afforded by a highly favorable student-to-faculty ratio.

Universities are composed of two or more colleges or schools, and they customarily offer a variety of graduate degree programs. Research and publishing are major aspects of their educational activities. Compared to the emphasis that most colleges place on teaching and advising students, some universities may be behind. But of course, many universities are concerned about both classroom teaching and treatment of students as individuals. Fortunately, some of the finest scholars on a university campus can also be among the best teachers. If your interest, say, is in English literature, and you would like to come into contact with as many renowned scholars as possible, then you might wish to seek out a major university with a fine English department. Do not depend, though, on having those professors as classroom teachers at the undergraduate level. Sometimes you might, but at other times your contact with them could be limited to occasional lectures in a large auditorium.

A major university could be a fantastic place for you. Quite surely you would find there the potential for high-quality learning, cultural, social, and athletic experiences. You would not have enough time to take part in more than a small portion of what exists to stimulate your mind and body. But you might also feel lost in the labyrinths of university life. Largeness and smallness are relative, of course. Gulliver in the land of Lilliputians was huge; in the land of Brobdingnagians he was tiny. The University of Vermont has about 10,000 undergraduate and graduate students. To some people the university would seem impossibly megalithic, a place where the individual student would get lost in the crowd. To others, the university would represent a folksy kind of place where people get to know one another and spread out on the grass to chat and study in the welcome springtime sun. It is not so much the size, or perhaps even the type, of the institution that is important but the size and type of its total effect on you as related to your needs.

Public or Private

Adult readers of this book who come from certain parts of the country may remember from their early days an intellectual snobbery that tended to separate private from public institutions. For instance, in one popular conception of education, public colleges were thought to train teachers and farmers, not educate young men and women. Those colleges, and other state schools, were not intellectually rigorous enough to suit the tastes of a segment of our society that was conditioned to send their children all the way across the country if necessary to enter an Ivy League school.

Some of that snobbery still exists. Unfortunately, some of the public colleges seem to have given ammunition to their critics from the private sector. They have defended themselves against charges of low academic standards not by seriously attempting to elevate those standards, but by using the excuse that their mission is to provide the greatest possible access to higher education.

Of the more than 3,000 colleges and universities (to include branch campuses) in the United States, slightly more than half are privately controlled. However, four out of every five students attend public institutions. Of the 60 largest institutions, only five are private. All of those in the top 25 are public, with enrollments from 30,000 to over 60,000. The University of Minnesota, Minneapolis-St. Paul, is the largest public institution with 64,000 students. New York University is the largest private institution with about 33,000 students.

At the two-year college level, the differential in numbers of institutions and enrollments is even more striking. Of over 1,100 two-year colleges, about 900 are public and somewhat more than 200 are private. Only about 3 of every 100 students attend a private as compared to public two-year institution.

The average tuition and fees at public institutions are about one-fifth of that at their private counterparts. (As you will see in chapter 6, the average actual cost differential to you, though, may be not as great as you think it might be.)

If you are considering large universities, the question of public or private as related to quality does not make much sense. (Is the University of Southern California, a private institution, better or worse than the University of California at Berkeley, a public institution? Would anyone really care to spend time on such an inquiry?) Even in the case of small colleges we would urge that considerations other than public or private control should determine your choice. Whereas some states have not done as good a job as others in ensuring appropriate quality in their public institutions, the administrations of some private institutions have also been remiss. The quality of education attainable in an institution does not depend so much on the nature of control, public or private, as it does on the long-term quality of that control.

Reputation and Accreditation

Reputation is an elusive thing. It defies precise definition, enumeration of its components, and prediction of its effects. Yet it exists, and it is powerful. It may draw a new student through a college's gates without any previous direct contact being initiated by the college. We are convinced that good colleges, as well as good restaurants and good books, are most often marketed more effectively by casual word than by forms of deliberate advertising. A single student who feels good about what he is getting or has gotten at a college can be worth far more to the college than the classiest advertisement.

The reputation of a college's degree can have great financial, social, and personal significance for its holder. A degree from college A may be worth more in the marketplace than one from college B. Your standing in certain social circles may relate to the degree you hold. Also, the way you feel about your school may affect the way you feel about yourself, which in turn may affect important aspects of your life not directly related to your schooling.

Loss of reputation by a college is a sad thing to see. In the late 1960s and early 1970s, some colleges and universities responded to pressures for greater access to higher education by initiating an open-admission policy. Virtually any student who wished to enroll could do so. Not past level of achievement but level of performance once enrolled was supposed to be the standard by which the student would be measured. Predictably, the level of performance in thousands of cases turned out not to be satisfactory. Yet students were allowed to advance until an outcry from concerned students, faculty, administrators, legislators, and the public itself forced some improvement. Tens of thousands of alumni of those institutions, graduated in the days when high standards prevailed, understandably are upset about what happened. They believe that the degree they earned in a better day was seriously degraded and that they were cheated by their alma mater.

Reputation derives from the degree of quality maintained through the years. Obviously you would like to choose the best-quality school at which you can be successful. But do you have any way of making an informed choice, since quality and reputation are such nebulous matters?

We think an indicator of reputation for the institution as a whole may be available to the person who has no other indicator, but it cannot be used too precisely. That indicator is the average SAT scores, or other entrance examination scores. If you find two institutions that are reasonably comparable in size, type, and program offerings, and they have at least 50 points separating their median SAT scores, the institution with the higher scores may be of better quality. A college either tends gradually to adjust its admissions and teaching standards to meet its students' capabilities, or it sets standards and expects its students to meet them. Either way, SATs may be at least a rough measure of expectation of student performance and, hence, the quality of the system. You will find average SATs in several of the college guides in your library. If you are aware that even apparently similar institutions can vary a great deal from one another in mission and programs, and don't expect too much, you may find SAT comparison to be of some help to you.

In the previous chapter we discussed accreditation as it applies to programs within a college. (Also see Appendix A.) We stressed that the lack of accreditation of a program does not necessarily imply a poor-quality program or that you would be endangering your career by enrolling in it. When we examine *institutional* accreditation status, though, we find very different circumstances. The status of institutional accreditation of a college of your choice is vitally important to you. Whereas it may be true that a very few high-quality institutions do not desire accreditation and would quite certainly get it if they wished, one can safely say that no degree mills are accredited by accrediting groups recognized by the Council on Postsecondary Accreditation (COPA) or by the United States government.

In addition to listing accredited institutions, COPA lists candidates for accreditation. In order to achieve candidate status, an institution is rigorously screened by the accrediting body. If the institution is young, and is a candidate, you are probably safe in choosing it, since, normally, achievement of candidate status leads to full accreditation. But do check out the matter carefully with the school.

Most people never think to investigate the accreditation status of the college or university they are considering, and most get by with it because the large majority of institutions with campuses are reputable. But don't trust to luck. Look in the college's catalog for a statement regarding accreditation status, or if you want to be certain, check in ACE's *Accredited Institutions of Postsecondary Education* or in the federal government's directory, *Accredited Postsecondary Institutions and Programs*. You wouldn't want to discover someday that your degree is a source of pain rather than pride.

Instruction

Could any factor be more important to you in choosing the right college than quality of instruction? Yet, of all the elements we discuss in this chapter, this is among the most difficult for you to judge. Quality of instruction may vary enormously even within departments, so how can anyone make meaningful comparisons between departments, much less institutions? Educators may be able to get a reasonably good idea of levels of quality within their institution and may even be able to make some meaningful comparisons with other institutions. But how can you, the prospective student, do the same?

In comparing colleges, make some phone calls or visits and ask about faculty quality. Usually near the end of a college catalog you will find a list of faculty and credentials. How do the academic credentials you find there compare with those of faculty at the other schools you are considering? If you note a discrepancy among schools, ask why this is so. Especially if you are considering a university, inquire about the amount of emphasis by the faculty on teaching and advising as compared to scholarship.

The student-to-faculty ratio will give you a quantitative measure of how much attention you can expect as an individual. If lower-level courses (often listed as 100- and 200-level courses) habitually carry an enrollment of more than about 30 students, this is an indicator that you ought to question how serious the college is about providing individual attention to its students. Large lecture courses are all right if they will constitute a small portion of your total curriculum, but if they appear to be numerous, question why this is so.

Curriculum variety and flexibility are especially important to the adult student, yet these are often areas of weakness in adult evening and weekend programs. Ask about the total number of majors offered in these programs as compared to the total number in the day divisions. Then compare the percentages among the schools you are evaluating. The higher the percentage, the greater the curriculum variety and flexibility you are likely to find. This is so because courses, especially at the lower levels, often service more than one major. The more majors you find, the more choice you will probably have in selecting courses that fit your schedule. Don't assume that a university is naturally going to offer you more curriculum variety and flexibility than a small college. The university might give relatively scant attention to the needs of adults whereas the college might try hard to serve its adult students.

In assessing the answers you get to these inquiries on quality of instruction, you will recognize that people associated with colleges and universities usually present their institution favorably. Sometimes, though, a staff or faculty member or a student will tell a different kind of story, one that comes from honesty, perhaps, or maybe from bitterness, and you have to take this attitude into consideration.

Some Other Concerns

Credit Policies

This matter of importance in choosing a college will be treated in detail in chapter 4.

Costs of College and Financial Aid

Money is almost always a major factor in an adult's choice of a college. When faced with a choice between a college costing, say, $25 a credit and one where tuition per credit is $100 or more, the decision for many adults may seem cut and dried. When the selection of a college is based simply on a comparison of tuition and fees, though, the result is often a poor decision. You should check with the financial aid office of each college you are considering in order to determine what assistance, if any, is available from the school. Depending upon policies for transfer and noncollegiate credit awards, coupled with the amount of financial aid available, a degree could cost less at a college where the tuition is high than at a school where tuition is lower. Much more on financing your degree will be covered in chapter 6.

Facilities, Services, and Attitudes

In many ways throughout this book we treat the question of college facilities, services, and attitudes as related to you, the adult student. We suggest that you deliberately draft a checklist of concerns. If child care is important to you, for instance, put it high on your list. Add your library concerns and anything else that may trouble you. Then as you make your calls or visits, your list of questions will grow, just as will the answers, as you speak with students, faculty, and administrators. And soon the picture will become clearer: College B offers more of what you need in regard to facilities, services, and manners of treating you than does college A.

Cultural, Social, and Fraternal Activities

Colleges and universities often are the hub of community cultural life, especially in small cities and towns. The college you choose might very well have an art gallery, a museum of natural history, classic and avant-garde film series, and music and theater series. Social and fraternal possibilities are endless, from small groups with specific interests to large gatherings with diverse interests. Fraternities and sororities exist on some campuses specifically for adult students. If cultural, social, and fraternal activities are important in your choice of college, the dean of students, director of continuing education, or head of the student government should be able to give you the information you need for seeking out groups for further investigation.

Accommodation to the Needs of the Disabled

by S. TAPPER BRAGG
Mr. Bragg, a disabled person, is a graduate of Hofstra University, Hempstead, New York, at the undergraduate, graduate, and law school levels.

In addition to all the other factors involved in choosing a college, physically disabled individuals must consider whether institutions in which they are interested can accommodate their special needs. Before making a final choice, a disabled applicant should visit the college or university to determine whether he or she can function properly in the physical environment of the campus. A personal interview with an appropriate administrator is highly desirable, if not essential, to allow the college official to become familiar with any special needs that the applicant may have and to allow the potential student to sense the attitude of the administration to the disabled.

The twin goals of a program for physically disabled college and university students should be to make the campus accessible to them and to make it possible for them to complete an academic curriculum. Handicapped individuals are expected to meet the same admissions and retention standards as any other students. The sole reason for providing special facilities and services is to compensate for or remove any barriers beyond the student's control that may unfairly hinder academic performance. Physical facilities should be modified as necessary to accommodate the disabled. Attention must be given to ramps and elevators, restrooms, public telephones, drinking fountains, parking places, and the marking of locations in Braille.

If note-taking is a problem, one possible solution is to ask a fellow student to provide carbon or photo copies of his or her notes. With permission of the instructor, a student might be allowed to record lectures on tape.

Disabled students may need additional time and/or the use of an electric typewriter to complete examinations. It may be possible for the institution to arrange for volunteer writers, provided by local service organizations, to whom examination answers may be dictated. Non-traditional students, however, should be aware that these volunteers are generally not available in the evening or on weekends when many of them take courses. It may, therefore, be necessary to reschedule exam-inations at a mutually convenient time. Will the institution be receptive to such special arrangements?

Nontraditional students for whom transportation is a problem may wish to live on campus. Those who do should be certain that residence halls meet their needs. If the institution permits, severely disabled stu-dents may hire private attendants to assist them. Some colleges and universities hire other students to provide their disabled colleagues with limited assistance in activities of daily living.

Mr. Leonard DuBoff, a sightless Hofstra University graduate who now teaches law, has suggested that blind students can acquire texts in Braille or talking-book form from the college library's interlibrary loan program or the National Council of Jewish Women. The American Foundation for the Blind can supply a drawing kit that converts illustra-tions into raised-line drawings. An entire afternoon or evening may be set aside to work in the library with a reader when preparing a research project, and papers may be written with the aid of tape recorders.

Unfortunately, college programs for the deaf and hard of hearing are in their infancy. Among the services provided by some institutions are note-takers, classroom sign-language interpreters, special counseling, and sign-language classes for staff members.

Disability is no barrier to successful participation in cocurricular activities. Physically handicapped students frequently assume leading roles in student government, campus media, institutional governance, and academic and social organizations. Some colleges provide outlets for the athletic interests of their disabled students through such activi-ties as wheelchair basketball, wheelchair football, archery, swimming, track and field, table tennis, and square dancing.

The first contact of many able-bodied persons with the disabled often takes place on a college campus. While some adjustments may be needed on both sides, interaction between the disabled and able tends to develop easily, and discrimination is not a significant problem. A fellow student should not feel hurt when assistance offered to a disabled individual is refused. Most disabled persons prefer to act independently whenever possible. On the other hand, they usually rec-ognize when assistance is needed, and in those cases, disabled persons may gladly accept aid or even request it. The general campus population should neither fear nor feel awkward in encounters with their disabled counterparts. With a little experience, people will soon find that contact with a physically handicapped person need not be a source of trauma.

In choosing a college, a disabled student should carefully assess each campus in terms of its ability to meet both educational and physical needs. The following publications should be useful both to disabled persons who are choosing a college and to college administrators charged with developing and supervising programs for the disabled:

> *Accessibility Modifications,* by Ronald L. Mace, available from the North Carolina Department of Insurance, Special Office of the Handicapped, P. O. Box 26387, Raleigh, NC 27611.

> *Campus Advocacy: How to Start an OPIDS,* a guide that describes the steps for campuses to take in order to activate service programs for disabled students. Available from the Office to Promote Independence of Disabled Students, Activities Center, The University of Georgia, Memorial Hall, Athens, GA 30602. Single copy free.

Extension Centers

Remember the days when the only place you could take a college course was on a college campus? If you were fortunate enough to live within a reasonable distance of the campus, you might have been able to squeeze out enough time from your busy schedule to sit in on a class two or three times a week. But if you had to commute 45 minutes to an hour or more each way, forget it!

Fortunately for many adults today, that situation has changed. If you live in a medium-sized or large metropolitan area, and are not fortunate enough to live near a college campus, there is almost certain to be an off-campus college center or satellite within reach. Waning enrollments on campus have encouraged many colleges and universities to reach out to the adult market and establish programs in community centers, libraries, and school buildings that had been closed.

While most college campuses offer reasonably good facilities and services, those at extension centers should be checked out. Will you be sitting for up to three hours in chairs intended for children? Are the classrooms well lighted and air conditioned? Will necessary instructional aids (chalkboards, projectors, screens) be on hand? Is parking convenient and adequate? Will required course books be sold at the off-campus location? Will you have easy access to library services? Is there a snack bar or at least a vending service provided? Each of such factors affects your comfort, convenience, or ability to learn. If you do encounter problems while attending classes at an off-campus location, don't hesitate to complain, and encourage your classmates to do the same.

Be especially cautious when considering extension centers operated by other than local institutions. Horror stories are abundant. For example, students have been promised a full program only to find later that the center in fact has been giving them inferior instruction for only part of a curriculum, the rest of which must be taken on the main campus that is several states distant. Several states have begun to crack down on the abuses of extension centers. The process of gaining quality control, though, probably will take years. In the meantime, you should recognize that extension centers can be a real boon for you when well operated by a high-quality institution. Or they can be the source of real trouble. Investigate the circumstances carefully when you consider an extension center among your college choices.

Visiting Prospective College Campuses

College catalogs, brochures, and bulletins provide valuable sources of information about programs, course offerings, and student services, and they should be examined. But a truer picture of what a college has to offer you might be obtained through a well-planned visit to the campus.

Be sure to visit at a time when classes are in full session. The only advantage of visiting a campus during intersession is the ease with which you will find a parking space. It is best to set aside two full days if possible (or at least one day) since you will need ample time to visit various campus facilities and talk to some key people. The following are among the places you might want to include in your tour:

- Admissions office
- Financial aid office
- Office of the dean of continuing education or nontraditional adult programs
- Office of the academic department head in the field of your interest
- Office of the evening or nontraditional students' organization
- Career placement and counseling office
- Offices of program coordinators responsible for awarding credit for life experience, noncollegiate courses, and proficiency examinations
- Library and other research facilities
- Computer center (if applicable)
- Bookstore
- Student center

- Child-care facilities (if applicable)
- Dormitories (if applicable)
- Cafeteria
- Athletic and recreational facilities
- Classrooms, lecture halls, and laboratories

You would be wise to list all of the places you would like to visit in the order of their importance to you, and to follow this sequence as closely as possible during your tour. Then if you run out of time, you will at least have visited the most important places. You might also be prepared to take notes, and you should collect as much relevant printed literature as possible. This information will enable you to reflect upon your visit later and make a more objective comparison to other colleges. Finally, if you wish to meet with a specific person, you should call a week or two in advance and make an appointment.

Some colleges will permit a visitor to sit in on a class as an observer. While this might provide some insight, it may consume too much valuable time, and observing a class is a hit-or-miss proposition. No college has all good or all bad professors, and all professors have good and bad days. You might use your time more effectively by questioning several adult students who have spent some time in the program you are considering.

The most important objective of your visit should be to acquire a sense of how well the college fits your particular needs and interests—both personal and academic. Factors you should consider carefully are the general attitude toward nontraditional learning and the programs and facilities available to accommodate the special needs of adult students. These could make a big difference in your potential success as an adult in college.

■■■ STUDENT PROFILE ■■■

Arlene LeBlanc

Learning was rather difficult for me, so having to leave school at 15 years of age proved to be no problem. My ability as a "jack-of-all-trades" saw me through a ten-year period. Love, marriage, and two children occupied me for the next ten years. During this time at home I realized how little I knew and how much I wanted to learn.

At 36 years of age I started studying French, took some aptitude tests, and wrote to England for my school marks. The test scores proved quite low, and my marks came back from England with this written across the page: "Shows marked weakness." Just after receiving this nice bit of information I failed a French exam. So I sat back, patted myself on the back, and said, "Well, Arlene, you tried." I couldn't handle the failure. It just seemed to reinforce how poorly I did in school.

Two years later my discontent at not learning anything was stronger than ever. It was now or never. I enrolled in a course for adults wishing to return to school. After receiving lots of confidence from a superb teacher, I started searching again for an appropriate school programme.

With no particular degree in mind and not wanting to enter university (too costly and too scary), my choices were limited. Evening courses are very tiring for me, so I was really looking for a daytime programme. A preuniversity college in the area said they would accept me during the day, but I didn't have the nerve to sit in a classroom with 17- and 18-year-olds.

Trying to find the right programme at a convenient college proved frustrating, but finally everything worked out. Dawson College here in Montreal has set up a tuition-free programme for mature students. It's a daytime course of two full days a week, leaving time for family and studying. It is not too heavy a course, which is ideal for people like me who need to be eased back into the educational structure. The programme incorporates basic study skills, basic math, and group behavior. The course boosts one's confidence while teaching one how to study again. The course can lead to a one-year preparatory science programme, which in turn can lead to a diploma. The responsibility lies with the individual to do as much or as little as he or she wishes, but most students take their responsibility seriously.

I am most impressed with the helpful resources available at Dawson. The college offers learning centers where one can go for help in writing book reports and term papers, in reading skills, and in other academic areas. All the professors are very approachable, and there are guidance counselors on staff to help out with any kind of problem. School was never like this when I was young!

My children are amazed that I should want to go back to school, but I try to impress upon them that one is never too old to learn. Even if one does not have a particular degree in mind, I feel that learning for learning's sake is a goal in itself.

My best-laid plans for balancing home life, traveling time, and studies sometimes go awry, but I find this to be a plus as each individual in the family accepts more responsibility. This in turn makes for a more caring atmosphere.

To sum it all up, I would say that it is rewarding to be back at school regardless of where or what it leads to. My plans for the future? The possibilities are endless. I will continue taking academic courses to increase my knowledge.

There is a big, wide world out there and I intend to be part of it.

4

Getting Credit for What You Already Know

How can I get a degree in the shortest possible time?

A Degree May Be Closer Than You Realize

Traditionally, earning a bachelor's degree required four years of full-time college attendance. An adult carrying a typical part-time load of two 3-credit courses each semester was able to earn only 12 credits a year. At that rate, a conventional four-year bachelor's degree took *ten years* to complete! Many adults have earned college degrees the slow way; perhaps you know or have heard of someone who has struggled through many years of night school to finish college. Yet many of these people had already acquired consider-able knowledge of their academic discipline through life experience. Stories have been told of top business executives sitting through basic management courses that they would probably be able to teach as effectively as the professor. Imagine an accomplished professional artist taking Drawing 1, a journalist taking English Composition 1, or a musician taking Introduction to Music! At one time, such absurd re-quirements were not unheard of for adults.

Fortunately, most colleges today provide means for individuals to demonstrate and document college-level knowledge and receive equiv-alent course credit. By taking advantage of credit for noncollegiate instruction, proficiency examinations, and special life-learning assess-ments, adults with no previous college credits may be able to earn an associate degree within as little as 18 months and a bachelor's degree within as little as three years. Coauthor Charles McCabe completed all of the requirements for his degree in less than two and a half years by taking advantage of the credit policies outlined in this chapter.

Transfer Credits

Transfer policies vary, and different policies may apply for different programs at a single college. Transfer credit for previous college course work is generally granted under the following conditions:

1. Courses must have been completed at an accredited college or university (with rare exceptions).

2. Credit will not ordinarily be granted for courses passed with a grade of less than C or C−; however, some institutions will accept a D if it is offset by an A or a B in another course.

3. Most colleges have a residence requirement of at least 30 credits; that is, 30 credits must be earned at that college. Usually those credits must also be the final credits earned toward the degree. Since many baccalaureate degrees require 120 credits, course work accepted for transfer usually will not exceed 90 credits.

4. Full credit (usually not to exceed 64 semester hours) is ordinarily transferable if you have an associate degree, regardless of how long ago it was earned. State universities often guarantee admission to transfer students from public two-year colleges in the same state. The guarantee does not, however, ensure admission to a specified college or a specified curriculum.

5. Course work completed more than ten years prior to admission is often nontransferable; however, special adult degree programs usually do not impose a time limit.

6. For advanced standing to be granted, courses must usually be deemed "appropriate" or "suitable" to fulfill a requirement or elective of the degree program to which the student is being admitted.

7. A limitation, often 30 hours, is usually placed on the number of credits that may be transferred for correspondence college courses (and noncollegiate instruction). Often the same holds true for standardized proficiency examinations (see page 57). Usually institutions review scores of examinations submitted for transfer credit, and even if one school accepts a score for credit, another may not if the score is low.

8. Official transcripts from all institutions previously attended must be sent to the college for evaluation of proposed transfer credits.

Credit for Noncollegiate Instruction: Military Training, Company Training, Continuing Education, Correspondence Courses

Several sources exist for credit for noncollegiate instruction. For instance, most colleges award credit for certain in-service course work completed by service personnel and veterans. Credit for military service training courses and work experiences, when granted, is usually based on the recommendations outlined in *Guide to the Evaluation of Edu-*

cational Experiences in the Armed Services, a publication of the American Council on Education. Many institutions will also grant some credit for physical education to matriculated students who are service members or veterans of active military service.

The Defense Activity for Non-Traditional Education Support (DANTES—formerly known as the United States Armed Forces Institute, or USAFI) is an educational service that provides support to the voluntary educational programs of all the military services. Over 7,000 independent study courses from 58 regionally accredited colleges and universities are available to service personnel through the DANTES Independent Study Support System. While the majority of the courses available through this system are applicable to undergraduate degree programs, 28 of the participating colleges offer courses at the high school level, and 10 offer graduate-level courses. The *DANTES Independent Study Catalog,* available at education offices of military installations, is the key to the independent study system. The catalog lists the participating colleges, the available courses, and the necessary course information.

All of the proficiency examinations described later in this chapter are available through DANTES. In addition, DANTES administers its own DANTES Subject Standardized Tests (DSSTs). The DSST Program is a series of examinations in vocational-technical areas. The DSSTs have been evaluated by the American Council on Education for academic credit recommendations. DANTES also administers professional certification examinations. Testing through the DANTES program, however, is available only to active-duty personnel.

Through formal agreements with nationally recognized certification organizations, DANTES is authorized to administer the certification examinations of the following groups:

- American Association of Medical Assistants
- American Medical Technologists
- Institute for the Certification of Engineering Technicians
- National Institute for Automotive Service Excellence
- Institute for Certification of Computer Professionals
- International Society for Clinical Laboratory Technicians
- Institute for Certified Professional Managers
- American Society for Quality Control
- National Association of Social Workers
- Administrative Management Society

A transcript of the grades and scores you may have earned through courses and examinations formerly offered by the United States Armed Forces Institute (USAFI), as well as scores earned through examinations offered by DANTES, are available through the DANTES Transcript Service, maintained by the Educational Testing Service (ETS) in Princeton, New Jersey. Both active-duty service members and veterans who took courses and tests through USAFI may apply to have their transcripts sent from ETS to the colleges and universities of their choice. For grades and scores earned prior to July 1, 1974, write to: ETS, Box 2879, Princeton, NJ 08541; no charge. For examinations completed after that date, send $2.00 to ETS, Box 2819, Princeton, NJ 08541.

An increasing number of colleges and universities, particularly those offering special adult programs, have adopted policies to permit credit for certain "in-house" training or continuing education courses given by your employer. The usual criteria for determining if noncollegiate sponsored instruction qualifies for college credit are: (1) College-level conceptual knowledge and/or specialized skills must have been taught; (2) the instructor must have been qualified to teach the course; (3) requirements must have been imposed for successful completion; and (4) classroom attendance must usually have been involved, although specialized independent study followed by a proctored exam may qualify. Basically, the course must have content equivalent to that which might also be found in a course offered by a college or university.

Examples of employer-sponsored instruction that might qualify for college credit are company in-house management seminars, police academy training, technical training provided in various industries, and hospital laboratory courses.

Many courses in continuing education could also qualify for college credit. A few examples are courses in effective speaking and human relations from Dale Carnegie & Associates, Inc.; income tax preparation courses offered by H & R Block, Inc.; real estate courses sponsored by a local board of realtors; finance courses offered by a local chapter of the American Institute of Banking; and various computer courses conducted by the Xerox Corporation.

Successful completion of such courses must be documented by a certificate of attendance or a letter from the sponsoring organization. You might also be asked to submit your course books and notes, if available, to further substantiate the course content. A syllabus, or course outline, prepared by the sponsoring organization will probably be required. Faculty members are usually called upon to evaluate noncollegiate courses and make recommendations as to how much, if any, credit should be granted.

Correspondence courses may also be evaluated for degree credit even if they were not taken through an accredited college. Many private correspondence schools offer fine courses that might be acceptable for degree credit.

The references applicable to credit for noncollegiate instruction are *The National Guide to Credit Recommendations for Noncollegiate Courses* (the latest edition, published by the American Council on

Education, lists credit recommendations for over 500 courses by over 40 organizations in several states except New York) and *A Guide to Educational Programs in Noncollegiate Organizations* (published by the University of the State of New York, it lists 800 courses conducted by some 70 organizations in New York State). Taken together, these two guides document the ever-increasing sources of credit available to you for certain courses taken in noncollegiate settings. College libraries and admissions offices are likely to have copies of these basic references.

Proficiency Tests to Document College-Level Learning: AP, ACT PEP, CPE, REDE, CLEP, GRE, Departmental Exams

Proficiency examinations can enable you to accelerate significantly your progress toward a degree. Thirty credits earned by examination may represent one year of full-time college attendance plus thousands of dollars in college costs. When you consider the potential benefits, proficiency examinations are often well worth the effort. Knowledge you have acquired through life experience or independent study in some subject commonly taught in college can often be documented by taking a test and achieving a score equal to or better than the average (based on scores achieved by college students who have completed a course in that subject). You may even receive credit equivalent to that college course. Although your practical knowledge may be limited, if you have an aptitude for the subject you can probably learn enough by studying a college text or review book to pass the exam. A wide variety of qualifying exams is available through several nationally recognized programs.

Advanced Placement (AP) Program

The Advanced Placement (AP) Program of the College Board is intended for high school students. Courses are given at high schools to prepare students for the AP exams, which, if passed, may entitle them to up to one year's advanced standing in college. Three-hour AP exams are given in May on several introductory college courses in the humanities, social sciences, physical sciences, languages, the arts, and mathematics. Arrangements to take AP exams must be made several months before the test date. Anyone can take the exams, even those who have not taken AP preparation courses and are not in high school; therefore, adults are eligible. While most colleges recognize the exams, they often disagree as to what constitutes an acceptable grade for granting credit. Some colleges will exempt students who pass AP exams from introductory course requirements, but will not allow credit. Other schools require that you repeat a similar exam after admission to validate your grade. Before taking AP exams it is wise to check out your college's (or prospective college's) policies. For information on college policies, see the latest edition of the College Board's *College Placement and Credit by Examination*. AP course description booklets, which include sample questions and a list of participating colleges, may also be purchased from the College Board, P. O. Box 2815, Princeton, NJ 08541. These publications are available in many libraries and guidance counselors' offices.

Proficiency Examination Program of the American College Testing Program (ACT PEP); College Proficiency Examination (CPE) and Regents External Degree Examination (REDE) of the Regents External Degree Program

ACT PEP examinations, like CLEP tests (described in the following section), are oriented more toward experiential learning than learning derived from classroom instruction. A variety of ACT PEP exams are offered to test conceptual knowledge in many aspects of business, social, and professional services. Unlike CLEP, study guides for ACT PEP tests are available. ACT PEP exams, though, may not be as widely recognized as CLEP exams. If your college will award credit for ACT PEP exams, you should write for a free booklet and registration packet to: ACT Proficiency Examination Program, P. O. Box 168, Iowa City, IA 52243. These examinations are the same as those offered in New York State as CPE-REDE (College Proficiency Examination and Regents External Degree Examination). For information, write to: RED-CPE Program, Cultural Education Center, Albany, NY 12230.

Incidentally, if you took an examination to gain admission to college, you might be eligible for advanced standing or equivalent course credit. The ACT Assessment Program (commonly called the ACT) of the American College Testing Program or the Achievement Tests of the College Board are used by some colleges to assess experiential learning. If you've taken such exams, you should determine if your college will evaluate the results for possible credit.

College-Level Examination Program (CLEP)

The College-Level Examination Program (CLEP) is designed specifically to document college-level knowledge acquired through life learning or independent study. This program of the College Board was founded on the premise that nontraditional learning is a viable alternative to classroom study—what you know is more important than how you learned it. The acceptance of CLEP is widespread; not only are CLEP exams used by colleges as criteria for granting credit but CLEP exam scores have also been employed by business, industry, and government as a measure of competence for licensing and as a criterion for advancement.

Many adult students with whom we have corresponded have expressed enthusiasm about CLEP. Coauthor Charles McCabe earned 18 CLEP credits. He thought that was quite good, then heard from Dawn Logan who earned 60 credits from CLEP.

You too may be able to earn CLEP credits and save yourself considerable time and money. To find out, you can obtain the free booklet, "CLEP Fact Sheet," by writing to: CLEP, Box 2815, Princeton, NJ 08541. As the College Board explains, "The tests are not easy; this booklet will give you an idea of their difficulty and your chances. But don't sell yourself short. If you are within striking distance, you can take steps to get yourself ready."

Two kinds of CLEP tests are administered, the general examinations and the subject examinations. The CLEP general examinations cover subjects usually studied by college freshmen and sophomores as a foundation for upper-division course work. Five general examinations, each taking 90 minutes, are offered. The exams cover English composition, mathematics, natural sciences, social sciences, and humanities. You may take only one or any combination of the general exams. All exams are entirely multiple choice; however, the English composition exam provides for an optional essay in lieu of the second half of the test. Credit granted by participating colleges for an acceptable score is usually 6 credits for each general exam or up to 30 credits for the entire battery of tests. CLEP tests are given the third week of each month, except for the English composition with essay examination, which is given only in October and June.

CLEP subject examinations are achievement tests covering a wide range of undergraduate courses. They are entirely multiple-choice, 90-minute tests. In addition, with few exceptions, each has an optional 90-minute essay that may or may not be required by the college from which credit is being sought. Credit for each subject exam varies; usually either 3 or 6 credits are granted for each test on which a passing score is achieved. The following subject areas are covered: business, dental auxiliary education, education, humanities, medical technology, nursing, sciences, and social sciences.

Each college has its own policies as to which exams are accepted, how many credits are granted, and what constitutes an acceptable test score. However, the Commission on Educational Credit of the American Council on Education provides general recommendations that are followed in many instances.

After reading the booklet "CLEP Fact Sheet," which briefly outlines the content of exams in the above areas, you may decide to take a CLEP exam or two. Or you might want to obtain more specific information by ordering the College Board booklet, "CLEP General and

Subject Examinations: Descriptions and Sample Questions." You can also request a free packet of registration information material consisting of a list of CLEP test centers, and registration information and forms. You may also want to consult the current edition of *College Placement and Credit by Examination*. This publication from the College Board "reports the policies of more than 1,500 colleges and universities toward granting placement and credit through Advanced Placement and CLEP. Also included are the policies of institutions that use the College Board Achievement Tests and the Test of Standard Written English for placement purposes."

Graduate Record Examination (GRE) Advanced Tests

GRE Advanced Tests were developed by the Educational Testing Service as devices for helping graduate schools assess students' undergraduate knowledge. Some external degree programs, though, use the tests to award substantial blocks of undergraduate credit in major subject areas. Information about the GRE Advanced Tests is available from Graduate Record Examination, Educational Testing Service, Princeton, NJ 08541.

Preparation for any of these standard proficiency tests is important. Rosemarie Sunderland, who reduced the time for a B.A. from eight years to less than half that time by taking proficiency exams, gives some practical advice: "While it is most important to know the test subject well, getting to know the location of the testing facility beforehand is also extremely important. On a pretest visit, looking for parking facilities, the building, and the rooms to be used for the exams will later save time and nerves. Arriving at the testing center without extra tension helps you to keep a clear head."

Departmental Exams

Many colleges permit students to take exams prepared by faculty members and receive credit for, and/or exemption from, specific courses offered by the college. Sometimes standard waiver examinations have already been developed for certain courses, and suggested study guides are provided to interested students. Some colleges may allow a matriculated student to take an advanced credit examination in any course offered by the school. However, the college might require that other course requirements, such as term papers and special projects, also be fulfilled to receive equivalent course credit. Departmental exams are often discouraged by faculty members who may view them as an unwarranted concession, or a threat to their livelihood, or simply an undesirable extra burden. Consequently, such exams are often unreasonably difficult. However, this is not always the case; if you have a good understanding of the subject matter, you have nothing to lose by ·asking the department chairman or faculty member for permission to take an exam to demonstrate that you have already mastered the course content. This is often referred to as "challenging" a course.

Caution should be exercised to avoid duplication of credits when taking proficiency exams. If you already have a course on your transcript or plan to take a course entitled Accounting I, for example, you would not also be granted credit for the CLEP Introductory Accounting subject exam. Duplication of credits through proficiency examination, life-learning assessment, noncollegiate course evaluation, and regular course work is a common dilemma encountered by adults in college. For this reason it is important to determine early in your adult college career which examinations you may be able to receive credit for. You would be wise to begin preparing for and taking these tests as soon as possible so you can plan your remaining courses without risk of duplication.

Credit for Experiential Learning

Special assessment of experiential learning is another way you might get degree credit from your college. It can be tailored by your college to your specific circumstances and designed to measure the degree of college-level knowledge you have acquired from your life experiences in several categories that might include:

Career

An executive secretary earned 23 credits in business law, communications, economics, finance, advertising, and personnel administration, all because of her previous work experience.

Volunteer work

A woman devoted much of her time to volunteer work for a hospital and several civic and religious organizations in her community (serving in responsible leadership positions). She earned a total of 21 credits in business, economics, political studies, psychology, and religion.

Travel

A woman loved to travel. Whether she was visiting the pyramids or some town not too far from her home, she looked for unusual things to see and do, and people to meet. She always kept notes and, upon her return from a trip, wrote a short travel column for her church's monthly newsletter. She received 16 credits for sociology and journalism based on the excellence of her columns across the years, supplemented by her detailed notes on lifestyles of people.

Unsponsored Independent Study

A handicapped woman, unable to travel, nevertheless "visited" many countries. Concentrating her efforts on one country at a time, with the special aid of her public library, she ordered books, movies, and filmstrips. With language tapes and tutoring she learned the language of the country she was "visiting," and she invited a foreign student from that country to live in her home while he or she was attending a university in the city. Her only "charges" to the student were conversations in the student's language. When she decided to get a degree, she was awarded substantial credit in the areas of language, literature, art history, political science, history, and several other disciplines.

Stephanie Phillips of Milford, Connecticut, was active in community theater. She says: "Prior to a careful reading of my college catalog, I never realized categorizing those experiences could eventually earn me three college credits."

These are typical examples of the innumerable forms of experiential learning for which colleges and universities throughout the United States have awarded credit. You, as an adult, have probably acquired knowledge equivalent to college-level learning through your life experiences. Some of this knowledge probably can be rewarded with college credit. The Council for the Advancement of Experiential Learning (CAEL) will help you locate colleges that will give such credit. Call (800) 638-7813 (toll free) or write CAEL, Lakefront North, Suite 300, Columbia, MD 21044. CAEL also publishes a directory, *Opportunities for Prior Learning Credit*, as well as several other helpful guides. Write for their publications list. Another book that might be of help is *I Can: A Tool for Assessing Skills Acquired Through Volunteer Experience* (Ramco Associates, 228 East 45th Street, New York, NY 10017). A program of the American College Testing Program, called COMP (College Outcomes Measures Project), provides an objective approach to evaluating general education knowledge for the purpose of awarding college credit. For more information, write to ACT, P. O. Box 168, Iowa City, IA 52243.

Documenting Experiential Learning

Understandably, you will not automatically get college credit for life experiences. You must be able to document what you have accomplished.

Varying procedures are designated by colleges to allow adult students to demonstrate the nature and extent of their life learning. Typically, the student prepares a portfolio for each academic area or subject in which life-learning credit is sought.

One student prepared nine life-experience portfolios because he wanted to be sure of receiving maximum credit. Each portfolio highlighted a different aspect of his ten-year career as a business executive and related that experience to specific academic areas. Each portfolio consisted of four sections:

- A concise cumulative life-learning outline listing positions held, special assignments, and appointments that related to the academic category
- A specific life-learning outline detailing the relevant duties and responsibilities involved in each of the posts listed in section one
- A brief objective summary of the nature of the life experience
- A subjective essay demonstrating personal growth and conceptual knowledge gained as a result of the life experience

Documentation accompanying the portfolios included:

- Letters from a former superior and a business associate verifying positions held and dates of employment, duties and activities, achievements, and expertise developed
- Copies of professional certificates and awards of recognition
- Copies of intracompany and outside correspondence (including a number of complimentary letters received from superiors)
- Samples of reports prepared, in-house newsletters edited, and training materials and company policies developed

This student's final award totaled 66 credits. Although the university's policy allowed for a maximum of only 30 life-experience credits toward its B.A. degree requirement, all 66 credits were posted on his college transcript, which would later be reviewed by potential employers and graduate schools. Perhaps most significantly, though, 30 credits represented one year of full-time study for him, and savings in tuition alone of more than $3,000.

Most colleges use alternative methods of demonstrating life learning in lieu of, or in addition to, written portfolios. The Regents External Degree Program uses a special assessment process—an individually designed examination (usually oral) that can be accompanied by a portfolio of the candidate's written or artistic products. The College of Public and Community Service at the University of Massachusetts at Boston accepts a variety of methods, including written portfolios, oral examinations, analysis of a project, and on-site evaluation. Thomas A. Edison College in New Jersey requires a student to demonstrate proficiency through oral or written reports, submission of a portfolio, performances, or "other appropriate means." In any case, it probably would be a good idea to review your college's undergraduate catalog and identify any courses related to your life experience.

You may want to submit additional supportive material, such as copies of correspondence, samples of your literary or technical work, or examples of your artwork. In the case of foreign languages, music, or the performing arts, you will probably be asked to demonstrate your proficiency. Colleges normally require documentation of work experience and accomplishments. This usually means that you must submit letters from present and past employers detailing dates of employment and positions held, and verifying specific achievements. Documentation might also take other forms such as articles in newspapers or periodicals, copies of theater or concert programs, tape recordings, videotapes, and official records or documents. In addition, you might be interviewed by the evaluator.

The key to relating life experience to college learning is to establish that the experience resulted in your acquiring conceptual knowledge. Conceptual knowledge should not be confused with skill, which is the ability to carry out some function or activity, although there is sometimes a fine line separating the two. For example, the ability of an experienced tax-return preparer to complete accurate tax returns may not demonstrate knowledge of the fundamental concepts of our tax structure (an integral part of most college tax courses).

It is best to undertake the evaluation process as soon after matriculation as possible because your life-learning credit award could duplicate courses you've already taken. And it might also have a bearing on which courses you should take to satisfy specific degree requirements. One student at an Arkansas college put off his life-experience evaluation until he was 6 credits short of his B.A. degree, only to discover in dismay that his life experience award for education totaled 18 credits. (He had developed and taught a course for businessmen.) Had he not procrastinated, he would have avoided two semesters of part-time study and saved over $1,200 in tuition. This highlights an important point: The credit you may receive from life learning equals time and money—often, a lot of both.

In this chapter we have tried to show you that your degree may be closer than you realize. As an adult you have a significant advantage over younger students. Because you have lived longer and have already had credit-worthy courses or experiences, you should be getting at least some credit for what you already know.

5
Getting Accepted by a College

How do I apply, and how can I enhance my chances of being accepted?

Admission Prospects

If you are worried about getting accepted at college, you shouldn't be. Don't be apprehensive about the detailed admissions criteria outlined in most college catalogs, such as high school study prerequisites, recommendations, and college admission test scores. The chances are good that such requirements may not even apply to you as an adult, and if they do, alternative means of satisfying them are probably available.

Of course, merely being an adult will not guarantee you admission to the college of your choice. The screening process for admission to top schools is highly selective for all candidates since the number of qualified applicants far exceeds the number that can reasonably be accommodated. Yet adults have been admitted to prestigious schools. The *New York Times* carried an article by Harry Gersh who was admitted to Harvard as a freshman at age 63. Mr. Gersh explained: "I bothered the admissions office until they agreed to let me in." Then the *Times* provided a follow-up three years later when Mr. Gersh graduated—*magna cum laude!* The point is, if you are as qualified as the competition (and many adults are), you stand a good chance of being admitted to the college of your choice.

Entrance Requirements for Adults

Many colleges and universities have established special (written or unwritten) admissions criteria for adults. The following excerpt from a recent catalog of Towson State University in Maryland is typical:

Mature Adults Policy
Towson State . . . guarantees admission to a mature student regardless of the student's previous academic records or standing. Students are required

to have a high school diploma or equivalency, and have a three-year break in their formal education in order to be admitted under this policy. Applicants are required to submit a formal application and official transcripts of any and all academic work attempted, but are excused from entrance test requirements.

Towson State, like many other postsecondary institutions, has recognized that an academic record as an adolescent frequently bears little relationship to an individual's academic potential as an adult. Even if a college you are considering does not have a "mature adults policy," you can probably still enroll as a nonmatriculated or "special" student and take courses for credit. At a later date the college would assess how well you are doing, and then if you are qualified for matriculation based on your college performance, the credits will be applied toward your degree.

Obtaining a High School Equivalency Diploma

You do not have to be a high school graduate in order to enroll at many colleges. You may qualify either by demonstrating your capacity for doing college-level work as just described, or by passing a high school equivalency examination.

The state education department of some states such as New Jersey have provisions to award high school equivalency diplomas to individuals without requiring them to take a test. The diploma goes to residents who successfully complete at least 24 credits of college course work. Your state may have a similar provision. Even if the college you wish to attend will not allow you to take courses without being matriculated, you might be able to take your first 24 credits at another local college and then transfer. If this option is not available to you, or if you prefer to become matriculated right away, you can take the high school equivalency examination.

This examination, more widely known as the GED (General Educational Development) test, is administered nationally at various times throughout the year. Information on the GED and locations of test centers can be obtained from your local high school or state education department.

The GED examination is made up of five individual tests in the following categories: writing skills, social studies, natural sciences, reading comprehension, and mathematics. Each test takes two hours, and the entire series of five tests is administered over a two-day period. You can prepare for the GED test by obtaining a study guide from your library or bookstore. After passing the GED test, you will receive a certificate that is the legal equivalent of a regular high school diploma.

Applications: Forms, Essays, Presenting Career and Life Experience Most Effectively

Undergraduate admission application forms for most colleges and universities are fairly short and straightforward. They are generally divided into four sections: (1) a statement of the program, location, and status for which you are applying; (2) personal information about yourself; (3) details of your academic background and credentials; and (4) supplementary information needed as input for the admissions committee's decision.

In addition you may be asked to complete a financial aid application (if requesting aid) and a student information sheet containing a summary of certain data from your application (used for classification and statistical purposes). These supplements to your application may or may not have bearing on the institution's admission decision.

Transcripts of your highest level of schooling are usually required (but often for adults merely as a formality). These may be difficult to get because of the time elapsed, but usually not impossible.

In the supplementary information section you should list any significant continuing education courses you have successfully completed, including employer and armed forces training programs. Any professional certifications earned such as teaching, nursing, or real estate licenses should also be mentioned. You might also consider attaching a copy of your résumé or a short autobiography and copies of any awards or letters of commendation you've received. If you have any doubt as to the strength of your academic credentials, you might consider enclosing an essay written to demonstrate your strong motivation to pursue a college education at this stage in your life. In the essay you could comment on your previous academic, employment, or personal experiences and the ways in which you feel they relate to your current desire to attend college. If you submit an essay it should be grammatically correct and carefully written and rewritten to be clear and concise. Otherwise, the essay might be detrimental rather than helpful to your admission chances. Ask someone who is a good writer to critique your essay, then have it typed and proofread. Keep a copy for possible later use.

Letters of Recommendation: Whom to Ask, How to Ask

Letters of recommendation are not usually required for admission to colleges at the undergraduate level. However, some colleges, particularly the most selective ones, may request them. Since it is probably not possible or practical for you to look up former teachers, the college will probably allow you to submit letters from other individuals who know you. Present or past superiors at work, or professional acquaintances, can usually comment on your potential ability to do college-level work. If you happen to know a college professor, his recommendation might be ideal. Normally, you should ask someone who is a college graduate since that person would know from experience what qualities are required to succeed as a college student. Obviously, it is best to find someone who has achieved a high professional station in life, such as a doctor, lawyer, top executive, or legislator. The person you choose should know you fairly well and respect you.

Composing a good letter of recommendation can be a difficult and time-consuming task. You should do whatever you can to lessen the effort required by the writer. Be specific about what the letter should include, such as how long the person has known you, in what capacity, why the person is qualified to comment on your ability to do college-level work, and statements attesting to your ability, motivation, and discipline. Some schools may eliminate this problem by providing a form with specific questions to be answered by the person recommending you.

College Entrance Examinations: College Board SAT and Achievement Tests; ACT

Although some colleges do not require standard admission tests for adults, some will want to see your scores on one of the two nationally recognized college entrance examinations: the College Board's Scholastic Aptitude Test (SAT) or the American College Testing Program's exam (ACT Assessment). Some colleges give applicants the option of submitting scores from either the SAT or the ACT, while others specify one test or the other. Some of the more selective schools also require College Board Achievement Tests, which are designed to measure proficiency in specific subjects. English composition is frequently one of the required tests. Other subject tests cover history and social studies, literature, mathematics, sciences, and various foreign languages.

The SAT is divided into five sections; two are in verbal skills, two are in mathematics, and a fifth, which does not count toward scores, may be in either verbal or math skills. The questions are all multiple choice, and you are given 30 minutes to complete each section. In addition, the half-hour Test of Standard Written English is given along with the SAT to determine placement at the appropriate level in a freshman English course. The test does not affect your SAT score. The mathematical sections of the SAT include questions on algebra, elementary geometry, and arithmetic, while the verbal sections include reading comprehension, antonyms, analogies, and sentence completions. Information and registration forms for the SAT and College Board Achievement Tests can be obtained from high school guidance counselors or by writing to the College Board Admissions Testing Program, Box 592, Princeton, NJ 08541.

The ACT Assessment consists of the following four separate tests: English usage, mathematics usage, social studies reading, and natural sciences reading. You are given 35 to 50 minutes to complete each test, and the questions, like those on the SAT, are all multiple choice. The questions focus on analytical and problem-solving skills and also require some general subject knowledge. ACT information and registration forms are available from high school counselors or from ACT Registration, P. O. Box 414, Iowa City, IA 52243.

Barbara Dunn of George Mason University, Fairfax, Virginia, describes her experience in taking the SAT:

> A visit to the local university yielded a week's worth of reading in the form of literature, catalogs, and application blanks, and started the process of reentry after I had been out of school for 25 years. Because I wanted to be a regular day student, I would have to take the SAT at the local high school. Fortunately, my son was a student at the same school and also was taking his SAT, so I was familiar with the application procedure. He was relieved when we were assigned separate dates for the test, but I wasn't. I would have been glad to have had someone to lean on, even my own unfriendly, embarrassed teenager. On a Saturday morning, I arrived at the school cafeteria with my sharpened pencils and settled into a folding chair. Luckily for me, my son's calculus teacher was there, and she was good moral support. Whenever I would start to get numb, my attention would drift and I'd look up, and she would wink at me and smile. Finally, it was over and there was nothing to do but go home and wait for the grades to be mailed. It was all worthwhile—my scores allowed me to enter George Mason University.

Since Barbara took that test in Virginia, a New York State "truth in testing law" has required testing services to provide students with post-test disclosure of the questions, their answers, and scores. The Educational Testing Service (a nonprofit agency that administers various standard tests) later endorsed the principles of the law on a national basis. No longer do students have to remain in the dark as to why they got a particular score.

Can you prepare yourself to score higher on the entrance examinations? This is a hotly debated issue. The Federal Trade Commission conducted a study that showed that "underachievers might be helped by coaching to improve their test scores by an average of 25 points on both the verbal and mathematical portions of the Scholastic Aptitude Test. . . . Both the College Board, which sponsors the SAT, and the Educational Testing Service, which administers it, said after release of the report they remain convinced that most of the 1.5 million students who take the test each year cannot be helped by coaching programs"

(*Higher Education and National Affairs*, American Council on Education, vol. 27, no. 22, June 1, 1979).

You can find preparation courses advertised in the newspapers of many large cities. Some people say that such courses can merely help you to become familiar with the test format and that you could do this at much less cost by studying one of the various available books that contain sample questions. It may be true that you cannot quickly overcome problems such as poor reading comprehension and poor math skills, but a good test preparation course might teach you some valuable techniques to lessen such shortcomings. Certainly, the minimum you should do to prepare for the test is to familiarize yourself with the format and to practice answering some sample questions. If you are unhappy with your scores the first time around, you may take the tests again. However, the testing services will present all scores to the college admission office. Colleges have different procedures when presented with several scores; some consider only the highest while others may also take the low scores into consideration.

Remember, however, that many colleges have special admissions criteria for adults. Even if the admissions policy clearly stipulates that SAT or ACT scores are required of all applicants, you might want to request an exception. As a mature adult, your aptitude for college-level study can probably be determined by an evaluation of your experience and achievements in life.

Deadlines in the Admissions Calendar

Your timing may be very important to you as an adult pursuing a college degree. Consider John, a young business executive from Philadelphia who finally accepted the idea that his lack of a college education was a major bar to career advancement. He had decided to apply to a famous school of business. He knew he had plenty of time before the September semester, and since it was just before Christmas he decided to wait until after the holidays to begin preparing his application. This turned out to be a serious mistake. The deadline for submission was January 1st for September admissions, and he could not get an extension—the school was already overflowing with applications. Now John would have to wait another year to apply. Since he was already concerned about completing his degree before his age began to make a difference to potential employers, he decided he could not wait. As a result of his ignorance of deadlines in the admissions calendar of that institution, he ended up enrolling in a lesser school that had a later admissions deadline. He always regretted missing his chance to apply to that other school of business.

Many colleges accept enrollments twice a year, in the fall and spring. Colleges on trimester or quarter systems often admit students three or four times a year, at the start of each semester. Some colleges accept applications after their stated deadline. Also, a large percentage of colleges have a "rolling" admissions policy, which means that applications will be considered as soon as they are received and decisions on admission are rendered soon thereafter.

You should note the admissions deadline as soon as you decide to apply. This is especially important if you want to attend a selective school since they are usually firm on their deadlines. Also, you will need sufficient time to do a good job on your application and have your transcripts and any other necessary documents mailed to the college.

Personal Interviews

Interviews at most colleges are not usually part of the selection process, but they may be for special adult programs. An interview is often the best way to evaluate the motivation and potential success of an adult college applicant.

If you are asked to come for an interview, be prepared to comment on why you want to go to college at this point in your life and why you are interested in that particular college. The motivation you display through your response to these questions could overcome a great deal of deficiency in your academic record.

You should also come prepared to ask specific questions. This will enable you to be somewhat in control of the interview and will demonstrate your thoughtful concern about choosing this particular college and one of its programs.

The success of your interview depends on the impressions you make. Favorable impressions are formed by projecting confidence, by having a good appearance, and by being straightforward. Confidence, of course, cannot be easily faked. If you are well prepared, well groomed, neatly dressed, and on time, you will probably be as confident as you can hope to be. Casual dress on college campuses today is accepted. What is appropriate for daily life on campus, though, may not be suitable for an adult going on an important interview. It is best, we believe, to be open and honest. The admissions officer will most likely appreciate your candor and be just as straightforward with you. This approach should make the interview a more pleasant experience for both of you.

For Those Who Decide at the Last Minute

If you decide at the last minute that you want to go to college, you have an option called "walk-on." It occurs during the two- or three-week period starting just before school opens, continuing through registration, and ending just after registration. Sometimes even very good schools discover quite late that their projections of enrollment are not being met. If you show up during this period you might be accepted. Probably you will be asked to get your transcripts and SATs or ACTs sent later.

The "walk-on" may be possible but usually only up to the "add date"—the last day for added courses (which is announced in the college calendar). You might be allowed to get in shortly after that date, but with each passing day your chances diminish since you are missing classes at the beginning of the term.

One note of caution: You should try to get your application processed so you can enroll as a matriculated student even if you have not decided upon a major. In general, nonmatriculated students are ineligible for most sources of financial aid.

STUDENT PROFILE
Mildred Troupe

I grew up in the rural area of southern Georgia. Actually, woods is a better characterization of the area where I was reared. Our nearest neighbor was two miles away. However, I had plenty of company. My family was a relatively large one—five brothers and seven sisters. I was the sixth child.

As a high school student, it had always been my desire to continue my education by going to college. But I had to forego my desire for a college education after my high school graduation due to a family crisis, and later, as a result of my ever-changing work shift. When I finally got to college, it was a dream come true.

When I was 16 years old my mother died. At that time, there were nine of us still at home. The youngest—my baby brother—was three months old. I was the second oldest at home. My mother had taught every member of the family who could understand the importance of accepting responsibility. Her teachings were instrumental in keeping us together.

When I graduated from high school it was my turn to take over the responsibility of managing the household. After a year and a half of carrying out my obligations, my father remarried. Subsequently I moved to Brooklyn, New York, in hopes of pursuing a career and a life of my own. At that time, college was the farthest thing from my mind.

There I was, a naive young girl from Fitzgerald, Georgia—experiencing a culture shock and filled with anxiety—determined to succeed. Less than three weeks after I arrived in Brooklyn, I started work as a long-distance telephone operator. Advancing in my job was now uppermost in my mind, and that is exactly what I did. Within four years, I was promoted to assistant manager.

Advancement in my job was not the only thing I had accomplished. Being out in the business world aided in transforming a taciturn young Southern girl into an assertive woman.

Hungry for a change and a day shift, I accepted a lateral transfer into the sales department as a service adviser. Initially the work was challenging and gave me a great sense of accomplishment. But before I realized it, the saddest thing that can happen to an individual happened to me: I became complacent.

The encouragement of my supervisor to attend college was unsuccessful. For only a high school graduate, I made an excellent salary. Why should I go to college?

After two years as a service adviser I became bored and discontented. I watched the college graduates in my department being promoted; some had less job knowledge than I. The limited upward mobility for noncollege graduates, boredom, and an innate thirst for knowledge rekindled my high school desire to attend college.

I selected Pace University's two-and-a-half-year National Council of Negro Women (NCNW) program, which awards an associate of arts degree. Several acquaintances had attended this program, and all of them spoke highly of it. Applying was much easier than I expected it would be. I was relieved to learn that no admissions test was required, just an interview. And my application was completed in one day—I had visualized much red tape. Much of the paperwork was handled by the NCNW staff, who were very cooperative and supportive throughout my college experience. I was even allowed to begin classes as an unmatriculated student pending receipt of my high school transcript by the admissions office.

The ten-week cycled program combines liberal arts and business subjects. And the classes are scheduled conveniently—I attend two nights a week and one Saturday a month.

Before I started college, I established scholastic goals. I planned to strive for straight A's, and accept not less than B's. I realized my goals were high, but I have always been a believer in a person's ability to accomplish anything he or she wants to.

When I entered college, I experienced the same anxiety I felt when I applied for my job with the New York Telephone Company. My fears were soon dispelled. Many of the students in my class worked for the same company as I, two of whom I had known before entering college. We developed an instant camaraderie.

Adjusting to college life is not easy, but the rewards are great. The time I spent studying and doing homework has paid off. After almost two years, I am still maintaining my initial scholastic goal of straight A's. A price tag cannot be placed on what I have learned. Deciding to enter college was the turning point of my life. I intend to continue for my bachelor of arts degree.

6

Financing a Degree

How can I possibly pay for it?

by CAROL MACKINTOSH
Director of Financial Aid
Utica College of Syracuse University, Utica, New York
and GLENN PERRONE
University Director of Student Financial Assistance
Pace University, New York, New York

Financial Aid

One aspect of going to college that concerns adult students greatly is the question of expense. You may find yourself wondering not only how you can afford tuition and books, but also how you can support yourself and your family if you have one. Many adults give up education because they don't know that there is financial aid to help pay for college and living expenses or because they simply don't know where to get application forms or how to fill them out. Preventing that waste is what this chapter is all about.

The primary goal of financial aid programs is to provide access and opportunity to those students who could not otherwise attend college without monetary assistance. The complexity of financial aid programs, though, has brought with it a great deal of confusion regarding the application processes associated with the many and varied assistance sources that are at a student's disposal. To avail themselves of financial aid programs, college students must apply for them amid a maze of forms, acronyms, instructions, and requests for information.

Fortunately, the college or university nearest you almost certainly will have a financial aid office to help you. (All institutions administering federal funds are required to have one.) Even if you are not planning to attend that institution, you probably will find this office willing to advise you. Someone in the office will help you explore options and provide you with information on current government, college, and private sources of aid and how to apply for it. There is no better way to get specific financial aid information than to visit the financial aid office of the colleges you are considering attending. However, this chapter and the Financial Aid References at the end of it provide you with sufficient general information about financial aid to enable you to prepare intelligently for such a visit or even to "go it on your own" until you actually register at the college where you have been accepted.

Qualifying for Financial Aid

The most common way to qualify is to document your financial need. We'll turn to this crucial question of documented need in a few minutes. Meanwhile, we'll explore other avenues.

Although the preponderance of financial aid is available to meet need, some grants (often called scholarships) are given to students in recognition of academic, athletic, artistic, or other abilities. Some colleges also have special funds targeted to help certain groups. For example, many colleges have opportunity programs for students who have poor or unusual academic backgrounds and who are in extreme financial need. Many also have special returning-student or women's grants designed for older students. Often colleges offer senior citizens free tuition. You should state your special circumstances and ask the colleges in which you have interest to send you information on such programs to see if you qualify.

Other than the above, there are five general sources of money you may be able to use while you are a student. Each of these categories of funds requires research to see if you qualify. To aid you in the process, here are some facts on these five sources.

1. Aid from Employers

Many employers make funds available for employees to improve their job skills, usually reimbursing them for courses satisfactorily completed (or sometimes only for those completed with a grade of B or higher). Lynn Gallagher of Baldwin-Wallace College, Berea, Ohio, began taking college courses when she discovered that part of her employer's benefit program included tuition refunds. The personnel office should be able to tell you if student aid programs exist at your place of employment.

Colleges and universities in particular frequently offer their employees tuition remission benefits. This means that if you are employed at such an institution, you would be able to take courses free or at reduced tuition at that institution or possibly even at another one. Benefits may extend also to your spouse and children. Some adults have taken jobs at educational institutions specifically to qualify for this aid. Consider the financial impact of having your entire family educated at no or reduced tuition! That may be of greater value than your salary for several years.

2. Aid from Professional Organizations, Businesses, and Other Agencies

Professional organizations, businesses, and other groups sometimes offer aid to their members, or to families of their members, or to potential members, or simply to deserving people. For example, a professional women's organization might make educational funds available to women who are seeking to enter that professional field. Sabina Leonard of Trocaire College in Buffalo, New York, says: "There are a lot of grants that go unused every year simply because people don't know about them. I found that a letter to a congressman works wonders. My congressman sent me a list of companies and organizations that make grants available. My girl friend and I sent letters to each company, and she received a $300 yearly grant from Clairol through the Business and Professional Women's Association."

You should search for such sources. (See Financial Aid References, end of chapter.) In particular, check with organizations to which you or your spouse belong.

3. Aid from Social Agencies

Some social agencies provide funds to students even if the primary function of the agency has nothing to do with education. It is wise to investigate carefully your rights with each sort of agency. Unfortunately, we have discovered that counselors in some agencies simply do not know what educational aid they administer. The college's financial aid counselor may be able to give you advice concerning local interpretations of laws within the agencies with which you are involved. However, you will be responsible for actual application for aid from the agency. Below are some major agency sources of aid to students:

Veterans Administration

Benefits are available to veterans with other than dishonorable discharges. The benefits for which a veteran may be eligible depend on when he or she was in the service and if he or she incurred any disability. In certain cases, spouses of veterans with service-connected death or permanent disability are eligible for veterans' educational benefits. Your local Veterans Administration regional office can help you find out exactly which programs are available to you.

Vocational Rehabilitation

Funds are available for students who have a physical or mental impairment that will put a limitation on employment. If you have such an impairment, you should make arrangements to meet with a vocational rehabilitation counselor who can usually be found through your state or territory government. You will be required to have a medical examination and may also be asked for financial information.

Aid to Native Americans

Aid is available through the U.S. Bureau of Indian Affairs for both four-year college programs and vocational training. Application forms are available from the Bureau of Indian Affairs Office in the Department of the Interior. If you are one-fourth Indian, Eskimo, or Aleut, are enrolled as a member of a tribe, band, or group, and have financial need, you should pursue this aid. Many states also have aid programs for Native Americans. You should contact your state government concerning Native American programs.

Social Security

In the past, educational benefits were provided for dependents of deceased or disabled parents. This program will be phased out by 1985. The only programs that may be helpful to older students are widow or widower benefits for parents. If you are a widow or widower with children, you should see your local Social Security office.

Social Services

Funds may be available to help you support your children, particularly if you are a single parent. In many social service agencies, there is a work incentive program. Under this program, it is possible to receive vocational training from a postsecondary school for about one year. If you are considering a program such as licensed practical nurse studies or secretarial science, and you receive welfare, you should ask about work training.

Food Stamps

Often students can qualify under the Food Stamp Program. Check with your local social service agency.

4. Aid Available to Students in Specialized Fields

Some money is available to students who intend to pursue certain professions immediately after graduation. On the national level, these programs include nursing programs and Reserve Officers' Training Corps. Details of eligibility are given in Major Sources of Undergraduate Financial Aid at the end of this chapter.

Some states and colleges have specialized aid for students taking certain academic majors. Ask either the college you are considering or your state education department to inform you if such aid is available.

5. Aid from Lending Institutions

Two kinds of loan programs are available to students who are enrolled at least half-time in a participating postsecondary school. The Guaranteed Student Loan (GSL), which generally comes from a commercial bank, credit union, savings and loan association, or other lender, is available to all students with financial need, as determined by the appropriate needs-analysis formula. Students may qualify under formulas that financial aid officers are qualified to interpret for you.

If an independent student (one not dependent on parents for financial aid) fails to qualify for the GSL under the formulas, the student may apply for a loan under the second loan program, Auxiliary Loans to Assist Students (ALAS). The ALAS loan carries higher interest and a more immediate payback period. It should be considered only after the possibility of getting a GSL has been thoroughly explored.

Having outlined several ways you may qualify for aid, we want to remind you that most students qualify for aid by demonstrating financial need. Therefore, the remainder of this chapter will be devoted to an explanation of how you apply, how the need system works, and what kinds of aid are available.

Applying for Financial Aid

To document financial need, most colleges request a statement of a family's financial strength. Factors such as income, assets, size of a family, number of family members in college, and indebtedness play a role in determining a given student's ability to pay for college expenses. Many students typically apply to more than one college, particularly new students. Consequently, for the convenience of student and college alike, most institutions ask that prospective students use either the Financial Aid Form (FAF), published and processed by the College Scholarship Service, Princeton, NJ 08541, the Family Financial Statement (FFS), published and processed by the American College Testing Program, Iowa City, IA 52243, or the Application for Federal Student Aid, processed under the auspices of the federal government. Any of these services will provide your financial information to the colleges you designate, eliminating the necessity for you to file numerous financial aid applications. Because of processing time, you should complete one of these forms as soon as you know you are going to enroll, even if you have not been accepted at a college. Forms can be obtained from a high school guidance office, a college financial aid office, or the services at the addresses given.

Establishing Need

The vast majority of financial aid given by colleges and the federal and state governments in this country is granted only to meet documented financial need. Financial need is defined as the difference between your cost of going to a particular college and the money you (and your spouse, if you have one) can provide.

As the first step in establishing need, the college that intends to offer you admission will establish your cost of going to that school. This cost itemization for each incoming student who applies for aid is called the student's budget. The budget will include the cost of tuition and books, and living expenses such as food, housing, transportation, child care, and so forth. These budgets vary from college to college according to the student's tuition, and even within colleges according to the student's living situation.

Consider the case of Julia, a divorced woman with two children to support, living expenses of $5,100, a $3,200 tuition expense, and a $300 cost for books at college X. Her total budget at college X is $8,600. Julia's budget would be different at college Y where the tuition is $700, and she needs $300 additional transportation money because college Y is farther from her home. Her total budget at college Y would be $6,400: $700 for tuition, $300 for books, and $5,400 for living expenses.

	College X	College Y
Tuition	$3,200	$ 700
Books	300	300
Living Expenses	5,100	5,400
Budget	$8,600	$6,400

As the second step in establishing need, after the budget is set, a college will decide what money is available from you (and your spouse) to meet college expenses, according to the information you have provided on an FAF, FFS, or Application for Federal Student Aid form. In Julia's case, colleges X and Y would consider her net income of $1,000 and the $2,400 she receives in child support as money available to meet her expenses. Since she has no major assets, owns no home, and has no major indebtedness, these factors are not considered. At both colleges X and Y, Julia would have a family contribution of $3,400 (net income of $1,000 plus child support of $2,400).

Only after a budget is established and your contribution has been figured can the college determine if you have financial need. If your contribution is less than the budget, you are eligible for aid. The higher the budget, the more likely you are to have need. In Julia's case, she has different needs at the different colleges due to the difference in the budgets.

	College X	College Y
Budget	$8,600	$6,400
Family Contribution	3,400	3,400
Documented need, or eligibility for aid	$5,200	$3,000

It is important to note a few things here. Budgets vary from school to school, but, generally, family contribution does not change from school to school. Since the amount of financial aid that you can receive is a function of the college's budget and your ability to contribute monies toward that budget, you may qualify for more aid at a college with high tuition than at a college with low tuition. In Julia's case, she qualifies for $5,200 in aid at the high-cost school and $3,000 at the low-cost school. Thus an "expensive" college might be your better bargain. *Do not assume you can't afford to go to a quality institution.*

Types of Aid Available to Meet Need

Financial aid to meet need takes the form of either a grant, a loan, a part-time job, or some combination of these three. Grants (or scholarships) are direct awards, and repayment is not required. Loans are funds that must be repaid. Loans are usually guaranteed by some agency and offered at low interest; repayment is usually due after you leave college. Part-time employment provides an opportunity to earn money. The college decides whether to give a grant, a loan, part-time employment, or a package that consists of a combination of types of aid. Our friend Julia could receive the following types of packages:

	School X	School Y
Budget	$8,600	$6,400
Family Contribution	3,400	3,400
Need	$5,200	$3,000
Grant	$3,200	$1,000
Loan	1,200	1,000
Employment	800	1,000
Package	$5,200	$3,000

In making up a financial aid package, the financial aid office first tries to help the student qualify for federal- and state-government grants that are student-based, meaning that the student applies directly to the government for consideration. To be eligible for these sorts of grants, you must have financial need and be attending an approved undergraduate institution on at least a half-time basis.

The federal student-based grant is called the Pell Grant, currently authorized in amounts from $200 to $2,600 per year. The maximum amount that actually is available in any one year, though, may vary with congressional appropriations and quite certainly is going to be significantly lower than $2,600. Part-time students have their awards proportionately reduced from the maximum yearly entitlement. You may apply for the Pell Grant using the FAF or FFS described above or by using a special Application for Federal Student Aid.

State student-based grant programs vary from state to state according to constitutional, legislative, or policy restrictions. For example, the most generous state aid programs exist in California (through the California Aid Commission Programs), Pennsylvania (the Pennsylvania Higher Education Grant Program), and New York (the Tuition Assistance Program). Because of the wide variations in state programs, as well as application procedures, you should direct your inquiries to the financial aid officer at your local college or to your local state scholarship agency. (See Appendix B.)

After helping the student apply for student-based aid from the federal and state governments, the financial aid office will refer the student to agencies from which she or he may receive funds. The agencies most often referred to were described earlier: the Veterans Administration, Vocational Rehabilitation, Bureau of Indian Affairs, Social Security, or social services.

Once all the sources from outside the college are exhausted, the financial aid office will begin to consider giving the student aid that is administered by the college. The most common forms of aid follow.

Supplemental Educational Opportunity Grant (SEOG)

The Supplemental Educational Opportunity Grant is for students who have been determined to have financial need and who, without the grant, would be unable to pursue or continue their higher education. This grant program is funded by the federal government and administered by the college. This means that, within the federal guidelines, the college decides who gets the money and how much. The awards currently range from $200 to $2,000, but these amounts may change, so check with a financial aid officer.

College Grants

These grants are funded and administered by the college. They are usually described in the college catalog or in the college's financial aid brochure.

National Direct Student Loan (NDSL)

This loan is jointly funded by the federal government and the college. There is no interest on the loan while a student is in school. Repayment with low interest begins six months after the student leaves school. If you enter certain fields of teaching or teach in designated schools, some or all of your loan may not require repayment.

College Work-Study (CWS)

This employment program is jointly funded by the federal government and the college. It provides part-time jobs for eligible students in private or public nonprofit organizations such as the college's campus library, a local hospital, or a youth agency. CWS is designed to provide a flow of income to assist students in meeting everyday educational expenses. Usually the salary received will be based on the current minimum wage, but it may also be a function of the type of work that is assigned and the ability of the student to perform that work.

In addition to aid programs, you may also be able to obtain employment at or near the college. Campus employment is funded entirely by the college and usually provides part-time employment on campus. Also, a wide variety of off-campus opportunities probably exists, particularly when a student is at a college located in or near an urban area. Additionally, cooperative education programs are available at many colleges. The popularity of the alternating employment/study feature of these programs seems to be growing. For more information regarding off-campus job opportunities, contact your college's employment/career planning center, financial aid office, or personnel office.

The financial aid packages that students receive vary greatly depending on the resources of a given student and the types of aid funds available. Following are three sample student packages that demonstrate the sort of differences that are possible at a school considering three students, each with a $7,000 budget:

		Student A	Student B	Student C
Budget		$7,000	$7,000	$7,000
Family Contribution		1,000	2,000	4,000
Documented Need		$6,000	$5,000	$3,000
Student-Based	Pell Grant	$1,800	$1,300	$ 800
Aid	State Grant	200	100	0
	Social Security	$ 0	$ 0	$ 0
	Veterans' Benefits	0	2,400	0
Agencies and Programs	Social Services	0	0	0
	Vocational Rehabilitation	500	0	2,000
	Work Incentive	0	0	0
	Indian Affairs	0	0	0

		Student A	Student B	Student C
	SEOG	$ 500	$ 0	$ 0
College- Administered Funds	College Grant	1,000	200	200
	NDSL	1,000	500	0
	CWS	1,000	0	0
	Campus Employment	0	500	0

After the financial aid office has exhausted its resources or if a student is unable to establish need, the office will refer the student to the Guaranteed Student Loan and/or a loan from the Auxiliary Loans to Assist Students program. These loans are the ones described above that come from a lending institution. In many instances, even if a student's need is met by student-based aid, agencies and programs, and the college, the student will be able to obtain these loans to supplement his or her financial aid.

If You Cannot Establish Need

If you cannot establish your financial need according to the prescribed procedures, yet you know you have need, you should be aware that you can discuss your situation with the staff of the financial aid office and they will help you find alternatives. There are several points you should talk over if you find yourself in this situation:

1. Was the budget used by the financial aid office realistic? If you can justify a higher budget, you may qualify for aid or additional aid.

2. Was the contribution expected of you (and your spouse) too high? Should it be adjusted due to some unusual noncollege expense you are facing?

3. Many colleges have payment plans that allow students to make their tuition payments over the entire semester rather than in one large payment at registration. The interest or bookkeeping charges are usually minimal. The plans are worth exploring if you don't receive aid or if you receive less aid than necessary to pay your tuition at registration.

A Few Final Points on Financial Aid

If you decide to continue your education and if you decide to pursue financial aid, the list of reminders below will help you through the complex world of financial aid. Most of these pointers apply whether you choose to attend part-time or full-time.

1. Make an appointment to meet a financial aid counselor at the college you are interested in attending if you can travel to it; otherwise ask a counselor at a nearby college for assistance. As Sabina Leonard of Trocaire College puts it: "The main thing to remember is that no one can help unless you are willing to swallow your pride and let them know you need help."

   You may not be eligible to receive financial aid from every source that you consider, but you most decidedly will not get aid from those programs that you do not know exist, or for which you don't apply.

2. Read the college catalogs for financial aid deadlines and make sure that you meet them.

3. Complete the Financial Aid Form, the Family Financial Statement, or the Application for Federal Student Aid described earlier. Complete any other forms you may be given by the financial aid office.

4. Provide the college with all the documents it requests. Tax forms, letters from social agencies, and separation or divorce papers are among the forms often requested.

5. See any people outside the college in agencies or organizations that may be of help to you.

6. Reply to all mail you receive and keep copies. Never change an address without letting the financial aid office know.

7. If you decide you will need a Guaranteed Student Loan or a loan from the Auxiliary Loans to Assist Students program, apply six to eight weeks before you start college.

8. Once enrolled, you must reapply for financial aid each academic year since funding levels, eligibility criteria, and family circumstances invariably change from one year to the next.

9. If you are offered aid in a package that you cannot take advantage of—for example, part-time employment that is not possible because you would have to pay a baby-sitter—you should discuss changing types of aid in your package.

10. The details of some of the financial aid programs offered nationally are outlined at the end of this chapter, but of course are subject to legislative changes. However, while a reauthorization of the Higher Education Act undoubtedly will make changes in the administration of most federal assistance programs, the spirit and intent of the programs will likely remain intact. Although the data were current at the time this book was published, you may want to check details for any subsequent changes that might have occurred.

11. Federal toll-free numbers for information on student aid are: (800) 638–6700 (from all states except Maryland) or (800) 492–6602 (from Maryland).

The process for filing for financial aid is by no means a simple one, but the task is not as arduous and confusing as it seems at first glance. The methods of paying for your college education demand just as much of your time and attention as the choice of a college itself and the prospective field of study.

Fortunately, you need not struggle with paying your education without the guidance of a financial aid official. Whether you attend a public or a private college, live on campus or are a commuter, financial aid officers are committed to meeting your financial requirements to attend their institution.

Income Tax Deductions

As an employed or self-employed individual you may, under certain circumstances, claim an income tax deduction for qualifying educational expenses. However, if you are not currently engaged in a business or profession, even though you may be going to college to become qualified for employment, your educational expense is *not* deductible, according to the Internal Revenue Service (IRS).

To qualify, your curriculum must comply with one of the following two conditions listed in *Your Federal Income Tax*, a taxpayer's guide published annually by the IRS. You may deduct expenses that:

1. Meet the express requirements of your employer, or the requirements of law or regulations, for keeping your salary, status, or employment; or

2. Maintain or improve skills required in performing the duties of your present employment, trade, or business.

The IRS points out that qualifying expenses may be deducted even though you may be pursuing a degree. But only those courses that directly relate to your occupation qualify, regardless of whether or not they are part of your degree requirements.

Assuming you meet the above requirements, allowable educational expenses include tuition, books, supplies, and course-related fees and expenses. In addition, if you go to school during the same day that you go to work, you may deduct the cost that you incur in traveling between your school and work locations. (Commuting between your school or work location and your home is not deductible.) This transportation expense is allowable even if you make an incidental side trip home or elsewhere, but the distance must be computed as if you had gone directly between your job and school locations.

Allowable transportation expenses include the cost of operating your car, or the current standard mileage rate allowed by the IRS, plus parking fees and tolls. If you use public transportation, you may deduct your actual fares. The entire cost of a trip away from home for qualifying educational purposes may also be deducted as explained by the IRS (*Your Federal Income Tax*):

> If you travel away from home primarily to obtain education, the expenses of which are deductible, you may deduct your expenditures for travel, meals, and lodging while away from home. However, if you engage in incidental personal activities, you may not deduct the part of your expenses used for personal activities.

In addition to educational and travel expenses, you may be eligible for a tax credit for child care or disabled-dependent care. To qualify, you must meet the following conditions outlined in *Your Federal Income Tax* published by the IRS:

1. You must be married and must file a joint tax return (using form 1040) with your spouse.
2. You must be a full-time student for each of any five months during the tax year.
3. You must pay someone (other than your spouse or a person you can claim as your dependent) to care for your dependent who is disabled or under age 15.
4. Your qualifying dependent must live with you in a home that you maintain.
5. Your child-care and disabled-dependent care expenses must be incurred to allow your spouse to work.
6. Your spouse must have income from work during the year.

If you meet these requirements, you may claim a tax credit equal to 30 percent of your work-related expenses. The yearly work-related expenses, however, are limited to $2,400 for one qualifying dependent or $4,800 for the care of two or more qualifying persons. Therefore, you may reduce your tax liability in any year by up to $720 for one dependent or $1,440 if the expenses are for the care of two or more people. This credit is not merely a deduction from taxable income but, rather, a *direct credit* that reduces your taxes dollar for dollar.

Additional information on educational and related travel deductions, and child-care and disabled-dependent care credit, as well as single copies of *Your Federal Income Tax*, may be obtained free from your local IRS office. Deductible categories and amounts may change, so check with your local IRS office or income tax adviser for the latest data.

Major Sources of Undergraduate Financial Aid

Name	Type of Aid	Amount Available	Available for Part-Time Study (6 hours or more)
Pell Grant (formerly Basic Educational Opportunity Grant— BEOG)	G	$200-$2,600 per year.* Total varies by appropriation and also from college to college.	Yes
Supplemental Educational Opportunity Grant (SEOG)	G	$200-$2,000 per year	Yes**
National Direct Student Loan (NDSL)	L	Undergraduate student: $1,500 per year; $6,000 total. Graduate student, to include undergraduate amounts: $12,000 total.	Yes
College Work-Study (CWS)	J	Open	Yes**
State Student Incentive Grant (SSIG—name varies from state to state)	G	Varies from state to state.	Varies from state to state.
Guaranteed Student Loan (GSL)	L	Dependent student: $2,500 per year; $12,500 total. Independent student: $2,600 per year; $12,500 total. Graduate student: $5,000 per year; $25,000 total, to include undergraduate amounts.	Yes

Terms	Source of Funds	Application Sent to
Enrolled in eligible institution/making satisfactory progress.	Federal Government	Federal Government or its contractor
Enrolled in eligible institution/making satisfactory progress.	Federal Government	College
Enrolled in eligible institution/making satisfactory progress. No interest charged during school or for 6-month grace period afterward or during military service; 5% interest on unpaid balance once repayment begins.	Federal Government and College	College
Enrolled in eligible institution/making satisfactory progress.	Federal Government and College	College
Varies from state to state.	State and Federal Governments	Varies from state to state.
Enrolled in eligible institution/making satisfactory progress. No interest charged during school or for 6-month grace period afterwards; 9% interest on unpaid balance once repayment begins; 1% insurance premium is deducted from the original loan. An origination fee of at least 5% of the loan is payable to the lending institution at the time the loan is disbursed.	Lending Institutions	Lending Institution and College

Name	Type of Aid	Amount Available	Available for Part-Time Study (6 hours or more)
Auxiliary Loans to Assist Students (ALAS)	L	Independent undergraduate student: up to $2,500 per year; $12,500 total (in combination with GSL). Graduate student: $3,000 per year; $15,000 total (in addition to GSL).	Yes
Nursing Student Loan	L	$2,500 per year; $10,000 total.	Yes
Reserve Officers' Training Corps (ROTC)***	G	For 4-, 3-, 2-, 1-year scholarship students: full tuition, fees, books. $100 per month subsistence for last two years of study. All students: Approximately $600 for summer camp in junior year.	No
Nursing Scholarship	G	$2,000 per year	Yes

*Actual amount of award varies according to congressional appropriation, year by year.

**Also available for less than 6 semester hours of study.

***Facts given are for Army ROTC. Data for Navy and Air Force somewhat different. Details on these programs and Marine Corps Platoon Leaders Course available from nearest recruiter or campus ROTC office.

Terms	Source of Funds	Application Sent to
12-14% interest payment begins within 60 days after the loan is granted, but full-time students are eligible for a deferment. ALAS is available to independent students and also to parents of dependent students.	Lending Institutions	Lending Institution and College
Enrolled in eligible institution/making satisfactory progress. No interest charged during school or for 6-month grace period afterward or during military service. 4% interest on unpaid balance once repayment begins.	Federal Government and College	College
Scholarship students must be under 26 years of age upon graduation; nonscholarship under 28 with waiver possible for prior service. 4 years of active duty for scholarship students upon graduation; for other students, active duty for training for 3-6 months or 3 years of active duty.	Federal Government	Federal Government
Enrolled in eligible institution/making satisfactory progress. Student must have exceptional financial need.	Federal Government	College

Note: Data were current as book went to press. Program details may change as a result of legislation or executive action. Check with a financial aid officer for the most up-to-date information.

CODE: L = LOAN
      G = GRANT
      J = JOB

Financial Aid References

Free Brochures and Pamphlets

"The Basic Grant Formula," "Federal Financial Aid for Men and Women Resuming Their Education or Training," "Federal Student Financial Aid: Where Do You Fit In?" and "Student Consumers' Guide: Five Federal Financial Aid Programs." Pell Grant Program, P. O. Box 84, Washington, DC 20044.

"Educational Financial Aid Sources for Women." Clairol Loving Care Scholarship Program, 345 Park Avenue, New York, NY 10022.

"Meeting College Costs." College Board Publication Orders, P. O. Box 2815, Princeton, NJ 08541.

"A Selected List of Fellowship Opportunities and Aids to Advanced Education for United States Citizens and Foreign Nationals." National Science Foundation Publications, Room 235, 1800 G Street, N.W., Washington, DC 20550.

"Undergraduate Programs of Cooperative Education in the United States and Canada." National Commission for Cooperative Education, 360 Huntington Avenue, Boston, MA 02115.

Students having problems with Pell Grants or needing general information on student financial aid can call (800) 638-6700 or, in Maryland only, (800) 492-6602.

Booklets and Books

After Scholarships, What? Creative Ways to Lower Your College Costs—and the Colleges That Offer Them ("Cost-cutting options at 1,600 four-year colleges and universities"). Paperback, $8.00.

The A's and B's of Academic Scholarships ("For the student who has combined SAT scores of 1000 or higher or a composite ACT of 20 plus"). Paperback, $2.50.

Don't Miss Out: The Ambitious Student's Guide to Scholarships and Loans ("Seventeen fact-filled chapters teach you what you should know about college financing." One of the best guides available). Paperback, $2.50.

How to Pay for College: An Introduction to Financial Planning for Applicants to Selective Colleges ("Explains how to accurately estimate college costs and presents case studies of aid packages awarded to four families"). Paperback, $1.25.

Your Own Financial Aid Factory: The Guide to Locating College Money ("Contains a wealth of information for the college-bound and their parents. . . . The information on how to get loans, grants, and scholarships is well organized and easy to use"). Paperback, $5.95.

The five publications immediately above are available from Peterson's Guides, P. O. Box 2123, Princeton, NJ 08540. Books and booklets; new editions annually.

The College Blue Book: Scholarships, Fellowships, Grants, and Loans. New York: Macmillan Publishing Co., Inc., 866 Third Avenue, New York, NY 10022.

The College Cost Book, by the College Scholarship Service of the College Board. $8.95. *Paying for Your Education: A Guide for Adult Learners* (booklet). $3.50. College Board Publication Orders, P. O. Box 2815, Princeton, NJ 08541.

Need a Lift? American Legion's Education and Scholarship Program, P. O. Box 1055, Indianapolis, IN 46206.

Selected List of Postsecondary Education Opportunities for Minorities and Women. Superintendent of Documents, U.S. Government Printing Office, Washington, DC 20402. Booklet.

You may find these and other references in your local high school counseling office or library, or you may obtain them through interlibrary loan from your civic or college library.

7

Balancing Work, Family, and College Demands

How can I earn a living, be a part of a family, and go to college too?

by NANCY HAWKS
Summa cum laude *graduate of Adelphi University, Garden City, New York*

Time: A Priceless Commodity

Douglas E. Buck graduated from Whatcom Community College, then Evergreen State College, and is now making progress toward a master's degree at City College, Seattle, Washington. The questions facing you may be those he once asked himself: "How am I ever going to find extra time to go to school? If I do go to school, how much time will I have to spend doing homework and going to classes? I don't have extra time right now due to working and supporting a family. Or do I?"

Speaking from his own experience, Douglas states that "You actually have more time than you think you do. Your anxiety levels are high right now due to unanswered questions and the unsure feeling you get when you think about trying to put together work, family, and college demands."

When you return to school you will have to do some reorganizing of your life—maintaining previous schedules just won't work. Budgeting your time and energies is a must. As soon as you have made the decision to go to school, you might profit from analyzing your major activities and determining their relative importance. You will need to choose those you can eliminate entirely, pick the ones to be cut back, and decide which are to be retained because they are essential to you and the people around you. For instance, you may decide to relinquish your PTA duties and work less around the house, yet retain your place in the weekly tennis group since you consider it important to your physical and mental health. Despite how it sometimes seems, we are in charge of ourselves and how we spend our time. Unnecessary intrusions upon our precious time will not occur if we do not allow them to. A pleasant but firm "no" may be difficult to manage at first, but didn't a quick "yes" also begin as a habit?

A student at a California junior college, who is also the mother of three young boys, found studying difficult until she laid down the law: "I definitely discourage interruptions. The only information I want to receive is about anyone or anything on fire. Or if anyone is bleeding. And bloody noses don't count!"

Adult students need to create space for themselves in their daily existence—mental and emotional space. It will determine to some degree the success they will achieve as students. You might want to begin now and set aside a few hours of each day as strictly your own. Use this time to research a subject that interests you, or do some writing. If you feel that this is impossible, then perhaps your decision to return to school is a premature one.

Anne Seavey, an accounting student at Bentley College, Waltham, Massachusetts, says: "Time is the villain that must be dealt with if one is to succeed."

Time: villain or friend? Only *you* can decide which it's going to be.

Your Employer and You

Openness and understanding are important keys to a successful employer/employee relationship. If you are currently employed and plan to schedule your schooling around your work week there should be no conflict, but we think it is usually best to notify your employer of your plans.

Initially, the attitude of your employer toward you in your new role as a student may be negative. He or she may wonder whether you will be able to meet the demands of college work yet continue to be an effective employee. Your performance over a period of time will, of course, answer the question.

Purely by accident, a student in an Oklahoma college made a very positive connection with her employer from which they both benefited:

> I didn't tell a soul I had decided to go back to school until I had actually registered. Finally I mustered up my courage and told Hank, my supervisor, that I was now a part-time college student. As I was explaining I had worked out a schedule that wouldn't interfere with my hours on the job, I could see he was puzzled and somewhat annoyed. I felt very uncomfortable, even a little guilty, when I left his office. A few days later I was eating lunch at my desk and trying to wade through a tough reading assignment. I must have groaned out loud because Hank stopped short on his way out to lunch and asked what was the matter. I said, "This!" and I began

reading to him. When I finished the page he was smiling broadly. It turned out that he was totally familiar with the subject and began to explain it to me. When he had finished I realized that I understood it completely. I felt wonderful. So did Hank. And from that day on he's been my biggest booster. I think he's prouder of me than *me!*

It can be extremely difficult to juggle full-time employment with full-time schooling. If one or the other can be part-time, so much the better. An ideal job might be one in which you can spend some of your time on your studies. In the last century, several writers found work as customs agents, and turned out their masterpieces while waiting for a boat to come in. Have you ever considered taking a job as a night watchman where there are few rounds to make, or as a night clerk in a motel?

Fortunately, many students are employed by companies that have tuition-refund programs. And in some companies, employees are even released for part or full days so that school requirements can be met.

If you are unsure of your company's educational support program, or anticipate any type of work/school conflict and are uncertain about your employer's cooperation, we think you should speak to your supervisor or personnel officer as soon as possible. If you have decided to go to college, and early resolutions of potential problem areas in employment appear unlikely, you may be wise to begin seeking another job—one more compatible with your role as a student.

Your Family and You: Rights and Responsibilities

Most of us experience apprehension when we consider a major change in our lives. And it is not unusual that others—especially members of our family—will wonder just how such a change will affect them. While you are making the arrangements for your schooling you can help prepare those around for your new venture.

If you have not already done so, we suggest that you and your spouse discuss your plans at length. At the very least, higher education will mean an investment of time and money. There will be questions about household duties and responsibilities. Subsequent discussion might include children in the household since they, too, will be affected by new arrangements. Older children probably will be expected to assume additional chores. Child-care plans should be explained to younger children. Of course you may hear moans and groans, but they can be changed to expressions of support.

Linda Mitchell, who attends Brescia College in Owensboro, Kentucky, has four children. She says:

If I had to choose the toughest aspect about going to college it would be the adjustments in home life. Everyone in my family had to form new habits. I had to learn to use my time wisely; housework, cooking, and studying had to be intertwined without too much clashing. The kids took on more of the housework, and my husband had to get used to my absences. At first, there were a lot of head-on collisions, but we soon learned that by pulling together as a team we could keep things running *almost* smoothly. I found that if all members are involved there is less resentment and more willingness to help. As a result of our combined efforts we have formed a new closeness as a family. The gains have far outweighed the problems.

The degree of support and cooperation you will feel from your family will vary greatly, perhaps even from day to day. Disputes involving rights and responsibilities may sometimes seem insoluble. Your confidence in yourself will ebb and flow. Sabina Leonard is a nursing student and mother of five children who confesses that there were times when she broke down, cried, and declared that she would not attend another class: "I felt that it just wasn't worth the aggravation. But I always went back." Sabina believes that "making a go of college without family support is much more difficult, but not impossible."

Remember, you will not be able to be all things to everyone at all times. You can begin your college career with greater confidence if you begin now to prepare yourself and your family for your new role.

The Single Parent

Single parenting is a tough assignment under any circumstances since the single parent usually feels responsible for supplying all of his or her children's needs. Because there isn't a spouse to share the financial burdens as well as the daily chores, including child care, getting through school as a single parent can be a difficult and lonely endeavor. Ironically, it is the single parent who most frequently requires higher education to attain greater financial stability. A woman in New England explained her situation this way: "I married Phil during my sophomore year, dropped out of school, and took a secretarial job so *he* could finish. Now we are divorced, my skills are rusty, and I have no recent job experience. Besides, the pay scale around here for office work is just plain inadequate. One day last year I woke up and realized that my anger and bitterness were getting me nowhere. That's when I decided to go back and finish school. I hope that by next year I'll have my B.A. *and* a decent job."

Two important factors are sending women back to school: Marriages are being dissolved at a fast pace, and women are still outliving men during an age in which higher education for women has become widely accepted. Virginia Mills of Henderson, Kentucky, said: "After my husband died I was faced with the necessity of becoming self-supporting. I would have returned to an office job, but I wanted something more fulfilling. I decided to return to college to prepare for a job as a special education teacher. The youngest two of my three children could not understand why I simply didn't go out and take a job. I tried to explain that sometimes immediate gratification must be delayed so that a better life in the future may be attained."

Single parenting may be particularly difficult, at least psychologically if not financially, when that parent is a man. Depending upon the children's ages, either child care or supervision may have to be provided during the periods of his absence from home. Fortunately for the male single parent, he has been accustomed to drawing a salary, and usually does not have the added burden of getting a job. But if his budget does not allow for a housekeeper's salary, he will be a very busy man. What can we say? That women have long had to be both wage-earner and housekeeper, that they have succeeded in the roles of single parent and student, so men can too? That's probably of little comfort to some men, but there are numerous cases of success.

Under certain circumstances, being a single parent can be a plus. There is one less role to fill. You do not have a husband or wife to please, cater to, or consider. Your leisure time is more your own. Naturally your social life will be somewhat curtailed, but this too can be turned into an advantage. Certainly you will become more selective since you won't be accepting invitations out of sheer boredom. As an adult college student you won't have *time* to be bored!

"I really stop and think about accepting a date, now that I'm back in school," explained Dottie, of Omaha, Nebraska. "If I'm really interested in the person, I'll find the time. If not, my excuse of an early morning class, or an upcoming test, or the necessity of spending some time with my children is quite satisfactory. I don't hurt anyone's feelings. Besides, my reason for not being available is probably true!"

Child Care

Several types of child care are available to most parents who elect to return to school. Your decision about which kind is most suitable for both you and your child might be based upon such factors as the age of the child, care hours necessary, availability of care, cost, and, finally, your personal preference. Early investigation of the various options can save time and minimize confusion later.

The following are major areas that you will probably wish to explore.

Cooperative Child Care

This is a kind of barter system that can be either informal or structured. You may be able to make reciprocal arrangements with the mother of one of your child's playmates to take turns "sitting" for one another. This is an excellent way of introducing the young child to the idea of being away from you since he or she will be in familiar surroundings. A more formal exchange of child care involves a group of parents who rotate child care among themselves. Each parent is required to contribute a certain amount of time or, in some instances, a fee so that qualified staff may be hired.

Private In-Home Care

The advantage of this arrangement is that the child remains at home and maintains a more normal schedule. A lack of playmates may be a disadvantage. Also, this type of care can be quite costly. If you cannot make your own arrangements for a reliable person, check into the possibilities of an agency. Several are usually listed in the telephone directory of a large city. Be sure to investigate their requirements for their employees.

Family Day-Care Homes

This type of group care is a common arrangement for children under three years of age. The care giver is usually a woman who prefers to earn money at home. In some states certain requirements must be met in order to obtain a license to provide day care in the private home.

Community Day-Care Centers

The advantage of a center is that the service is usually more stable since substitute teachers can be called in when necessary. These centers usually provide group care for children three years of age and up. Inspected and licensed, they are usually run by a professional director. They may be located through welfare agencies, the Community Chest, churches, settlement houses, or Head Start programs.

Private Nursery Schools

Usually limited to the three-to-five-year age group, nursery schools tend to emphasize the preparation of the preschooler for future formal education. They often provide transportation (at additional cost), and their daily and hourly sessions are flexible.

College Child-Care Centers

Many colleges and universities have established child-care centers on their campuses to accommodate students with young children. These centers are often sponsored by the school's education department or by the parents in the campus community. In the latter case, the adult student either volunteers his or her services during times of no class commitments or pays a nominal fee.

Once you have selected your preference in child care, it may be a good idea to make some trial runs. If a private sitter sounds right for you and your child, begin interviewing candidates and using them. Observe the interaction between those persons and your child. If out-of-home care appeals to you, why not visit various facilities, bringing your child with you and leaving him or her for short periods?

In any case, no matter what arrangements you finally make, it would be good insurance to have a backup child-care plan in mind. You might need it.

Marriage Partners at College Together

Reluctance of some adults about going to college may be partly due to apprehensions of competing with fellow students. It is a possibility that you will encounter some rivalry and occasional instances of one-up-manship. It is more likely, however, that feelings of friendship, or at least friendly competition, will prevail.

Many classes evolve into minisocieties with members sharing a "we're all in this together" feeling. Books, papers, and notes can become positively dog-eared from being passed around. Not just pens, but shoulders to cry on, may be freely loaned. Such interdependence often produces great warmth.

If it is good that adult students are willing to help one another, it must be especially good when those adult students happen to be married to one another. Mark and Dee Scanlon, parents of two small girls, attend Roger Williams College in Bristol, Rhode Island. They note: "To maintain some sort of routine at home, you might each consider attending college on different nights, thus permitting the children to have at least one parent at home. This gives each parent the opportunity to help his or her children with any school problems and projects that they might have. And after the children are in bed, there's time alone for studying or other activities. If it is possible for a husband and wife to attend college together, they can find it to be a very enjoyable experience."

Jayne and Paul Castle of Stockton, California, the parents of four children (three of whom live at home), also attend college together. Paul goes to California State College, Stanislaus, Extension in Stockton two nights a week, and both Jayne and Paul are part-time students at San Joaquin Delta College in Stockton, where they are both active in the Evening Student Association. Paul is employed full-time and Jayne operates a child-care business in their home. The Castles describe some of the unique problems they've encountered in attending college simultaneously and some of the solutions they've come up with:

Our 8-year-old daughter is quite proud that every member of our family goes to school, and our 17-year-old son has changed his mind about not going to college since we've both enrolled. But being parents, marriage partners, and college students all at once has not been easy. Our biggest problems are coordinating our schedules and finding time to spend together. Jayne keeps a calendar listing both of our activities so that we don't take two cars to campus at the same time. We have established a rendezvous point at one of the campus snack bars where we can meet before and after classes. Our joint involvement in the Evening Student Association has provided the opportunity to share common interests every other Friday, as well as to travel together (sometimes with the children) to conferences and conventions. It is interesting to note that six of the nine directors of the Evening Student Association are actually three married couples. We feel our joint college involvement has enhanced our marriage and family relationships.

Establishing Your Home Study Area

It may be time to start thinking about finding a niche somewhere in your home where you will be able to study in relative privacy. You can plan it now, or if you are already enrolled and awaiting entry, begin to set it up.

The two essential elements of a home study area are sufficient space and a conducive study atmosphere. Rosemarie Sunderland, a graduate of the College of New Rochelle in New York State, reflects:

You need to know yourself well enough to decide whether you concentrate best with total quiet or regular, routine noises or music drowning out these noises. Once you know this much, you need a place where you can come as close as possible to your ideal setting. Though the space may be small and compact, it must be set aside just for studying and be yours throughout the course of your studies. Even five minutes can be used constructively if you don't have to run around first cleaning an edge of a table and scrounging for a pencil. Try to plan your study area as carefully as you would plan for a dinner party or a poker game. You don't want to be caught short of anything! If you can, set up your area as far away from the main traffic of the home as possible lest you be caught in a traffic jam—or many of them!

If space is at a premium in your home—as it is with most of us—you will probably have to draw on your imagination to create it. Are there children who would survive if they were doubled up for the duration of your school career, thus freeing up a bedroom? Or how about finishing off a portion of the attic or cellar? The garage might yield a corner that could be insulated, with the addition of an electric heater for very cold days. Perhaps a section of a room can be partitioned off either permanently or temporarily with a screen. We heard of a man appropriating the playhouse that his daughter had outgrown.

And how about the woman in Florida who spent most of her study time in her son's backyard tree house? (She "bought" it from him with a new ten-speed bicycle.) Her neighbors thought she was a little strange, but she got excellent grades on the papers she wrote among the leaves.

To equip your home study area, we suggest the following items:

- Typewriter—in good condition, with a new ribbon
- Wastebasket
- English handbook
- Dictionary—recent edition
- Thesaurus—also recent
- Pens, pencils, felt-tipped highlighting markers—for underlining important points in your textbooks
- Scratch paper (children's past school papers and notices are ideal)
- Typewriter paper—of good quality, preferably erasable
- Folders—either plastic or cardboard, for research papers
- Stapler, hole puncher, paper clips

Rosemarie Sunderland thinks that you need a chair "comfortable enough to study in, but uncomfortable enough to keep you awake."

The next step in establishing your study area may be to educate your family not to disturb your study equipment. Few things are more frustrating than reaching for something that isn't there. "My family finally learned not to borrow *anything* of mine," related one Texas student. "But only after I made repeated threats of death, destruction—even divorce!"

In time you will probably learn to study anywhere you happen to be. But your home study area will be your base—a very important one.

Now we come back to the question posed at the beginning of the chapter: "How can I earn a living, be part of a family, and go to college too?" We could answer, "With difficulty." And in many respects that would be true. The college experience, as reflected in these past chapters, can be a complex one, of course. But many, many adults in the United States, in Canada, and indeed all over the world are involved in that experience. And in being involved, in coping, they are growing as individuals, continually developing more of their capacity to be the persons they can be. Will *you* become one of those adult students?

Penny Meek

My education has been sporadic, to say the least. My last full year of public school was the ninth grade in Colorado. In the middle of my sophomore year I quit school to get married. Later I passed the GED and got my high school diploma.

Six years later, with a little girl and a baby boy, we were living in northern California. I decided to go to a junior college nearby. I was timid at first, but my self-esteem was reinforced when I received high grades for my first courses. That summer we moved to Colorado where my husband set up a business in which I helped. I thought about entering college, but the combination of helping in a business, caring for two small children, being a housewife, and going to school at the same time was just too much to handle. I didn't go.

Two years later we moved to Kansas and started a new business while my husband taught school at the same time. I went to work for the Topeka school system as an educational aide working with special education children. During one of the four years as an aide I worked with emotionally disturbed children. The teacher, a very special lady, taught me some valuable lessons about living. One of these lessons was to look at my potential and self-worth and at my value to society. A day didn't go by that she didn't tell me to go back to school and get my education. I thought about it.

Some years later we moved back to Colorado. Finally I decided to go to school and find out about my potential. After being out of school for seven years I entered Colorado Mountain College, a small community college of 1,500 students. I was intimidated at first by the fresh young students right out of high school. But I had to take the risk of going, even if it meant failure; otherwise, I wouldn't find out where my potential lay.

By the end of the first quarter I had learned two things: one, I didn't fail, in fact I earned straight A's; and two, the most important lesson of all, being older gave me maturity and life experience that the young students didn't possess. This realization quickly balanced any lack of self-confidence.

By the second quarter I had formulated goals and plans. I like working with people and helping people, so I made a degree in sociology and/or psychology my goal. Then I started thinking about how I could go to a four-year institution for my B.A. and still maintain a traditional family life. My husband, thank goodness, is flexible. Aside from helping with the housework and the children while holding down his own job and teaching on the side, he encouraged me to take all the necessary emotional and physical steps to start working toward my goal.

The two years at CMC were a period of growth for our marriage, as a family and as individuals. We had to reevaluate our individual and joint expectations and goals. We found at different times each of us had to give a little more than we normally might have. As a result, I feel we developed a nontraditional marriage and family. When I said I wanted to go on to the University of Denver and would not take second best, my husband supported me.

During my last year at CMC I held several jobs. One of my favorites was working as a volunteer on the Child Protection Team for Lake County; another was as the Outreach Counselor for Lake County. The counseling job was particularly rewarding as I met several people like myself who were struggling with the decision about going back to school.

In addition to juggling family responsibilities, jobs, and studying, I served on various committees in town and on the college campus. All of this meant budgeting my time carefully and wisely so I still had time for my family and for social outlets. Sometimes this meant doing several things at once. For example, while doing the wash on a Sunday afternoon I might also be cooking a meal with my papers to the side so that I could study for my Monday morning biology test. Or I might drive to school or work while my husband quizzed me on the material I had to know for my anthropology class.

This past spring I graduated from Colorado Mountain College with a very high grade-point average, a certificate indicating I was listed in *Who's Who in American Junior Colleges*, and an award for academic achievement. Now I'm looking forward to entering the University of Denver with a scholarship.

Part II

Succeeding

The weeks, months, perhaps years of your deciding and preparing are over. No longer do you have to worry about what program to take and what college to attend. *You are in college.* Your goal now is to succeed, and the remainder of this book is designed to help you to this goal.

8

Registering for Courses and Going to Classes

How much can I handle? What can I expect in those first few weeks?

Opening of the Academic Year

T hose first days in college will be among the most intensive and memorable (or perhaps we should say unforgettable) days of your life. On that first day or evening of the fall term, you will probably experience excitement, anxiety, confusion, exhaustion, frustration—many things—and all in a jumble. Faculty are moving offices, advising students, trying to get the bookstore to perform the miracle of making all the course texts appear on the shelves on time. Students are scrambling to do all things at once. If you find yourself befuddled, you are not at fault. It's the system.

Should you enter college at a period other than the beginning of the academic year, you will avoid some of the hustle and bustle. Those openings after intersessions come easier. Faculty have settled into the year's routine of teaching and committee duties, and students have taken care of many registration matters by preregistering in the previous term. Don't worry that you may have missed something; just be patient. The opening of a new year will soon be upon you, and there will be sufficient confusion on campus for you to share in it.

Considering Types of Classes

Even in these experimental times, traditional types of class settings are still the most common: Students come face to face with a professor in a lecture hall, classroom, seminar room, laboratory, or studio.

Lectures

Students in a university often are shocked by the lecture hall when they first encounter it. In registering for Physics 101 they had no idea that in going to class they would be plunged into a horde of jostling people seeking the same goal, room 303. This destination had been merely a piece of miscellaneous information that looked innocuous enough on their course schedule, but it now turns out to be a cavern capable of swallowing 500 people. The student who struggles to a seat and sees a few seats vacant will be little comforted to discover she has only 347 others to compete against instead of the capacity crowd of 500.

If you face a similar circumstance, do not lose heart. The professor will probably lecture once a week, and you will take notes. And then, perhaps twice a week you will go to a classroom and meet with a teaching assistant who will likely be a graduate student. The lecturer may allow some questions in the lecture hall, but most of your dialog will be with the teaching assistant in class. And except for the few common tests given in the course you will not be competing against the 347 but against those in the classroom.

The disadvantages of the lecture hall are evident. As part of a mass you get little, if any, attention to your needs. The professor is basically a teaching tool, a conveyor of information, often less stimulating than a good book on the subject. Yet, for various reasons, some of them valid, the lecture-hall method persists.

Your real advantage in the lecture-hall course is studying with others and comparing lecture notes. Since the professor in the lecture hall is primarily an information disseminator, notes are particularly important. If common tests are given to the whole class of 348 students, the questions quite certainly will be centered primarily on major points covered in the lectures. The questions will probably be objective so they can be graded by key, and not too difficult (if, in fact, you have the basics well in mind). The large lecture-hall experience is most often an exercise in intensive listening, careful comparing of notes with others, and precise relation of the lecture material to that in the course textbook. Do not get behind, be diligent, and get an A.

Class Sections

The classroom of 15 to 40 or so people is probably going to be your most common type of learning experience throughout college. In registering for a course that has several sections (common for lower-level courses), sometimes you will have a choice of a course section with a relatively small number of students in it, or one that is almost closed out with the maximum enrollment. If registrations are nearly complete, class sizes might tell you something. Is the smaller class at a less desirable hour—say 8:00 A.M. as compared to 9:00 A.M. or 10:00 A.M.? If so, and you can stand the early hour, register with confidence. If, however, the smaller class is given during prime time, watch out. Students who didn't register for this small section may know something you don't about the professor. If, before registering, you can take time to investigate reasons for the difference in section sizes, do so. If not, your safest choice would be the larger section.

Seminars

Seminars are expensive for the college, so they are usually reserved for upper-level courses where attrition and specialization make the seminar more common. But there may be some lower-level seminars. If you know the professor, and you are confident you can operate effectively under the pressure of performance among a small number of students, fine. You will probably get a lot out of the experience. But if grades are important to you, and neither of those other conditions applies, you would do well to pass up the seminar and register instead for a course in some other type of class setting.

Labs

Labs can be fun, and this is fortunate because they can also be a lot of work. Whether your lab is for science, engineering, psychology, or some other subject, you may get a lot of satisfaction from your hands-on experience—testing classroom theory against physical realities.

If you have had no experience with labs or have had bad experiences, you should wait a semester, if you can, to take a lab course. This will give you time to investigate the nature of the lab and learn some of the tricks of the trade from other students before you have to commit yourself.

Someone might advise you to split your lecture and lab; that is, take the lecture this semester, and the lab next semester. The problem with this solution is that in the next semester you will probably have to restudy lecture material, and this is not the most efficient utilization of your time.

Studio and Physical Education Courses

Studio courses are usually "guts"—easy courses. Sure, there are exceptions, and we apologize to the professors who make fine arts studios a real challenge. But the facts are generally these: Professors of studio courses usually are performance, not theory, oriented. They are often nontraditional and distrustful of a grading system, *any* grading system. (How do you grade a painting? What would you give the *Mona Lisa*?) It is easier for these professors to give A's and B's than to try to explain the vague distinctions that may separate the higher from the lower grades. You may have a good time, meet some fine people, and discover latent talent, which is all for the best. A studio course could be just what you need for a change of pace and an assured "pass" in an otherwise difficult schedule.

You ought not to neglect, too, that other marvelous gut, the physical education course. Attend almost every period, have a good game of volleyball or badminton, get an A and one credit. And don't feel guilty about it. The intellectual work you are doing in other courses more than makes up for the lack of it in P.E. Keen mind, healthy body. You owe it to yourself.

Independent Study

Independent study is an alternative to the classroom, so we want to come back to this topic from chapter 2 in another context. Independent study has usually been reserved for above-average students. However, some institutions offer standard courses on an independent-study basis to any student who, for some valid reason, cannot take the course at the regular time. Students are often allowed extra credit for continued independent study of some aspect of the subject they found particularly interesting after completing a conventional course. Credit may also be allowed for conducting research to assist a professor who is undertaking a special project, perhaps a survey or a scientific experiment. Independent-study credit was earned by Charles McCabe and some contributing authors for work on this book.

Independent-study courses can often be found in the college's bulletin following listings of conventional courses. However, if no such courses are listed, don't assume that independent study is not available. Ask a faculty member, if you know one, or the department head.

Assessing How Much to Take

Anne Seavey of Bentley College in Waltham, Massachusetts, says:

> A working adult student has to be highly motivated or he wouldn't be going to school. Even so, each person should take only the number of courses he can handle, considering the amount of time he has available to spend on those courses. Attending class is the easy part. It is the hours of homework—the reading, the writing, the research, and the studying for exams—that takes the most time. Difficult, too, is sacrificing social activities or having to be satisfied with a messy house because time is needed for studying.

A natural tendency for an adult student is to want to get the certificate, diploma, or degree as quickly as possible. Perhaps you have a promotion waiting or a career change impending. Perhaps you have taken a leave of absence from work for a predetermined period of time and feel you must finish your degree on schedule. Or your college may allow one or two tuition-free overload credits per semester, and your degree will cost less if you take an overload and finish early. Many other reasons might be impelling you to assume a large course load. Before you hoist this burden on your back, though, consider very carefully whether you are able to carry it well to the end of the journey.

If this is your first experience in college, and you elected to go part-time at the beginning even though full-time was a viable option, you probably made a wise choice. If you believe you can manage three courses in three nights per week, you might be better off to take two. Most adults find two courses to be a challenge when balanced with work, family, and other demands. Satisfaction and good grades in one or two courses at the start of part-time study will be more beneficial to you than barely passing while carrying a full-time credit load. You may need time to build your confidence. Take it if you can.

Choosing Courses (and Professors)

Choosing courses (and professors) wisely is important to your success. A good place to start is to make sure you need a particular course. Both first-time and returning adult students sometimes take courses for which they could later qualify to receive equivalent credit. Before registering, you should review chapter 4, Getting Credit for What You Already Know, and make a personal assessment of your potential noncollegiate credit awards.

You will probably be required to take a certain core of courses in your freshman and sophomore years. During your junior and senior years you will most likely have to take a specified group of courses to satisfy the degree requirements for your major. However, in your degree program a certain number of credits may be earned by taking courses as electives. You should also be aware that while two courses given at different times may carry the same title, no two courses will ever be exactly alike. The material you will cover, the way it will be presented, the knowledge you will acquire, and the enjoyment (or lack of it) you will derive from the course will be determined largely by your classmates and, particularly, by the professor.

The kind, not just the quantity, of courses you choose is important. One combination of courses may be impossible for you and another combination easy. And sometimes the difference is the inclusion or exclusion of a single course.

Ideally, before registration, you have already investigated the kinds of courses that will make up your semester load. You have consulted with your adviser, talked to adult students who have taken these courses, and conferred with as many of the course professors as possible. You know at least by reputation which courses are the guts and which are the backbreakers. Even armed with this kind of preparation, though, you are never assured of having selected the best combination. The gut course you chose to pad your program, Film as a Subversive Art taught by Professor Thompson, might become a real problem when at the last moment Professor Cut-'em-up Kowicki is substituted for good old Thompson. Don't panic, though. Registration procedure (which we'll come to shortly) should allow you to make adjustments in your schedule.

Beware, too, of the syndrome called "getting the required courses out of the way." Programs of study usually are designed to space required courses reasonably across the full number of years needed for graduation. It is difficult for students even to schedule required courses before the natural time for such courses has arrived. Yet, by straining, some students manage to do this, and many of them later regret it.

Required courses can be among the more challenging courses. If they are required, especially core courses at the lower level, a clientele is probably assured for the professors. They may not have to compete with their colleagues in attracting students to these courses, so they can be more demanding in their expectations of the students in them. To take a chance on putting too many difficult courses too early in your program, before you have developed the capability to handle them, does not make good sense.

You should utilize counselors, of course, but your best advice in planning your schedule may come from other students. Try to draw unbiased conclusions by looking for consistencies in what they tell you. Their impression of a professor often represents your most valuable information for making a decision about taking a course. A given professor might be considered easy when it comes to grades, but he might also be so boring that you will learn very little. The best professors will be interesting, reasonably demanding, and fair in determining grades. If you are going to invest 10 to 15 weeks of your time and a considerable sum of money in a college course, it makes good sense to find out as much as possible about the professor before you make the commitment.

Sampling Courses

But what do you do if the professor's name is not announced in advance? A tactic employed by some college students to decide among courses is to screen personally the professors after the semester begins. This can usually be accomplished by the students' registering for more courses than they plan to complete. After sitting in on every class for the first week, the students determine which courses and professors are most beneficial for them, then they drop the courses they believe would be to their disadvantage to continue. (To drop a course means to discontinue it in the first few days or weeks of classes; no record of it appears on your transcript.) As indicated in a previous section, you can usually withdraw from a course early in the semester without receiving a grade. However, some colleges require that you forfeit part of the tuition, so check this out. Remember Professor Cut-'em-up Kowicki, the professor you got by mistake when you thought you were signing up for a gut with good old Thompson? You can drop Kowicki and add someone else.

Another possibility for choosing professors is to sit in on a class or two this semester for courses you are considering taking in the future. Remember, it is the professor who will have the greatest impact on your success and enjoyment from a course.

Avoiding Closeouts

The best way to avoid being closed out of a course is to plan ahead. Word of a particularly good course or professor spreads quickly in student circles. If you want to get into a popular course, you should register as soon as registration opens. Even if you are undecided, you may still want to register for the course provided that your school has a withdrawal and refund policy. Admission to some courses may require that you obtain the professor's signature prior to registration.

After registering for your first semester, you should begin formulating plans for the next semester. Each semester thereafter you should make it a point to know well before registration opens exactly which courses will be offered and which courses you plan to take the following semester. If the course schedule has not been published, the department office or an individual professor may be able to tell you which courses are likely to be scheduled.

If your official status is that of a freshman or a sophomore, you may be given low priority for admission to certain courses required for graduation. The registrar's office may feel that you still have plenty of time to take such required courses prior to graduation; preference may, therefore, be given to upper-class majors. Should you find yourself closed out of a course, don't give up right away—there are ways to get admitted to closed classes. One possibility is to get permission directly from the course professor. If you can convince the professor that you absolutely must take *his* course *this* semester, he will probably make room for you. Another possibility is to find out from the registrar's office what "ceiling" was placed on enrollment, then attend the first session and count the students in the class. If someone is absent, you may be able to take his or her place.

Class Locations:
Avoiding Conflicts

Be sure to pay attention to the locations of the classes when scheduling more than one class on a given day. University campuses can cover a lot of real estate. Unless in all kinds of weather you enjoy running between distant buildings during the ten minutes that may separate class periods, take the time to check your tentative schedule against a campus map. With some prior planning and without detriment to your overall plan to get your degree, classes can often be grouped by location, deferring the one in a far-off building until a future semester. By then the class location itself may change to be more convenient for you, or your schedule may be more conducive to including it.

That First Class!

Now that we've covered possibilities for types of class encounters during both your first and your somewhat later college experiences, we come back to the thing itself—that first class! Rosemarie Sunderland of the College of New Rochelle reports: "I arrived for my first class in a state of fear that bordered on numbness. I was in, yet I had no idea what I had gotten myself *into*."

This anxiety is experienced by many adult students (and we'll look at it in more detail in chapter 11). If the adult student is entering a class containing younger students, the anxiety is heightened. Linda Mitchell of Brescia College in Ohio says: "I glanced around the room and was dismayed to find that I was the only 'older' student there. Turning back slowly toward my new biology professor, I really panicked when I realized that even *he* was younger than I."

Rosemarie and Linda weathered that first class experience and went on to succeed in college. Some adults—who knows how many— undoubtedly do not survive that shock, and drop out. Be prepared for anxiety. It may or may not come. If it does, remember that it is a natural element of life as an adult student, it lasts a very short time, and later you can joke about it as so many other students have done.

Understanding Professor and Student Relationships

How can I get the best grades or most satisfaction (both, I hope) from each course?

Grading Systems

Most colleges use a letter grading system or a grading scale of 0 to 4.0. However, many colleges incorporate variations into the predominant grading system. Since it is not possible to cover all systems, we will explain only the most common. You should check carefully your own college regulations.

Basic letter grades include A, B, C, D, P, F, I, and W. An A indicates superior performance, B is above average, C means satisfactory, and D indicates marginally acceptable performance (but still passing). However, a course in your major or minor area of concentration passed with a D may not be acceptable to fulfill your degree requirements. P is passing when the option of pass-fail is elected. The grade P also is commonly used to record credit for proficiency exams and noncollegiate courses. The grade of F is failing. The letter I (incomplete) may be recorded at the instructor's option when you have attended a course but for some reason did not complete all requirements.

The letter W indicates that you officially withdrew from the course before the deadline for withdrawing passed. (This deadline comes later in the term than the deadline for dropping a course.) If you feel certain you are going to fail a course, or receive a poor grade which will lower your average, you may wish to use the withdrawal option. At many colleges students are permitted to withdraw from any course during the first two-thirds of the semester. However, more than one or two W's on a student's transcript will probably raise questions in the minds of potential employers or graduate program admissions officers.

The pass-fail option can be a valuable alternative if you are taking a difficult course outside your major field. This election usually must be made by formal application prior to a specified deadline; some colleges do not permit the pass-fail option to be elected after the first class session. The advantage of pass-fail is that you can take a course for which you expect to receive a low passing grade without the risk of the poor grade appearing on your transcript and lowering your average. However, you should be aware that above-average achievement in the course will not be officially recognized, and the course will not count toward meeting the requirements for graduation with honors. Other possible disadvantages are that some schools will not accept pass-fail for transfer credit, and a potential employer may frown upon an applicant who has opted pass-fail if the election was made more than a few times. Nevertheless, wisely electing pass-fail for just one course might make the difference between graduation and graduation with honors.

Quality or Grade Points, and Honors

Quality-point average (QPA), or grade-point average (GPA), is a measure by which college students may be compared to determine eligibility for such things as academic honors, scholarships, graduate school admissions, and career opportunities. Each semester hour of completed graded course work is counted in computing the grade-point average. Usually, an A is worth 4.0 quality points per credit, B equals 3.0, C equals 2.0, D equals 1.0, and F equals 0. Pluses and minuses, when used, are given intermediate weights (A- equals 3.7, B+ equals 3.3). The number of credits you've earned for a given course is multiplied by the number of quality points you've earned per credit (determined by your course grade) to arrive at your total quality points earned for the course. Your total quality points for all graded courses completed is divided by your total graded semester hours attempted. The quotient is your current cumulative quality- or grade-point average.

Each semester you may have the opportunity to qualify for the dean's list by meeting the criteria of your college. The dean's list is usually open only to matriculated degree candidates who have completed a certain number of credits during a given semester with the required current semester grade-point average (usually 3.2 to 3.5). If you aspire to making the dean's list, check your college's catalog or bulletin to determine the requirements.

Graduation with honors should not concern you too early in your college career. There will be time to think about honors and honor societies as you get closer to completion of your degree requirements. (These topics are covered in chapter 13, Reassessing Goals and Performance.) For now, you would be wise to concentrate on the present and simply do your best in each course.

So You Want to Be a Straight-A Student?

by DENNIS GERARD ELLIS
A graduate of Dutchess Community College, Poughkeepsie, New York (A.A.S. in Business, GPA 4.0; rank in and size of class, 1/754); Pace University, Pleasantville, New York (B.B.A.; GPA 4.0; rank in and size of class, 1/650); currently enrolled at Cornell Law School

Straight A's. Sound impossible? Or at the very least, highly improbable? Well, it need not be either, for this pinnacle of academic success has been reached by many adult students and can be reached by you! Although everyone does not achieve all A's, there is absolutely no reason everyone cannot strive for them. This striving is, in itself, the key to academic success.

Many students enter college with a fear of failure. Unfortunately, this fear often leads them into the establishment of passing as their primary goal. Thus, they concentrate their efforts toward obtaining any grade except an F. Aiming for such small goals leads to underachievement. I propose that you settle for nothing less than a straight-A average as your goal. Granted, you may not achieve your goal, but your straight-A motivation and output will be reflected in A's and B's instead of the C's and D's that your short-sighted peers will receive.

I agree with Nancy Hawks of Adelphi University who says: "Adult students joke about grades a lot. But I'll let you in on a secret. They are damned important to us. Our high grades are signals of our **Success!**"

Here are some reasons that I consider important enough to justify working toward high grades:

1. **Honors and awards:** They become a permanent part of your college record and are conclusive evidence of your success.

2. **Scholarships:** Nearly every four-year school has funds available for outstanding transferees, as does nearly every graduate-level school. Colleges want exceptional students, and grades are used by virtually every college in awarding scholarships.

3. **Graduate and professional schools:** Almost every good graduate or professional school requires a copy of your college transcript when considering you for admission. They also have questions on their applications regarding your rank in class and any honors or awards that you may have received. Although graduate studies may seem miles away or not in your plans at all, you may change your mind after a year or two of college. It is wise to prepare for that contingency now.

4. **New jobs or job advancement:** Many employers ask you to list your honors and awards or rank in class on their applications. Some even require college transcripts. An outstanding college record looks good in your employment file.

5. **Yourself:** Even if you can find no other reason to work toward good grades, the self-satisfaction that you will derive from top perform- ance is sufficient reason in itself. Prove to yourself that you can excel. Prove to yourself that you can set high goals and work hard to attain them. To those of you who may believe that good grades are not an accurate measure of good performance and learning, I offer this to think about: Poor grades *are* indications of poor per- formance and *do* imply poor learning. Thus, for your own good, prove to yourself that you can meet the requirements of the system even if you are opposed to it. Finally, and most importantly, prove to yourself and to others that you are a winner. If you can develop within yourself the ability and motivation that it takes to become a winner, it will remain with you throughout your life.

If you motivate yourself toward reaching high goals, establish a plan of action, and fulfill that plan through hard work and ingenuity, you will succeed. Good luck!

Grades and Personal Satisfaction

Ideally, the student would earn an A+ in each course and be able to say, "This was the best course ever." The student would remember her exciting class preparations, invigorating participation in class discus- sions, fascinating research for papers or reports, and brilliant writing, and she would feel that she had not only gotten the best possible grade but also the highest level of satisfaction from her effort. Unfortunately, such a pleasant circumstance is enjoyed only rarely by college stu- dents. The best grades and most satisfaction from courses are not necessarily compatible.

At some early point in your college studies you might have to make a conscious and perhaps painful choice between getting a good grade and deriving the maximum satisfaction from a course. Many avenues can lead to such a choice. Perhaps you have become fascinated with a single aspect of the course and you find yourself irresistibly drawn farther, ever farther in pursuit of it. Then one day you realize you are not keeping up with assignments that seem dull in comparison to your explorations.

Or perhaps you often disagree strongly with your professor and itch to prove your points in class. You may discover that by disagreeing you have satisfied your commitment to personal integrity—at the cost of a good grade. Has the system been unfair to you in both circumstances?

Shouldn't you be allowed to explore a subject and not just keep up with assignments? Alas, when you chose to go to college you were given no guarantee that you would be treated fairly in every instance. Nor did anyone say that you could set the standards for what would constitute acceptable work in your courses.

If you find yourself having to make a choice between grades and satisfaction, and you are seriously disturbed by it, you need to review both your reasons for college study and your life goals. If, for instance, your primary reason originally was to expand your intellectual horizons, and this reason remains valid, then you may wish to commit yourself to achieving personal satisfaction even at the potential cost of receiving a lower grade than you could otherwise attain. But if your original reason, for example, was to enable you to go on for a higher degree, and your acceptance at one of the graduate or professional schools is dependent on high grades, then probably you are going to have to swallow hard and subordinate that urge for personal satisfaction to the demands of getting that A.

To be most successful in college, you should consider making your first course of study your professor, you, and the relationship that exists between the two of you. The rest of this chapter deals with interaction of professors and students, and some of the possible results and implications of that interaction.

Interaction of Students and Professors

by WILLIAM C. HAPONSKI
and PHILIP M. BACKLUND, Ph.D.
Assistant Professor of Communication
Central Washington University, Ellensburg, Washington

You are seated in your first class of the semester and the professor walks in. What do you know about this person right away? After 30 minutes of class? At the end of the class period? After two periods? Ten? Do you know this person at the end of the term?

How does the student sitting next to you interact with the professor? After several weeks does she enjoy the class and get good grades whereas you hate it and do poorly? If so, it is possible she has no more capability for enjoyment and good grades than you, that her I.Q. is no better, her background for taking the course is no better, her desire to do well no greater than yours. What, then, may account for the difference in success?

Possibly you and the student next to you look at the professor differently. Perhaps she sees in the professor a person who can be understood and appreciated as considerably more than a teaching resource such as a textbook or filmstrip.

Michelle entered a southern university as an 18-year-old freshman and dropped out as a 19-year-old sophomore. Sixteen years later she was back, taking again the second semester of her sophomore year. On her first day of her return to school she was seated in the same classroom, retaking a course she had failed earlier, listening to the same professor deliver the same litany: "If this is a typical class, as I imagine it will be, I can expect from you only one A, a few B's, several C's, and far too many D's and F's."

"You creep," Michelle uttered to herself, just as she had probably done 16 years earlier. Then she immediately retracted the silent reproach. She recalled that several of her earlier classmates had also believed that this woman, Professor Sutpen, was impossible, and they had not done well in her class. But some had succeeded in getting those few A's and B's from this grade-stingy professor. And this time, having learned some useful coping methods as an adult, Michelle decided she would be in the latter category.

Michelle found some students who had gotten those higher grades and asked them about the professor. Michelle also asked her adviser, and she even asked a librarian and a janitor about the woman. Carefully listening in class, Michelle tried to determine just what it was that Professor Sutpen expected from her students. She visited the professor during one of her office hours. Then after a few weeks, the woman Michelle was beginning to know seemed different from the professor she remembered from 16 years ago.

Michelle's attempt to understand and relate to the professor took a few hours extra during those early weeks in the course, precious hours she could have used in study. But through listening in class, not getting turned off by the professor's austere manner, and trying to meet the professor's expectations, Michelle discovered she actually enjoyed the course, and she got a good grade too.

Classroom Chemistry

For a moment now, assume that you are the professor, and you walk into your first class of the semester. You wonder, is your term with this class going to be pleasant or painful?

Every class is different. As a professor, you have noted that even sections of the same course have unique "personalities." Section A might be lively and B dull. These section personalities can last not just for a class meeting or two, but for an entire term.

There is a mysterious "chemistry" at work in college classrooms, and at the beginning of a semester a professor hopes that the formula will be a good one for the term. If this chemistry is right, you will benefit, as will most of the other students. If it is not, you can still benefit. But you may have to be more perceptive and work harder at it.

Many students don't realize they are the ones who control much of the chemistry in a class. Your behavior helps set class norms. For example, if from the beginning of the term you make an effort to be cooperative, diligent, and friendly, you will probably influence at least a few other students to act the same way. Only a few students are necessary to set a prevailing tone for a class, positive or negative. So rather than merely waiting to see what develops, perhaps you could actively involve yourself in creation of the class norms by behaving in the way you think is best for that class. Quite certainly your role in creating a pleasant class environment will not go unnoticed by the professor.

Undoubtedly you will have a bad professor at some time in your college life. You might be inclined to fight such a person. But fighting a professor throughout a term will bring you no good.

Even a bad professor will have *something* good to offer. Probably you sincerely appreciate Professor A's consistently good job. Try to do the same with the good parts of Professor B's generally bad job. Your positive attitude will be conveyed subtly to the professor. Every normal human being has need for a sense of self-worth. The student who enhances a professor's sense of worth will be appreciated by the professor whereas the student who diminishes it will not. At the end of the semester the professor may very well view you as one of the few students who made his efforts seem worthwhile.

Peer Pressure and Classroom Politics

Our attitudes and actions may be entirely different when we are acting alone from when we are part of a peer group. How we perceive information, draw inferences, make judgments, formulate ideas, and respond to stimuli can be, and often is, profoundly influenced by the phenomenon of group peer pressure. This power by which we seem bound is derived from our strong human need for acceptance by others—classmates, for example—with whom we identify, interact, and socialize. If we fail to conform to the norms of the group we risk rejection, and few people want to be treated as outcasts. On the other hand, is rejection always the consequence of nonconformity? And what is the price of conforming?

Students who have emerged as informal leaders through their assertiveness, either in class discussions or informal conversations, may plant seeds that grow into modes of behavior accepted by the group. You may find yourself in a student lounge listening to a dialog among your classmates such as the following:

"What do you think of the professor?" asks Joe.

"I think he's ridiculous," says Dave. "This course is a joke. All he wants to do is hear himself talk."

"Yes," chimes in Bonnie, "I'm very upset with that man. I have no idea what he is talking about."

"When I asked him the question about the text, he answered to my satisfaction," injects Frank. "He seems to know what he's talking about."

"Oh, he knows his subject," Dave retorts, "but every time someone questions his views he just shoots them down. I'm not going to open my mouth anymore. Let him do all the talking; that makes it easier for us."

"I agree," says Bonnie. "I'm not going to let him make me feel foolish again."

And so the classroom norm becomes silence. Any individual who violates the norm by asking questions risks being shunned or talked about by the other class members.

Obviously, refusal to ask questions in class is counterproductive to the learning process. Perhaps you or another classmate, recognizing the fallacy of this approach, might speak out and bring the others to their senses. Or someone might muster up enough courage to speak to the professor about the situation.

If peer pressure is contrary to your best interests, and you have been unsuccessful in getting the group to change its attitudes and actions, try to ignore that pressure. Although it is uncomfortable to jeopardize your status as an accepted member of the group, it is best to think and act in accordance with your own standards and beliefs. If you think a classmate is being unjustly critical of the professor, tactfully say so. If you feel like asking a question and you are convinced it is a good one, ask it. If you want to make an extra effort on an assignment, do it. You are investing your valuable time and money to learn. Don't let negative peer pressure prevent you from achieving your goals.

Another factor in dealing with other students is classroom politics. While the majority of students are forthright and hardworking, some are not, and they practice classroom politics as a substitute for honest effort.

Al, a glib retail department manager, was capable but lazy. His objective in college was the same as his goal at work: to get by with as little effort as possible. Like many astute politicians, what Al lacked in motivation and discipline he made up for with his ability to "talk a good game." Al made it a point to talk with the top performers in the class. In his convincing manner, he continually suggested that the course was a gut, and the reading assignments could be easily skipped. Al told his classmates that he knew several people who had taken this course last semester. The professor, he explained, was lax on reading the case studies and lenient with grades; therefore, it wouldn't pay to put a lot of work into the cases. It wasn't until it was too late that Al's classmates realized their friendly adviser was merely trying to lower the peak of the curve in order to get a better grade himself.

Classroom politics can take several forms: student with student, student with professor, professor with student. The possible variations on the basic formats are endless. Be aware of the politics, and you will cope better with classroom circumstances.

Being on Time and Prepared for Class

Inherent to adult academic pursuits is a large measure of freedom to make choices and shape your academic pursuits around other less malleable aspects of your life. Let us say that you have a job, and your employer expects you to be at it until five o'clock each day. Then you have to enter unforgiving traffic, struggle your way home, fix supper for the family, enter traffic again, and appear at a six-thirty class. Let's further assume that you used to spend your weekends immersed in family life—taking the children to their lessons, taking them to a museum, or to the zoo. They have come to assume that you are theirs, at least until school begins again for them on Monday. These patterns—remaining at your employment until five o'clock, devoting your weekends to your children—previously were no problem. But now you find yourself frequently late for class because of the traffic and your family responsibilities, and often unprepared because of activities during the weekend with your children. Does the professor understand?

He may not. Students entering class late can be a serious distraction to the professor and the class, and students unprepared to participate waste the time of professors and classmates alike. You assume that your professor will earn his salary that is derived from your tuition money by being on time and prepared for class regardless of the normal demands of his personal life. Why should he not assume that you will earn your good grade at least partially through promptness and preparation?

Discuss anticipated problems of this nature with your professor. He may accept your chronic tardiness if he knows that you absolutely cannot prevent it. And he may accept your occasional unpreparedness because of family situations, again especially if he knows of a specific reason for it. It is quite certainly better to let your professor know ahead of time that you may have a problem than it is to take your chances he won't notice, or that he won't care because he understands.

When to Open and Shut Your Mouth

Many good politicians have a keen sense of timing. They know when to speak and when to say nothing. Furthermore, when they do speak they have a sense of purpose; they attempt to score points. The student in the classroom or in conference with a professor should realize that speaking does not necessarily equate with good communication. A student who *communicates* well with the professor and her classmates is likely to get a great deal of satisfaction from the course as well as a good grade.

In classroom communication, quantity is a poor substitute for quality. Gauging the degree of classroom participation that will allow you to be an effective class member is important to you. Most professors (and students) don't appreciate "spring butts," the students who cannot restrain themselves, and all too frequently bounce about in their chairs with fervent, though vacuous, answers. On the other hand, neither do professors have any reason to admire "zombies," those classroom creatures whose only sign of being alive is getting up to go home after class.

The size of the class itself is a factor in a desirable degree of individual student participation. In a large class of 30 or more students, each student's opportunity for participation is quite limited. Consequently, in order to communicate well you have no need to offer an answer to the bulk of the questions the professor poses to the class. You can afford to let most of them go by and wait to participate until the moment is *right for you*. The same applies to asking him questions. An occasional intelligent, articulate question inserted at the right time is often more valuable than an answer. Anne Seavey of Bentley College says: "If a person listens carefully and concentrates on what is being said yet still doesn't understand something, that is the time to ask questions. Chances are, a number of other students have also missed the point."

Ann Girndt, also of Bentley, provides another dimension to asking questions: "One of my most humorous experiences occurred during a literature class. The professor had outlined the course requirements, which included a subjective report. Subjective report! What in the world was the professor talking about? I listened attentively. The professor had finished explaining, but I was still in the dark. When asked if there were any questions, I responded by saying, 'I've heard every word you have said, but I don't understand what is required.' Although the class roared with laughter, the professor understood my predicament. This time the detailed explanation enabled me to grasp what was required. Later, I did successfully comply."

In a small class such as a seminar of six to twelve people, good classroom communication is even more critical for you. An ideal seminar, in terms of communication, might be one in which each student was always well prepared and eager to contribute, but sensitive to the needs of other students to contribute and benefit from the professor's contributions. You will not likely impress either your professor or your classmates by wasting their time with rambling discourse, or at the other extreme, by saying nothing when it is clearly your time to add something to the seminar.

When You Think You're in Trouble

Has any student gone through a degree program and yet escaped the sick feeling that accompanies the suspicion he has not done as well in a course as he could have? Highly unlikely. Unless you are an unusual student, sooner or later you are going to be in trouble, or at least think you are. What should you do? Try to ignore your feelings in the hope you may be wrong? Launch a crash study program? Pray?

Such solutions might work. But a better approach probably would be first to analyze your performance as objectively as possible in order to define your strengths and weaknesses, then discuss the situation with your professor.

Psychologically, you have an advantage. The student who asks for help becomes known to his professor as a *person*, not just a name on a roster or a face in a class. The professor might be able to put an F beside a name, but to fail a *person* is quite another matter.

Whether you talk with your professor informally before or after class, or more formally in his office, be concise. Time is an asset in short supply with professors. Take notes if necessary, and ask for clarification of unclear points. No matter how sincere your desire to improve, unless you understand him and then act on his advice, you are wasting his time and risking further difficulty when he later inquires about your progress.

So, when you're in trouble, or think you are, review matters carefully, then, if warranted, talk to your professor and follow up with action. In doing so you may find that you have converted yourself from a name on a roster to a person who is important to him.

10

Developing Essential Educational Skills

*How important are: organization of time? study habits? reading?
writing? mathematics? speaking? listening? use of the library? note-taking?
taking exams? Can I improve?*

Organizing Your Time and Concentrating Effectively

Every hour, virtually every minute of your daily life, must be used effectively in order that you may enjoy the greatest possible degree of success in college. In this chapter we will focus on that part of your time devoted to study.

A human being, like an organization, runs better at certain times than at others. With the extra demands of school upon you, you should try to determine what have been the peaks and valleys of your work efficiency in the past. As a student, you will want to make your peaks as high as possible and minimize the depth of your valleys.

When do you do your best, most creative work? In the morning? afternoon? evening? Your past life may provide you with important clues to determine your best study times. As much as possible, you will want to reserve those most productive periods of the day not for the easiest or most pleasant course work, but for your most demanding or creative work.

At the beginning of a term, you will want to determine as precisely as possible for each course the critical work that will be required of you. The weighting system each individual professor will use in arriving at a final course grade will be your guide. When you have evaluated the weighting system for each course, the major work for a term will break down into segments, probably three to six or seven blocks per course. For English 101 the critical elements might be: first paper (10 percent), second paper (10 percent), midterm exam (20 percent), term paper (30 percent), final exam (30 percent). For Biology 101 the segments might be: class quizzes (10 percent), midterm exam (10 percent), research paper (20 percent), final exam (20 percent), laboratory exercises (40 percent). As you survey the requirements for each course, some blocks may be missing since a professor is fuzzy about his requirements. But you will be able to define enough tasks so that you can sensibly plan your work. Later you will adjust your plan as you move through the semester becoming more familiar with the material and discovering what is easy and what is difficult for you. If English 101 and Biology 101 are of approximately equal importance to you, and the degree of difficulty for you is about the same, you would be foolish to use a large amount of your best study time for writing the second paper for English 101 (10 percent) and a small amount for the Biology 101 research paper (20 percent). You must be selective; you must keep course requirements and their true importance in the grading systems well in mind as you progress.

We asked Dennis Gerard Ellis, who wrote about being a straight-A student, to give us some thoughts on use of time. The material from here to the end of this section is the result.

I'll bet that many of you have never thought of the time you spend shaving, brushing your teeth, cleaning the house, and driving the car, as study time. If you were to add up all of the minutes of these and countless other routine tasks, you would have several hours of extra study time available each day. You will find that a simple device will enable you to learn while engaged in such tasks—the tape recorder.

For example, take your final outline and anything else you need to know for an exam and go over them aloud in front of a portable tape recorder. Be sure to include any thoughts related to the material that may come to mind while reading aloud. This verbal exercise is itself a valuable learning and reinforcement method. If you have a patient family who won't mind hearing what to them will be boring repetition, you are now prepared to study while performing all of your "thoughtless" (not requiring concentration) duties. You may even listen to your tape outside, while gardening or mowing the lawn (listening with an earphone). Indeed, the uses of this time-utilization device are limited solely by the extent of your ingenuity.

Another technique, which is slightly more flexible, is the use of index cards. You can write anything on them that you wish to learn for an exam. One method is to write key terms on one side and their explanations on the other. You can bring index cards to places where you cannot easily bring a tape recorder such as the supermarket, an elevator, or a boring PTA meeting.

You will be required to do a great deal of reading in most of your courses. While the average student who is an average reader can get through college and maintain average grades, the prospective straight-A student must become more than an average reader to maintain his excellence. He must become a speed reader. I recommend a formal speed-reading course or, at the very least, a survey of books on the topic in your college library. Naturally, speed reading cannot be used all of the time. Your reading speed should be flexible enough to adapt to the type of material that you are reading and your objective in reading it. For example, you will have to slow down for detailed, technical, or extremely difficult material. At least the speed reader has the option of slowing down or speeding up depending on the situation. The slow reader can only read at one speed—slowly!

Well, there you have it, three ways to make optimum use of your study time: tape recorder, index cards, and speed reading. If you are one of those who, when looking for time to study, can literally count the minutes available, these will make those minutes count!

Effective Study Techniques

Much of your study time will be with textbooks, and by now you have used many of them. But have you used them effectively? Perhaps you should take a fresh look at those objects that have become so familiar to you. Do you really know what to look for in a textbook, and how to look for it?

A high-quality textbook is like a road map. It leads the reader who knows how to use it to a destination.

Just as there are traffic signals and signs along the road to guide the traveler, there are indicators within a textbook to guide you. In writing a textbook an author has a main idea for the book and each chapter, supported by several essential parts in the development of those main ideas. Usually he outlines his material before he writes the chapters. It is natural that textbook writers think in terms of structure, and you can use this thinking to your advantage.

A textbook outline becomes converted into headings. The book title presents the topic area and as much guidance to the material therein as is feasible. Chapter headings, boldface headings for sections, and subheadings are all reflections of essential points in the outline. Within sections, italics or boldface type highlight crucial points. Also cue phrases are used much as headings. For example, you will see statements such as these: "Three kinds of...." "There were four causes for...." "The major concerns were first ... second ... and finally ...." Such cue phrases are followed by the three, four, or five points that were promised in the phrase itself.

In addition to words and phrases that give you an overview of the material, visual aids are important. (Chinese proverb: "One picture is worth more than ten thousand words.") Charts, maps, diagrams, pictures, and other illustrations do more than relieve the monotony of the printed page. Many writers consider them so essential they create or assemble their visual aids first, then write their text around these aids. Recognizing the value of textbook indicators, you are ready to get more out of a textbook than you may have gotten in the past.

In 1941 Francis P. Robinson published *Effective Study*, a useful book based on research by others and the author's experience with helping college students become more successful. Variations on his five-step method have been used effectively by writers and teachers to this day. Thomas F. Staton, for instance, outlines a similar method in his book, *How to Study*. (These books are included in the Bibliography of Study Aids at the end of this chapter.) The methods of these two authors are:

Survey Q3R (Robinson)	PQRST (Staton)
1. Survey	1. Preview
2. Question	2. Question
3. Read	3. Read
4. Recite	4. State
5. Review	5. Test

You can see how similar those two methods are, step by step. We also suggest a five-step approach: (1) get an overview, (2) ask questions, (3) read actively, (4) repeat important points, and (5) review continuously.

1. Get an Overview

No matter how conscientious you are about your studies, to begin a textbook at the first page of your reading assignment and proceed to the end of your first assignment, then to the end of your second, then your third, and so on, is a poor way to learn. By proceeding straightforwardly at approximately an even pace, you may not recognize major points, and even if you do, you may give them no more time than minor ones.

When you first get your textbook, familiarize yourself with it as a whole. The table of contents is the outline of the book. Survey this outline. Note the topics for each chapter and the progression of the chapters. In addition, note other material listed in the contents, such as the preface, foreword, introduction, list of diagrams, list of maps. At the end of the table of contents you may find listed a bibliography, a glossary, appendixes, an index. Now take the time to locate and preview all these latter sections of the book. Only by doing so can you get a good idea as to how helpful they will be during your study. Is the bibliography brief or extensive? Is it annotated? What about the glossary—how detailed does it seem to be? Is the index extensive? If so, it should be a significant aid for you.

Once you have surveyed the table of contents and previewed each of the sections of the text to determine the general content and extent of coverage, carefully read the preface, foreword, or introduction. It is here that the author will most succinctly tell you what he is doing, his purpose for doing it, and how he will go about his task. Thus he is providing you with the major framework for your study during the course.

The first paragraph of the introduction, "To the Student," in *Writing Themes About Literature* (Englewood Cliffs, N.J.: Prentice-Hall Inc., 4th ed., 1977) by Edgar V. Roberts illustrates the point:

> The chapters in this book are theme assignments based on a number of analytical approaches important in literary criticism. The assignments are presented in the hope of fulfilling two goals of English courses: (1) to write good themes, and (2) to assimilate great works of literature into the imagination. Negatively, the book aims to avoid themes that are no more than synopses of a work, vague statements of like or dislike, or biographies of an author. Positively, the book aims to raise your standards of judging literature—and therefore your ability to appreciate good literature—by requiring you to apply, in well-prepared themes, the techniques of good reading.

With such excellent guidance, a student should not flounder around in Roberts's book, trying to discover what it is all about.

When you begin reading a chapter, employ the survey technique again. Note the chapter heading and subheadings. If there is a summary at the end of the chapter, read it. The summary provides the core of the material to be presented, and you will want to have this in mind before you read the rest of the text. Scan the illustrations and captions. The descriptive material associated with them in the text will be more meaningful later when you read it. Just below subheadings, usually near the beginning of the first paragraph, you may find key sentences that point the direction for the section. Look for them, and if you find them quickly, read them. This kind of survey or preview as a first step well equips you to continue your study.

2. Ask Questions

The good student is the curious student. He or she wants to know not just who and what, but why and how. This student is inquisitive about relationships between facts and ideas. Curiosity may have killed the cat, but it is also "one of the permanent and certain characteristics of a vigorous mind" (Samuel Johnson, *The Rambler*, March 12, 1751).

As you note the chapter title, topic headings, and subheadings, ask yourself what is likely to be included. Study is most effective when it is an active search to find answers to questions. Formulate your own questions from each heading, and let them guide your reading to find the answers.

For example, in volume 1 of Norman F. Cantor's *Western Civilization: Its Genesis and Destiny* (Glenview, Ill.: Scott, Foresman & Co., 1970), chapter 7 is entitled "The Rise of Medieval Culture." You might ponder that title and ask questions such as these: "What were some of the important aspects of medieval culture?" "How did these aspects develop and affect the people?" "What is implied by the term 'rise'?"

The first section heading is "The Romanesque World." "What is meant by Romanesque?" you might ask. "What is its relationship to rising medieval culture?" Equipped with this curiosity and these questions, you are ready to seek the answers by reading the sections. It is unlikely that you have asked irrelevant questions, but you will be able to pause and formulate new questions.

You have probably noticed that the author of a textbook will often place questions in the text. Usually these come at the end of the chapter for review purposes. Sometimes they come at or near the beginning of sections of the text. Regardless of their location and whether or not they are intended for review, use them also to guide your reading. You may be sure that these questions are central to the concepts presented. Additionally, they may be similar to the exam questions your professor will use.

Some texts are accompanied by a workbook, study guide, or instructor's manual. Your professor may not have ordered the study guide or workbook, but you can order it. Check your library or bookstore copy of *Books in Print* to determine what ancillary aids accompany your text. You may even be able to get the instructor's manual by writing to the publisher. A study guide, workbook, or instructor's manual can be a valuable tool in developing curiosity and a questioning attitude toward the course material.

3. Read Actively

How many times have you read several pages of a book only to realize suddenly that you have no idea of what you have read? Dismayed, you have had to turn back to the beginning and read the material again? To be effective, reading a text cannot be a passive plodding down a page, nor can it be done while daydreaming. It must be an active search to find answers to questions you and the author have raised.

Some people are avid readers of fiction and can analyze and relate to what they have read. These same people can be poor readers of texts. Why is this so? Fiction presents a world in which a cast of players sequentially go about their business of living. The reader can relate to the people and their thoughts and actions in that living world because the reader occupies a living world of his own that presents many similar experiences. The "world" of a text, though, is often not of people who are alive, at least during the time we read of them, as in fiction, but of people who are dead. Or the world of the text is a world of things: amoebas or Gothic cathedrals; or it is a world of past events: the Franco-Prussian War or the meeting between Chamberlain and Hitler. Through analysis and acts of imagination we have to enter into that world as fully as possible, handicapped initially by not knowing an amoeba or a Chamberlain as intimately as we can quickly come to know a character in a novel.

Reading a text well is an active exercise; it is a search for and reaction to material. It does not have the inherent excitement of a well-told story to keep your mind alert. The excitement may have to come from a different kind of discovery. New worlds exist in amoebas and Chamberlain. They are different from worlds you know, perhaps, but they can be no less exciting.

4. Repeat Important Points

Some of history's most intelligent people have claimed they really do not know what they think until they have said what they think. The mind receives countless impressions in short spaces of time. Living would be impossible for us if each impression were permanently recorded. Fortunately we forget the huge bulk of what stimulates our mental processes. But unfortunately we also forget much of what we would like to remember.

The mind has a short-term memory and a long-term memory. Tests have shown that most impressions that enter the mind are forgotten rapidly with the passage of time, and most of the forgetting occurs very soon after the impressions are received. Only those impressions that are particularly significant, or those that have been consciously formulated into ideas and selected for recall, become part of our long-term memory. So take an important step to store these impressions in your long-term memory: recite.

Yes, talk to yourself. Out loud, preferably. (Not just senile, but brilliant persons talk to themselves. "After all," quipped a renowned scientist, "who is more interesting to listen to than myself?") If you can't talk out loud, conduct an internal dialog with yourself. "Why is the Gothic cathedral so much higher than the Romanesque?" you ask after having read a section on medieval architecture. "Because, for one thing, the flying buttress took some stress off the walls and allowed them to be lighter and higher. For another . . . ," you continue to yourself, and in the process ensure that you really know what you have read. If you can't repeat the essence of what you have just read, don't expect some miraculous recall process to assist you on an exam some days or weeks later. If you can't say it, you don't know it.

5. Review Continuously

Immediately after reading, you should review your text markings or notes, expand them as necessary, commit to memory the main points, and try to understand relationships among important elements. You can't just "look over your notes"; you should actively try to remember, to reconstruct, to reflect on ideas and their relationships.

Then, periodically during the course of the term, you should review your learning. Review, to be most effective, must be a continuous process. It does much more than just help you recall a certain amount of material. It allows you to expand your body of learned material by posing new concepts, new questions, new tentative answers.

During your review you should keep a simple record of concepts with which you are having difficulty. To assist in learning a foreign language, one student used small packs of cards containing words and phrases, the translations of which she had written on the backs of the cards. In every spare moment she reviewed the cards, and every time she missed a word or phrase she would put a tick mark on the card. Periodically she culled out cards that gave her no trouble and reviewed them less frequently. As she encountered new words and phrases, she would make a new card and add it to the pack. After a period of time, using a continuous adding and culling process, she was left with only those cards to study that had a large number of ticks on them. By reviewing continuously those elements of language that caused her the most trouble, she became proficient in that language.

In summary, to be most effective, your review should begin immediately after reading your assignment. Then it should continue at intervals throughout the course. By spacing your review periods, by attempting always to put together a whole from the parts, your textbook study will become more effective.

In one college with both liberal arts and career programs, about 80 percent of the 62 courses of instruction used textbooks to which effective study methods such as those outlined could be applied. If you are like most college students, you will probably spend about half of your study time using such texts. And that is an excellent reason for you to use effective study methods.

Some courses, though, require study involving sources other than textbooks. Such sources might be essays, analytical articles, books of fiction or nonfiction, poetry, drama, and technical reviews. Many of the study techniques already discussed will apply to the reading of such material, but some will not. Certain disciplines require a highly systematic, progressive, painstaking approach to learning. For detailed guidance on how to study effectively in such fields as science, languages, and mathematics, and how to use sources other than texts, you can refer to any one of many excellent books treating the subject. See the annotated bibliography at the end of this chapter.

Reading

Good reading skills and good study skills are so closely related they are often taught together in developmental reading and study skills workshops. We use the term "workshops" often throughout our discussion of essential educational skills to emphasize the participative nature of these courses. In a reading class, students learn and immediately apply skills. Usually, they interact with the teacher and one another in a highly structured manner, and they sometimes use learning devices such as tachistoscopes and reading acceleration instruments.

Reading specialists agree that the most important factor in effective reading is motivation. This means that you, as an adult student, have an advantage. Excellent motivation, however, obviously does not ensure that a person will be an effective reader. And even if you are an effective reader, you probably have the capacity for a higher level of performance. We believe that virtually every adult student would benefit from a well-taught reading skills workshop.

"Reading efficiency" is a term used by specialists to measure performance. It is the rate of reading combined with the degree of understanding of written materials. Programs for developing reading efficiency usually are 10 to 30 hours long, spread across 3 to 10 weeks.

Years ago, many respected educators were convinced that a reading skills course would improve both the rate and comprehension of most students. Today reading specialists generally agree that for most students a reading skills course will bring about a dramatic increase in rate but will not significantly change comprehension. The higher rate, of course, means a higher reading efficiency. Various studies differ on the percentage of improvement for the average student, but a minimum of 200 percent increase in efficiency seems to be a reasonable claim.

Psychological, neurological, or physical problems may have impaired your ability to read effectively. Or you may have had unfortunate academic experiences that have contributed to poor reading efficiency. Or you may be reading effectively now, but you could develop even more of your capacity. Fortunately, many texts and workbooks that can help you are readily available through most libraries. (See the bibliography at the end of this chapter for only a few suggestions.) Better yet, reading skills workshops have become common in colleges and in many communities. A note of caution, however, is in order. If you are considering enrolling in any course other than one taught within a well-established college or a reputable private school, check it out carefully. When you do find a good program, the relatively small amount of time you spend in it may very well be one of your best educational investments.

Before we leave the matter of reading we should pause for a moment to consider the importance of vocabulary. Students who have not developed a curiosity about words are depriving themselves of the full value of any learning experience to be gained by reading. Too often we skip over words we don't know, such as "tachistoscope" in the first paragraph of this section. (Did you look it up?) Even if we pause to look up such a word that is so obviously uncommon, we sometimes assume we know what "common" words mean. And we really don't! We have seen them before, perhaps used them, yet don't recognize that we have been using them wrong for many years. The context of a word can help you, but there is no substitute for use of a dictionary.

Unfortunately, words are sometimes used improperly even by good writers. Curiosity about words—their denotations, connotations, associations—is at the root of improved reading efficiency.

Writing

In our schools, emphasis on reading skills begins to wane beyond the primary grades. Writing skills, however, receive continuing attention at least through the freshman year of college. In these times of low enrollments in the humanities, English professors still constitute a large percentage of the total college faculty, partly because of freshman composition requirements. Academe rests on the belief that effective writing is crucial to success in college. Your study and reading skills may be excellent, but if you cannot express yourself well in writing you have a terrible handicap. Look into the grading systems used by professors in a variety of college courses and you will find most often that a large portion of the course grades will be determined by the students' written material.

You may not be able to get from your college the help you need in some matters, but almost certainly you will find your college well equipped to help you become an effective writer. Basic or developmental writing courses have become common in college curriculums. Writing centers where you can get tutorial help are often open for much of the day and evening. These courses and centers will usually help you with the basics: sentence and paragraph construction, grammar, technical accuracy. In addition, the staff at the writing center often will provide more sophisticated services that you may want to use right up to graduation. Many students have learned to seek help habitually from the writing center in organizing and documenting term papers. The results, in terms of both their writing improvement and their grades, have been satisfying to them.

In a short section such as this, we cannot go into all of the detail some readers may need for their writing improvement. Many excellent texts will give you this kind of assistance. (*Writing with a Purpose* by James M. McCrimmon is one of the best. This book and several other writing aids are cited in the bibliography at the end of this chapter.) We do, however, wish to highlight two cardinal points of good writing.

The first relates to unity. To be satisfactory, any theme, technical report, research paper, or term paper must have unity. If the professor has to puzzle out what you are trying to say in a sentence, or worse, in a paragraph, or far worse, in the whole paper, you have caused him to waste his time. And that, for sure, is not good. You have also either created doubt as to whether you can think and express yourself adequately, or certainty that you cannot.

One of the most common forms of writing in college is the thesis paper. Your other types of writing assignments will be affected positively if you can consistently write a unified thesis paper.

A thesis paper initially draws its unity from a thesis sentence near the beginning of the paper. This sentence is a clear, concise statement of the conclusion you wish your professor to accept after you have properly developed your topic.

A thesis always contains a subject and your attitude about it. Your subject may be the effect of the passage of time in Wordsworth's poem, "Tintern Abbey," and you may write a long paper about your subject. But you have not written a thesis paper unless you have clearly expressed your *attitude* about your subject. That is, you must give the reader your considered judgment about an aspect of your topic. For example: *Thesis sentence*: The passage of time in "Tintern Abbey" enables the poet to "see into the life of things."

Your subject is "the passage of time in 'Tintern Abbey.' " Your attitude is your judgment that this passage enables the poet, as one line of the poem states, to "see into the life of things." Properly combined, your subject and attitude constitute a thesis, or a conclusion. Your whole paper will be built around this thesis.

Know your thesis. Do not forget your thesis. If necessary, print your thesis on a card and tape it to your typewriter. Do not let your thesis escape you while you are writing that paper. It is the source of unity, therefore, the source of your grade and your satisfaction.

An important step toward achieving unity is to develop your thesis properly. Not for one paragraph, not even for one sentence can you drift away from your thesis if your paper is to be unified. If you have a sense of thesis in you, you will understand that organizationally your thesis paper is a simple thing. It is a logical, orderly development of your conclusion about a particular matter.

In schematic form, a thesis paper may look like this:

First paragraph (introductory sentence(s), thesis sentence, amplification of introduction and/or thesis).

Second paragraph (topic sentence, development of topic).

Third paragraph (topic sentence, development of topic).

—and so on through the paragraphs to:

Last paragraph (topic sentence, development of topic). Summary or conclusion optional.

Somewhere in each paragraph there will be a key statement. This is the topic sentence, and it usually comes at or near the beginning of the paragraph. Sometimes for variety or emphasis it is placed at the end. It is the sentence around which the rest of the paragraph is built.

Each paragraph should have a reason for its existence and its place in the order of paragraphs. The second paragraph, for example, must relate directly to and develop the thesis. Furthermore, this paragraph should logically come next after the thesis; because of its nature it cannot be the third, tenth, or last paragraph. Succeeding paragraphs in turn must independently relate to and develop the thesis, and each should logically follow the preceding paragraph. And so on down the paper. A summary or conclusion may not be necessary, but if it is well done, it may add impact to the paper.

A good way to determine whether or not your paper is unified is to check each topic sentence against the thesis sentence. For each topic, ask: "Does it relate directly to the thesis? Does it develop the thesis? Is there a logical reason for its position in relation to the other topic sentences?" If the answer is "yes" to all three questions, you have an adequate framework for your paper.

The second cardinal point of good writing that we wish to emphasize is that the writer must always be a demanding, objective critic of his own work. After writing your draft, if you try to divorce yourself from your product, to look at your writing as if you were the professor who will be grading it, you will strengthen your paper. You will look for unity, as discussed above. You will ask yourself about each paragraph, each sentence, each key phrase: "Is it necessary? Is it the best possible expression of the ideas I wish to convey? Does it aid the logical flow of ideas?"

You may find, having asked these questions, that you will have to reorganize your paper. You may have to throw out sentences, paragraphs, sections over which you have labored. You must be able to do so. If something doesn't fit, you must change it or throw it out. To this point in your life if you have not truly been an objective critic of your work, and you have not been faced with these difficult decisions, the process can be painful. But your discomfort will diminish with practice, and your satisfaction with your product will grow.

Strive for unity, and be your own most incisive critic. These two points can guide you to better writing.

Mathematics

"Adult students are very concerned about their lack of basic mathematical skills," explained a math instructor. "And they shouldn't be. Compared to younger students, their insight and ability to reason mathematically are excellent. They do well in my classes."

Mathematics is central to the curriculum of most institutions of higher learning. And math anxiety is common to many students. It need not be a problem for you.

You have three recourses for improving your basic mathematical skills. First, as you encounter difficulty in your courses you can go back selectively to build your basic skills in order to solve specific problems. This approach saves time for the person who can keep himself firmly oriented on the goal of solving those problems. But it can also be ultimately frustrating since higher-level mathematical skills often require a broad basic understanding. Second, you can ask an instructor to recommend a self-help review book. Many good ones are available. These books often contain diagnostic tests that will help you concentrate on areas of weakness. Or third, you may be able to locate an instructor of basic mathematical skills, take a diagnostic test, and if you are found to be deficient, enroll in the course. For overcoming math anxiety or building basic skills, a mathematics workshop may be just what you need.

Speaking

by PHILIP M. BACKLUND
Assistant Professor of Communications
Central Washington University, Ellensburg, Washington

Previous sections have dealt with two other communication skills, reading and writing. These skills are clearly necessary to success in college and receive a great deal of attention in elementary and secondary schools. This section and the next discuss two equally important aspects of the communication process—speaking and listening.

These two activities occupy much of our waking time (estimates range as high as 73 percent), yet if you are like most students, you received little formal training in speaking and listening. However, a person's ability to communicate orally is being recognized more and more as an essential skill by educators and, of course, by employers. The person who can clearly organize his or her thoughts, speak clearly in most situations, and listen effectively to others has an excellent start toward success at school and work.

What are some of the skills in speaking that will help ensure success? We obviously can't cover all of them here, but we can sketch two of the most important skills, overcoming nervousness and speaking clearly. Also, we can refer you to some helpful books (see the bibliography at the end of this chapter).

Virtually everyone is afraid of getting up in front of an audience to speak. In fact, in a recent survey, public speaking was listed as the number one fear of Americans. So, if public speaking makes you nervous, you may take some comfort in knowing you're not alone. For many people, this nervousness extends to more informal speaking situations such as expressing an opinion in a classroom discussion or talking with professors and other figures of authority on campus. Many people find themselves quite tense in these situations, and that tension prevents them from being effective. Here are some ideas on how to overcome nervousness:

- Set a goal to *manage the tension*, not eliminate it. Even the best public speakers get nervous, but they can reduce tension to a manageable level.

- *Know what you want to say*. The more you know about the point you want to make, the clearer that point is to you, the more confidence you will have, and the more effective you will be.

- *Rehearse*. You would naturally assume that you would practice a public speech (in fact, good public speakers may practice ten to fifteen times for each speech), but you also can "practice" more informal speaking by mentally rehearsing the points you wish to make in class or in conference with your professor. That practice will also build confidence.

- *Take every opportunity to speak*. The more you do it, the better you will get. Set goals like speaking at least once in a group setting every day. Make a point of talking frequently to each of your professors. These activities will build both your confidence and your skill.

- This is more difficult, but try to *focus on the audience instead of yourself*. The more sensitivity you feel and show for the attitudes within the group, the more the group will respond to you and the less nervous you will probably feel.

A second area to work with is in actually saying or delivering what you want to say. Delivery includes such aspects as the rate of talk, volume, pitch, pronunciation, and grammatical appropriateness. Generally, people judge you against what is known as standard or "network" English. Many people develop language habits that are not "standard" such as using slang, shortened pronunciations, and various dialects. These habits are acceptable as the norm in some situations, but to be assured of success in most situations, you need to develop the skill of using standard English. Classes in voice and diction can help if you think you have a language pattern that may be cause for concern.

Lastly, you may want to consider taking a basic speech skills course. Such a course would provide information and give you practice in different kinds of speaking, usually in interpersonal communication, small group communication, and perhaps in public speaking. The most important part of this kind of class would be the feedback from the instructor and other students on your speaking performance.

Listening

by PHILIP M. BACKLUND

Your success in college is greatly dependent on your ability to gather information from a wide variety of sources and then give some form of it back to the professor in a paper, test, or discussion. The primary mode of gathering information is listening. In fact, we spend more time in listening than in any other mode of communication.

Researchers have classified many types of listening, and of these, the ones most relevant to the educational process include active listening, discriminating listening, and critical listening.

The difference between active and passive listening may seem obvious, but it is often overlooked. Good listeners are active listeners. They put a lot of energy into the listening process; they not only hear, but probe, analyze, and look to the speaker's nonverbal cues. In short, they work at listening. The passive listener, on the other hand, merely receives sounds with little recognition or personal involvement; he or she just happens to be present when someone is talking. So the first and most basic point about successful listening is the need to *work* at it.

As a student, you will find a lot of things to listen to, and separating the useful from the useless is called discriminating listening. This is listening for the purpose of understanding and remembering relevant information. This type of listening involves such skills as understanding the meaning of words from their context, listening for details, understanding the relationship of details to the main point, and listening to a question with intent to answer.

The third major type of listening behavior you will be engaged in is critical listening. In critical listening you are trying to analyze the ideas or evidence presented by the speaker and to make critical judgments about their value. You are trying to distinguish between fact and opinion, emotional and logical argument, and to detect bias or prejudice. In short, you respond in an evaluative manner, concentrating on specific points and choosing what to discard and what to retain. Good critical listening, used with active and discriminating listening, should assist you greatly in assimilating useful information.

Here are some guidelines on how to listen better:

1. Be mentally and physically prepared to listen.
2. Think about the topic or situation in advance when possible.
3. Try to guess the talker's intent or purpose.
4. Determine the value of the topic for you.
5. Concentrate—do not let your thoughts wander.
6. Listen for main ideas.

7. Become aware of your own biases and attitudes, and try to separate them from the speaker's message.

8. Reflect the message to the talker; give feedback to determine if you have heard accurately.

That advice is sometimes difficult to follow, but you can try. You can practice by working on one or two points at a time. For example, you might say to yourself, "Today I'm going to work on listening for main ideas and check to see if my own biases interfere." By doing a piece at a time, you can gradually build up your skill as a listener. A good listener is a valued person, both as a friend and as a student.

Unfortunately, advice and help with listening skills may not be as easy to get as help with writing problems. First check with the speech communication department. While they may not offer a specific course in listening, most speech courses have a listening component. Also check with the academic skills or learning center. For further work on listening, you might find one of the books listed at the end of the chapter to be helpful.

Using the Library (and Librarian)

Effective use of the library can improve your performance markedly and during a year save you hundreds of hours of study time. One of the first things you should do is to get your library's guide, usually a small pamphlet of great immediate and continuing value. Also, whether you use a civic or college library, you should arrange to take a tour of the facilities. Most college orientations include such a tour, but sometimes the tour is so cursory it amounts to little more than "Here is the circulation desk where you check out books, and here is the reference desk."

Libraries may seem complex to you, but they should not seem mysterious.

If you are basically at ease in the library but know you need to build library use skills, you might get by with a good library use handbook (see the bibliography at the end of the chapter). But if you find yourself in awe, not knowing really which way to turn, you need a library course.

Most colleges offer introductory courses in general library usage and in bibliographical work. These courses often are mini-courses whereby you may simultaneously make your future life in the college easier and earn a credit or two. The courses will include a description of the holdings, workings, and organization of the library, and use of general basic bibliographies as well as some special bibliographies.

If your college or civic library does not offer a course, ask a librarian to spend some time with you. It is unlikely you will be refused since librarians pride themselves (justly) on their service. A helpful librarian is a valuable ally against the oppression of too many papers or projects due all at once.

You should ask your librarian to enumerate the library resources in your area. Don't assume that the city and college libraries are your only assets. You might be surprised to find that the local Elks club has a fine collection of Welsh literature (a member donated his extensive holdings), and the Am Vets has a massive collection of pictures and books on the Italian campaign of World War II (a member was an Army public information specialist during the fighting). Special collections may be housed in your local historical society, in the museum on your campus, or in the chaplain's office. Much to the dismay of college librarians, who obviously would like to control all books in public use, many academic departments persist in maintaining small holdings, and the department secretary is the key that unlocks those treasures.

Three resources in the library must be used by virtually every student: the card catalog, the serials catalog, and the reference service. The card catalog is for locating books and is usually arranged alphabetically in three categories: author, title, subject (figure 1). Most small and moderate-sized libraries use the Dewey decimal system, but large research libraries, to include those on campuses, most often use the Library of Congress classification system because it facilitates subdividing categories (figure 2).

To find a book, you locate its call number in the card catalog, then locate the library map, which shows where the book is shelved. If the book is not there on the shelf, some students will quit in dismay and begin searching in the card catalog for a substitute. Instead, you first should begin looking on the shelf in the area where the book was supposed to be placed, since books of similar nature will be shelved together. If a satisfactory substitute cannot be found on the shelf, you should not give up but should ask the librarian to determine where the book you want is located. The librarian may discover that someone else has the book, and a "hold" can be placed on it for you when it is returned. If the book is overdue or lost, steps can be taken to get it for you. If the book is really important to you, you should find out where it is and take steps right away to get it quickly. It will not miraculously appear later today or tomorrow when you take your valuable time to search for it again. If the book is not listed in the card catalog, you can try interlibrary loan. The service is usually quick. In cases when you can get by with a substitute book on the subject, the reference librarian can help you locate the section where you can browse for a substitute.

Many students do not realize that libraries usually shelve oversize books in locations separate from smaller books of similar nature. If you see a + or ++ marking, or F (for folio), on the card in the card catalog, you must locate the oversize section, not the regular section. Art, music, travel, and highly illustrated cultural books are examples of volumes that might be placed in an oversize section.

Figure 1   Card Catalog: Title, Subject, Author

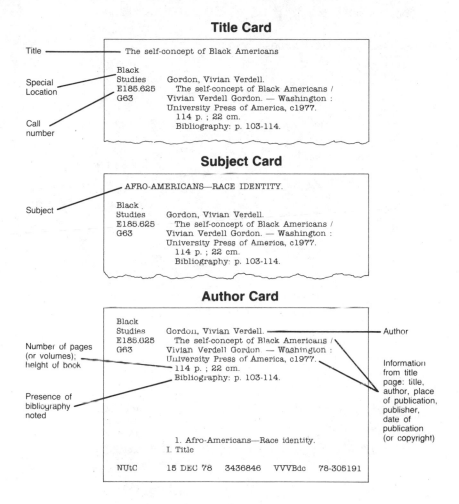

The serials catalog will guide you to periodical publications (popular magazines, scholarly journals, newspapers). Items will be listed by their official titles rather than the titles that appear on the cover of the publication and are sometimes abbreviated or translated (figure 3).

The reference desk, as the hub of reference services, is your most important source of information. Here the reference librarian not only can help you with the card catalog or serials catalog but will also direct you to encyclopedias, bibliographies, handbooks, directories, indexes, dictionaries, yearbooks, atlases, gazeteers, biographies, and guides of many kinds. Also, importantly, the reference librarian can help you with the mechanized information retrieval that is becoming increasingly necessary. If your research topic is the economics of Malaysia in the early

Figure 2 Basic Outlines of the Classification Systems with Examples of Subdivisions

Dewey Decimal Classification System

000 General
   030 General
      encyclopedias

100 Philosophy and Related
   150 Psychology
   160 Logic

200 Religion
   220 Bible

300 The Social Sciences
   330 Economics

400 Language
   420 English and
      Anglo Saxon

500 Pure Sciences
   530 Physics

600 Technology
   620 Engineering

700 The Arts
   750 Painting

800 Literature and Rhetoric
   810 American Literature

900 General Geography and
   History
   970 General History of
      North America

Library of Congress Classification System

A General Works
   AE Encyclopedias

B Philosophy and Religion
   BS Bible

C History—Auxiliary Sciences
   CB History of civilization

D History (except America)

E America and U.S. (General)

F U.S. local and other
   American nations

G Geography and Anthropology

H Social Sciences
   HB Economics

J Political Science

K Law

L Education

M Music

N Fine Arts
   ND Painting

P Language and Literature
   PA Classical languages and
      literature

Q Science
   QD Chemistry

R Medicine
   RD Surgery

S Agriculture

T Technology

U Military Science

V Naval Science

Z Bibliography

Figure 3　The Journal Index Entry

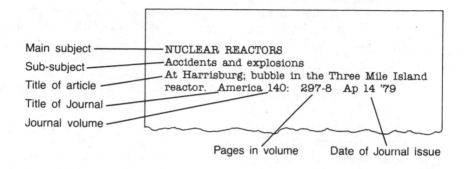

Main subject —————— NUCLEAR REACTORS
Sub-subject ————————— Accidents and explosions
Title of article ———————— At Harrisburg; bubble in the Three Mile Island
reactor. America 140: 297-8 Ap 14 '79
Title of Journal ——————
Journal volume ————————

Pages in volume　　　Date of Journal issue

twentieth century, the reference librarian will help you refine your topic sufficiently and categorize its elements to allow a computer search that will produce a printout of a bibliography of your topic. The reference librarian will also be able to guide you to language learning materials, microforms, slide, tape, and record collections, and many other audiovisual materials waiting to be used by you. You only need to know what is available, how to find it, and how to use it. Get your local library's guide pamphlet, get a library use handbook, take a course, and above all, use your librarian.

Taking Notes

Some people argue that taking notes interferes with listening in class and slows down studying at other times. In fact, experiments have shown that when one group of students only listens or reads intently and the other group takes notes or marks texts, there is little difference in their performance—provided that the examination is given immediately afterward.

　Forgetting, though, is our enemy. Three men heard a lecture, and the next day at lunch were discussing what a great lecture it was. One of them marveled at the speaker's acute insight into five problems in our society. Another of them agreed, and they started enumerating the points. They stopped, embarrassed. Between those two men they could come up with only two of the speaker's ideas. The third man, however, pulled out a notebook and supplied the other three points, and the men were then able to discuss all of the speaker's main ideas at some length. Without the notebook, they would have lost those points in the great sea of forgetting.

　After examining the conclusions of many other researchers into human memory, a distinguished psychologist found a basic theme: Unless detail is organized through reflection under meaningful categories, it is quickly forgotten. Notes, well-taken and reflected upon, are important aids against forgetting.

What form should your notes take? The proper answer seems to be: The form that is right for you, the one that allows you to reflect upon the material and to expand your knowledge of it. Study guides vary in suggested approaches. You may select from among those possibilities the methods that seem best suited to your general style. Rather than providing a shopping list of tips, we will concentrate on a few features of note-taking that seem to us most important.

"Taking notes" is the term we commonly use, but we probably should be saying "making notes." The difference is that making notes is an activity that goes beyond mere recording. It is an active and continuous process until the term is over. First, it involves attentive listening. In the mass of the instructor's words you should always try to select the main ideas and record the essence of them.

Then, after the lecture—as soon as possible—you should edit your notes. While the lecture is still in your memory, through your own system of symbols, underlining, or numbering, identify the major points and expand upon them by writing any necessary additional notes. If you omit this step of editing immediately after class, a step that should require only a few minutes of your time, you are seriously degrading the value of your note-taking.

A third stage in the process is to reflect, integrating in your mind the notes you take in class with all of your other aids to reflection on the course material. During the class itself the instructor may have referred several times to the textbook. You, the wise student, will have noted those places in the text for future reference. And during your study outside class you will have made some marks in your text, and perhaps some notes. Also you may have made notes relating to reading from other sources. During your periodic reviews you should try to draw all of this material together and reflect on what seem to be the main points. If you have listened attentively, then edited your notes, then reflected upon them, you have greatly enhanced your opportunity to perform well in the course.

Taking Tests

When you take tests, the quality of your preparation of course will affect your grade. So ask yourself some questions. Have you developed the habit of studying your past tests to determine not just what you missed but why? Have you kept up with your assignments and, using your notes and test markings, spaced your reviews to facilitate remembering? Through careful preparation, have you developed an attitude that this examination is going to be a challenge, yes, but certainly not a defeat? If you have done all of these things, you have taken major steps toward a good grade. Now your technique in actually taking the exam is the other ingredient of a successful outcome.

Several excellent guides will help you sharpen your technique. In most books on effective study, there will be a section on test-taking. Or, if you need more detailed treatment of the topic, you can buy a brief but incisive book such as *How to Take Tests* by Jason Millman and Walter Pauk (see bibliography, end of chapter). We will not go into methods of approaching various categories of test questions, such as a book on taking tests will do, but we will emphasize several important principles that apply to all categories.

Many students do poorly on tests because they do not properly size up the nature of the problem at hand. Concerned, nervous, perhaps even panicked, they start shakily with question one and work toward the end, trying to answer the questions sequentially with equal diligence to each and every question. If you take this approach, what happens if you run out of time and discover that the unanswered questions carry greater weight than the ones you have been carefully answering? Despite your good work on part of the test, you have only done a part, and your grade will reflect your lack of skill in taking tests.

Before you start to answer the questions, survey the entire test. The weighting system often is given, and you will want to identify the sections with the most weight. Note the recommended time if this guidance is provided. If not, knowing how long you have for the entire test, you can quickly sketch out a work schedule, allocating time to each of the sections in proportion to its weight. In making this tentative work schedule, allow time for checking and revising your work. About one-quarter to one-fifth of the total seems to work well for most students. It only takes a few minutes to prepare a schedule of progress through the exam, marking each section with the scheduled arrival time as a check on your actual progress when you begin answering the questions. It is time well spent.

The most common cause for poor performance, assuming that the student has prepared adequately, is *failure to read the problem*. First, you must read and understand the directions to each category of questions. This advice seems so obvious that you might wonder why it is necessary to emphasize the point. Yet, time after time, good students disappoint themselves on tests by failing to read directions. If, for example, you fail to note that the instructions allow more than one correct answer, you lose points when you choose only the best answer. And if the directions say answer A *and* B, and you misread them to say answer A *or* B, you lose points.

Reading the problem implies more, though, than just reading the directions, which are the mechanical means to a correct answer. Reading the problem implies also perceiving the thrust of the question asked so that you can attempt to answer the question *as it is stated*, not as you *think* it is stated or *wish* it were stated. Especially on essay questions, students tend to wander away from the point the professor wants answered or developed. Don't expect that the questions you asked yourself during your study of the course material will come out exactly that way on the exam. By asking those questions you have prepared yourself in a variety of related areas, and now you must tailor that preparation to meet the needs at hand: *answering the question the professor asked*. Sketching an outline of an answer will help you keep your writing relevant as it progresses. Don't be faced with this comment on your corrected exam paper: "That's a good answer, but unfortunately not to the question I asked." Not knowing an answer is a forgivable sin. If you simply don't know, write something and take your chances. Probably your vacuous answer will be worth more than a blank space would get you. What is nearly unforgivable, though, is to know, but through not reading the problem, to give the wrong answer. *Read the problem*.

The time you program for review and revision is important to your success, so guard against your encroachments on it. If you find during examinations that you are having to choose continually between completing additional test items and reviewing and revising, you probably are not attacking your exams well in terms of assessing the weight of individual parts and allocating the time you should spend on them.

Taking tests may not be the greatest entertainment in town, but you can get satisfaction from the results. Good preparation and technique bring better results.

■■■■ STUDENT PROFILE ■■■■
Ann H. Girndt

Graduation day has come and gone, but the memories of the events leading up to that day have not faded. After seven years, three months, and one week of hard, disciplined study, I finally earned a bachelor of science degree in accounting from Bentley College in Waltham, Massachusetts. I confess I couldn't help but feel overjoyed to hear the degree being conferred with honors. Truly it was a day of rejoicing.

Looking back over those eight years, I can easily identify the moment when the idea first came to me to enroll in a college accounting course. It was at work! I am a full-time employee in the Treasurer's Accounting Division of the First Church of Christ Scientist in Boston, Massachusetts. Seated at my desk one day, wondering how to improve the performance of my accounting duties, I became aware of a deep longing to express my gratitude for the privilege of working there by learning all that I could about accounting. Thus the desire was born to become as proficient as possible in the field of accounting. Never mind a degree. I hadn't even thought about that! Just concentrate on accounting courses and earn a certificate in accounting.

I selected Bentley College because of its excellent reputation in accounting and finance. Each semester I carried two subjects, except during the summer when classes met two nights a week for seven weeks and one subject was all I felt I could carry. During the fourth year I was confronted with the fact that the credits were adding up. It was at this point that I changed to a degree program.

Although it had been a very long time since I was last a student in a classroom, there were progressive steps that could be taken along the path of furthering my education. That is what I discovered during my first summer course in economics. Eagerly I attended the first night of lecture. Noticing those around me busily writing, I quickly followed suit. Shortly my pencil slowed. Did I hear the professor correctly? " . . . in the equation, let x and y represent. . . ." Dimly I recalled from more than 30 years ago a course in algebra. I realized I needed a good review. Evidently, Bentley College had anticipated such problems, because a noncredit basic math review course was offered. I enrolled in and completed the review, which enabled me to do well in the required math. Another source of help was a credit-free, six-week summer course in reading comprehension offered through the college's Division of Continuing Education.

By adhering to a regular course of study, I was able to achieve good results. I used the college library for study so much that it became known as my second home. I endeavored to pace myself by not overextending on commitments. Much like one shifting into low gear and then slowly starting to drive up a steep, winding, scenic mountain road, I settled back to enjoy the view along the way. Eventually I even became involved in a few college activities. Participating in the Evening Government Organization proved to be a most enjoyable learning experience. I value the friendships that I made among my fellow students. To sum it up, I thoroughly enjoyed my college experiences.

Annotated Bibliography of Study Aids

Effective Study

Apps, Jerold W. *Study Skills for Adults Returning to School*, 2nd ed. 1981. McGraw-Hill Book Co., 1221 Avenue of the Americas, New York, NY 10020. Paperback, 240 pp, $8.95. Includes chapters or sections on taking notes, listening, taking exams, reading, writing, thinking, vocabulary, library.

Crafts, Kathy, and Brenda Hauther. *Success in College: The Student's Guide to Good Grades*, rev. ed. 1981. Grove Press Inc., 196 West Houston Street, New York, NY 10014. Paperback, 192 pp, $3.95. Often hilarious, always irreverent, but ultimately sensible book. Written for the traditional student in a university setting, but some unorthodox study approaches may be applicable to the adult student. Pleasant, quick reading.

Osgood, Judy. *How to Beat the Grade Game*. 1978. Condor Publishing Company, Inc., 29 East Main Street, Westport, CT 06880. Paperback, 209 pp, $2.25. Chapters on skills in reading, writing, using library, note taking, taking exams, and sections on mathematics and other specific subjects.

Pauk, Walter. *How to Study in College*, 2nd ed. 1974. Houghton Mifflin Co., 2 Park Street, Boston, MA 02107. Paperback, 274 pp, $7.50. Written by the director of the Reading-Study Center, Cornell University. Gives students straightforward, practical instruction on how to tackle and overcome their special difficulties. Widely used in study strategies courses. Chapters on skills in reading, writing, mathematics, speaking, note taking, taking tests, and specialized skills such as studying science and foreign languages.

Robinson, Francis P. *Effective Study*, 4th ed. 1970. Harper & Row, Publishers Inc., 10 East 53rd Street, New York, NY 10022. Paper text ed., 304 pp, $11.95. SQ3R method of studying explained. Chapters on skills in reading, writing, mathematics.

Staton, Thomas F. *How to Study*, 6th ed. 1977. Distributor: How to Study, P. O. Box 6133, Montgomery, AL 36106. Paperback, 80 pp, $1.50. Less detailed than Pauk. PQRST method. Section on note-taking and chapter on taking tests.

Reading

Miller, Lyle L. *Increasing Reading Efficiency*, 4th ed. 1977. Holt, Rinehart & Winston School Publishing, 383 Madison Avenue, New York, NY 10017. Paper text ed., 333 pp, $11.95. A workbook devoted to reading exercises and comprehension tests.

Strange, Jack R., and Sallie Minter Strange. *Reading for Meaning in College and After*. 1972. Brooks/Cole Publishing Co. Paperback, out of print (get through library). Focuses on reading for comprehension; not a book on speed reading. Chapters on studying textbooks, essays and other books, scientific and critical articles, literature.

Writing

Blumenthal, Joseph C. *English Twenty-Two Hundred*, 3rd ed. 1981. Harcourt Brace Jovanovich Inc., 757 Third Avenue, New York, NY 10017. Paper text ed., $9.50. Also, *English Twenty-Six Hundred*, 5th ed., 1981, $9.95; *English Thirty-Two Hundred*, 3rd ed., 1981, $10.95. "Each text is a programmed course in grammar, sentence building, correct usage, and punctuation." Tests and answer keys available from publisher.

Gefvert, Constance, Richard Raspa, and Amy Richards. *Keys to American English*. 1975. Harcourt Brace Jovanovich Inc., 757 Third Avenue, New York, NY 10017. Paper text ed., 326 pp, $9.95. "For beginning freshman English classes who need work in the basic grammatical structures of 'standard English.'" Designed for students whose dialect is distinctly different from the standard. Can be used independently, but better used with help from teacher. Instructor's manual available.

McCrimmon, James M. *Writing with a Purpose*, 7th ed. 1980. Houghton Mifflin Co., 2 Park Street, Boston, MA 02107. Text ed., 501 pp, $12.50. Also available in short ed., $11.50. Instructor's guides, resource book available at extra cost. A classic text, used for many years in composition classes. Can be used independently. From use of individual words to writing research papers. Includes handbook of grammar and usage.

Technical Writing

Hays, Robert W. *Principles of Technical Writing*. 1965. Addison-Wesley Publishing Co. Inc., Reading, MA 01867. Hardcover, $13.95. A general guide for engineering, business, and other students.

Sherman, Theodore A., and Simon Johnson. *Modern Technical Writing*, 3rd ed. 1975. Prentice-Hall Inc., Englewood Cliffs, NJ 07632. Hardcover, $16.50. A general guide on reports, proposals, and business correspondence.

Mathematics

Carman, Robert A., and Marilyn J. Carman. *Basic Mathematical Skills: A Guided Approach*, 2nd ed. 1981. John Wiley & Sons Inc., 605 Third Avenue, New York, NY 10158. Paper text ed., 576 pp, $18.95. Good for brushup.

Watkins, John H. *Arithmetic and Algebra*. 1977. Harper & Row, Publishers Inc., 10 East 53rd Street, New York, NY 10022. Paper text ed., 515 pp, $17.50. Test booklet free. Techniques of problem solving in arithmetic and algebra.

Speaking and Listening

Adler, Ronald B. *Confidence in Communication: A Guide to Assertive and Social Skills*. 1979. Holt, Rinehart & Winston School Publishing, 383 Madison Avenue, New York, NY 10017. Paper text ed., 334 pp, $12.95. A clear, well-written book designed to help you analyze specific communication difficulties and to develop strategies for overcoming them. The book is designed to be self-instructional and self-paced.

Mager, Robert. *Goal Analysis*. 1972. Fearon • Pitman Publishers, Inc., 6 Davis Drive, Belmont, CA 94002. Paper text ed., 136 pp, $5.95. An entertaining, valuable guide for refining vague goals into specific behavioral targets. While the book is not designed for developing speaking skills, the techniques and methods lend themselves nicely to assisting in overcoming nervousness in speaking and in developing clearer, more understandable messages.

Weaver, Carl H. *Human Listening: Processes and Behaviors*. 1972. Bobbs-Merrill Co. Inc., Educational Publishing Division, 4300 West 62nd Street, Indianapolis, IN 46206. Paper text ed., 155 pp, $4.50. This text develops many different dimensions of theory concerning listening behavior, including clear descriptions of how the mind receives information. It also develops common pitfalls of listening and suggests ways of avoiding them. Additionally, it presents a number of exercises to develop skill in listening.

Using the Library

Downs, Robert B., and Clara D. Keller. *How to Do Library Research*, 2nd ed. 1975. University of Illinois Press, 54 East Gregory Drive, Box 5081, Station A, Champaign, IL 61820. Paperback, $3.45.

Gates, Jean K. *Guide to the Use of Books & Libraries*, 4th ed. 1979. McGraw-Hill Book Co., 1221 Avenue of the Americas, New York, NY 10020. Paper text ed., $6.95.

Lubans, John Jr. *Educating the Library User*. 1974. R. R. Bowker Co., Box 1807, Ann Arbor, MI 48107. Textbook, $17.95.

Taking Tests

Millman, Jason, and Walter Pauk. *How to Take Tests*. 1969. McGraw-Hill Book Co., 1221 Avenue of the Americas, New York, NY 10020. Paperback, $3.50.

11
Utilizing Resources for Coping

*What are my personal resources for coping,
and what college resources may help me?*

Resources

Resources for coping lie within you, around you in your home environment, and at your college. Your success will be directly related to how well you utilize those resources throughout your college career.

Adult Assets

Adults have many advantages over younger students. Comparing adults to traditional students, educators often list the following as strengths of adult students:

- More experience. As one adult student puts it, "Having lived longer and experienced more is the most important advantage an adult student has." This advantage gives adults a natural basis for discussions that is lacking in classes of younger students. The youngster in a history class may have only the most ludicrous notion of where Vietnam is, whereas the adult may have fought there. The adult has lived longer, probably read more, heard more, and talked more about matters that relate to classroom learning than has the traditional student.

- Greater eagerness to learn. Adults appreciate more what they have missed, and do not want to miss any more of life and learning.

- More intensive commitment. They are probably sacrificing more—time, money, energy—than the younger students, and they want to make that sacrifice worthwhile.

- Less time to waste. Too much time has already gone by, and they want to make wise use of what is left. They will organize, complete assignments, and follow through. They will spend more time on studies and avoid excessive socializing.

- Better sense of goals. Younger people often do not know where they are going. Experience points out directions, clarifies paths, identifies goals.

- More willingness to question. The general life experience of the adult student may be equal to that of the teacher. The adult student, therefore, is more prone to question the assumptions of the teacher, and those questions are likely to lead the class into more profound examination of material than is the case with the younger class of students. Teachers often find this profundity of exploration exciting. "I'd been saying the same thing for years to young students," one teacher said. "Then an adult student questioned me and I realized I was wrong. It was an exhilarating reawakening."

- Greater expectation of good teaching. The adult who has committed more of his own resources than the younger student expects good teaching. Teachers of adults are likely to be better prepared, and the student thereby benefits more.

- Greater appreciation upon completion. Once a successful learning experience has been completed, adults are more prone to express their sincere appreciation to the professor. Knowing this, and being after all only human, the professor usually is going to try very hard to make the course worthwhile for his adult students. "I will never forget the man who told me at the end of the term that my wonderful course and teaching had changed his life," said a professor from a college in southern Utah. "At that moment, I think I would have taken no salary for the rest of my teaching career if I could only have been assured of such a look on just one of my students' faces at the end of each of my courses."

- In short: Maturity, self-discipline, motivation are assets of adults.

Adult Liabilities

Two liabilities seem to be the chief causes of adult failure in college. Comparing adults to younger students, educators find the following to be one weakness of adult students:

- Greater susceptibility to fear of failure. The stakes seem higher to adults. With more to lose, with more insight into the consequences of failure, adults can inhibit their chances of success by succumbing to anxiety.

You, and we, recognize anxiety for the formidable enemy it can be, yet we know it can be overcome. Virginia Mills of Brescia College in

Kentucky says: "I would like to reassure an adult who has the desire to attend college not to let fear control her life."

Adults want so much to succeed they sometimes lose their perspective on college. In a previous chapter Dennis Gerard Ellis gave you some excellent advice on getting straight A's. Now we want to give you some advice on *not* getting straight A's: Put your performance in perspective. Did you do the best you could under the circumstances? Does a B, C, D, or even an F mean the end of everything for you? Many adults drop out of college before giving themselves a chance because they fear they have failed or soon will fail. Remember the race of the turtle and the hare? The turtle was behind in the beginning, but he did not equate that to failure, and he finally won the race. Among the multitude of adult students who have succeeded in getting their degrees are many, many examples of difficult, slow starts, overcome by perspective and patience.

The second liability is:

• Greater external pressure. Adults bring a more complex world with them to campus. They are subjected to a greater number of outside pressures to quit than are younger students.

Younger students are pressured by parents and friends to "stick it out." Adult students often find the reverse to be true. Women especially are susceptible to coercion.

"Why don't you stay home and act like a mother?" says the mother of an adult student.

"We can't afford any more of this tuition," says the husband.

"Mom, why don't I ever have any clean socks?" asks the teenage son.

And so on, and so on. One woman, normally a mild-mannered, soft-spoken person, gathered her family around her one evening—parents, husband, children. "I said to them, 'Now hear this! I want this degree, and you're going to start helping me get it. I'm doing something for me for once, and so help me God, if I have to, I'll walk out of that door and never come back in order to get it. Now which do you want?'" She got all of the overt and most of the subtle coercion stopped, and she graduated.

Self-Knowledge: Your Strengths and Weaknesses

Recognizing the assets and liabilities of adults in general should be helpful to you. But of even greater help is taking stock of yourself.

Sven, a chemistry major in an Ontario university, found that he had to make a conscious assessment of himself and act on it in order to succeed. After two semesters he was barely passing, yet he knew he could do better. Across the early months of the summer he took long walks to think the matter through. He knew he was not highly intelligent, but he had always had good common sense, and he was persistent in his approach to problems. He needed to be able to make his persistence more effective, he came to realize. Sven had been divorced two years before, and his ex-wife habitually dropped in to see him, sometimes bringing a boyfriend. Sven thought that he handled the situation well, that it did not bother him. But his long walks and conscious exploration of his strengths and weaknesses relative to his college work revealed that he was indeed bothered. He needed to be able to concentrate better across long periods of study time, and the frequent visits of his ex-wife not only cut into his available study time, but worse, disrupted his inner being despite his apparently tranquil exterior. Realizing this after his periods of introspection, Sven called her and terminated their relationship entirely. During the next semester, now liberated in mind, he was able to concentrate effectively on his studies and significantly improve his grades.

Perhaps if you believe you are not able to be objectively analytical of yourself you should see a psychologist. This person could test you and work with you in assessing your strengths and weaknesses. Your college may even have the capability to do this in the personal counseling office (more on this later). Insight into yourself is an excellent tool for coping with college, and one you should not neglect to use.

Interpersonal Relationships

You may know your strengths and weaknesses very well, but if you do not put this knowledge to use in interpersonal relationships it does you little practical good. "You" are not only the totality of individual qualities you possess when alone, but objectively "you" are those qualities and the impact you make on all other people.

It is to your advantage to affect professors, administrators, and other students positively. But how can you know their reactions to you?

First, by being alert, by being more aware of others than you ever have been, you can assess to a significant degree the nature of your interpersonal relationships. This does not mean that you have to be sugar sweet to everyone. It only means that you have to be effective in dealing with people.

Patricia was a student in a college in South Dakota, enrolled in a psychology class in behavior modification. Part of the course was lecture, part lab. The lab was intended as an extended practical exercise in actually modifying the behavior of the students. Each student, through testing, was first to identify an aspect of her personality for behavior modification, then work on the modification through lab exercises and encounters in daily situations. The lab was graded pass or fail, and the sole criterion for the grade was a practical test at the end of the course to determine if the chosen aspect of behavior had in fact been modified.

At the beginning of the course, tests had revealed that Patricia would become angry and attack others when criticized. She chose this aspect of her personality to modify. At the end of the term the professor gave his exam covering the lecture portion of the class, and he called Patricia into his office.

"I am sorry to say you got a C in the exam. Since you had been doing A work, I would like to hear your explanation. Did you slack off at the end of the course?"

Patricia flushed and said, "If I got a C the problem wasn't my answers. It was your questions. If you knew how to write comprehensible questions, I'd have gotten an A. Your questions were stupid!" She walked out.

A few days later she inquired about when she would be scheduled for the practical exam to complete the lab portion of the course.

"You already took the exam," the professor said. "You actually got an A in the lecture, and you got an F in the lab. You would do well, I think, to repeat the lab next semester."

Patricia had not learned to be effective in dealing with others. Even when her problem had been isolated and she had consciously worked at modifying this aspect of her behavior, she had not been alert to judge her potential effect on others. Her reply to her professor was intended to diminish, not enhance, his stature. Had this not been a laboratory situation he probably would have been offended, and Patricia still would have lost, not gained, from the encounter.

Another means of judging the effectiveness of interpersonal relationships is to ask others to give you their assessments. How do they think you affect others?

Your approach could be general: "Professor Kehrli, how did I do this past term?" This might eventually lead into an analysis of how she viewed your interaction with her and the class. But you might get a more meaningful answer if you apply insights to your personality and ask specific questions: "Professor Kehrli, I have been told that I often antagonize people by monopolizing class discussion. Did you feel that this was a problem this semester?" Professor Kehrli's answer, along with similar assessments, your analysis of them, and your behavior modification, could be an important ingredient to your success at college.

Family, Friends, Other Students as Helpers

When commenting on their college experiences, adult students almost always turn to the topic of helping and being helped. Many adults say essentially what Mary Lou Isernhagen of Kansas State University says:

"The encouragement I received from my family was an important factor in my decision to return to school and to stay in school to the completion."

In those cases where your family is not sympathetic to your problems, you may have to start making some withdrawals from that bank of family relationships to which you have been contributing all these years. Just as you have owed others, *they owe you*. It may be crucially important for you to let that fact sink in deeply: *They owe you*. Your investment in a college education is an investment in your family as well as yourself.

There are risks, of course, and a few adults have found they gained a degree and the many good things associated with it, but lost other things. In some cases, husbands and wives have turned against one another, and children against mothers or fathers, under the added stress of an adult in the family going to college. "My husband divorced me, and my children hold me responsible for it. But for the first time in my life I feel like something other than an adjunct to everyone else's existence. I am a person. *I am me!*" This woman who graduated from a university in Montreal had never worked outside the house until she went to college. Now she is the public relations officer for an organization in Quebec. "I create, I relate to others, I am alive!" She hopes that someday her husband and children will come to see that she, as well as they, deserved to be fulfilled as a person.

Friends, like family, can be a powerful resource for coping, or a detriment. A university psychologist suggests, "The friend who will give you a lift to school when your car is in the shop for repairs, who will take your children in an emergency, who will encourage you to persevere is the kind you will need. Just as you have to be selective and conservative with your time in order to study, you may have to focus your friendships more wisely. Don't invite trouble by hanging onto past friendships that you know to be detrimental to your success. Rather, seek friends who will be helpful. There are such people and, if you persist, it is quite likely you will find them."

Other adult students can aid you, perhaps more than you realize is possible. Carpools, shared baby-sitting, assistance with school work— these are obvious types of physical aid. Less obvious, perhaps, is the psychological uplift you can get from other students. Virginia Mills of Brescia College in Kentucky was tempted to quit because of extraordinary pressures that developed soon after her enrollment, but another student played a major role in keeping her in college: "Having made a good friend at Brescia helped me, and I was calmed by having a friend to share with." Said another adult student, "The encouragement I received from my classmates was one of the main reasons I was able to hold out. I made so many wonderful friends. I'll never forget them. It was like leaving a 'family' each time a class would end."

Some schools have programs of peer counseling that are greatly helpful to new students. Evelyn Greengross of the College of New Rochelle's School of New Resources tells about their Student Resource Center:

> Students very often feel isolated in their world with what they believe are problems unique to them. In reality they discover mutual problems, and very often their shared ideas lead to solutions or new discoveries that would not be possible otherwise. In a setting such as this, people feel free to discuss work-related or home-related problems that may strongly influence their school performance or general attitude toward life. In a student resource center, many students find that an empathetic listener helps them find their own solutions to problems that might otherwise have been destructive.

If your school has such a program, use it. If it doesn't, let the administration know, or perhaps even start one yourself.

College Resources: Getting Help

Few institutions in our society are as well equipped to assist people in coping with stress as is an educational institution, especially one with resident students. Although colleges and universities are not all organized alike, they do tend to have some elements in common, and an understanding of college structure and resources will assist you in getting help.

Under the president there may be one or more vice presidents, depending upon the size of the institution. Then come deans and directors of administrative offices. Reporting to the academic dean will be academic division or department chairpersons or directors.

Titles of officials vary, but functions are similar from one college to the next. The president will have help essentially in three areas: academic affairs, student affairs, and general administration, including, most importantly, business affairs. The next chapter will treat situations of student frustration with bureaucracy. Here, though, we will sketch the essential structure for helping you, assuming that it is operating reasonably well and the people in it want to help.

President

Busy person that he or she is, the president would never intentionally let a student go without needed help. The president may be the only person in the college structure who has the responsibility and authority to get office A and office B working together to solve your problems.

Administrative assistant to the president

The president may have an assistant who has the implied authority of the president, if not the direct authority himself, to get office A and office B working together to your benefit. Titles vary; the administrative assistant may be called something else, but the function of this person is to coordinate people and to follow through on problems, including yours.

Vice presidents and deans

The second ranking officer in the institution, often called the executive vice president, will have broad supervisory authority and may be able to help you as effectively as the president. Other vice presidents or deans generally want to help too (but unfortunately important things sometimes do not get done because students do not provide direct input to them).

Counseling Services

Any college, no matter how small, necessarily invests much of its resources in counseling. Whether or not counseling staffs are large, counseling services exist. At a four-year private college with an enrollment of 1,300 full-time and 2,000 part-time students, the president was considering a suggestion to integrate all counseling services on campus. He asked his administrative assistant to explore the matter and provide him with a list of all the people on campus involved in formal counseling of students. This president had been in office for several years, but when he received the list he was astounded. It contained almost *200* names.

"What is this?" he demanded of his assistant.

"You asked for everyone who does formal counseling. After you study it, tell me which names you want struck."

The list had been categorized with a summary of duties for each category. The categories included:

Primary:

- Faculty (92). Contracts require academic advising as integral to teaching duties.
- Academic Advising Office (2). Academic advising.
- Counseling Services (2). Personal counseling.
- Placement Services (1). Career and employment counseling.
- Health Care (2¼). Physical and mental care and counseling; part-time clinical psychologist.
- Dean of Students Office (3). Student affairs.
- Resident Assistants (22). Dormitory assistance and general counseling.
- Educational Opportunity Program (3). Special counseling for educationally and/or economically disadvantaged students.
- Financial Aid Office (2). Financial affairs.

- Registrar's Office (4). Academic records and regulations.
- Office of Continuing Education and Summer Sessions (2). Adult counseling.

Ancillary:

All academic administrators from the academic dean to program directors; all other chief administrators down to assistant directors; Admissions Office; Physical Education and Athletics Office; librarians; secretaries of all the above.

That seasoned president learned something that day. In his many years as a college administrator, he had never been as aware of the extent of counseling services on a college campus as he was when he surveyed that list. Similar resources exist on your campus to serve you.

Academic Advising

The academic advising process at its most basic level begins when you approach a professor after class and say, "Would you help me?" If this person cannot help, you have other resources. You could try your major adviser (or program adviser, faculty adviser, or program coordinator—there are many names for this person). He is available to ensure that you get the academic counsel you need in order to formulate and complete a viable course of studies in fulfillment of the requirements of your major. Some advisers are content never to see you; others insist on frequent meetings. Thank God if you have the latter. (One word of caution: Whereas colleges expect their advisers to act professionally, they usually warn you, "While you may seek the advice of a counselor, final responsibility for any decision reached or action taken *is yours*.") The student who does not seek periodic counsel with his or her major adviser is reckless with his or her destiny.

The academic advising office is another resource, and one too little used by most students. One of your first visits on campus as a student should be to this office. Probably the office will have a handout listing services and procedures. Read it, but don't stop there. Ask questions about the services and see as many of the advisers as you can, if only for a few minutes to introduce yourself. Who those people are and how they relate to you is important. You should assess their ability to help you so you can turn to them if you feel your major adviser does not or cannot give you the help you need.

Although most of your academic problems can be treated effectively by your classroom teacher, major adviser, or the academic advising office counselors, some cannot. These people can put you in contact, though, with department and division chairmen, the registrar, and the dean.

But, you say, you do not want to bother those busy people—better to suffer in silence. Nonsense. The dean, for example, may be the only person in academic administration with sufficient authority to help you. A college, like any other organization, has rules and regulations that govern its existence. But at certain levels, administrators may waive those rules and regulations in the interests of common sense, justice, or compassion. A dean will not lightly waive a requirement or counter a decision made at a lower level. Nor will he make a decision without input from others. Consequently, he will normally expect that you have taken your problem through channels. If you have done so, though, and are dissatisfied, it is his obligation to investigate the matter and act justly.

How often do individual student problems get to the dean's desk? More often than you think. And sometimes such problems are indicative of a weakness in the system that must be corrected. By persisting and utilizing your college resources for academic advising, you may not only have helped yourself, but all the students of the college for years to come.

Financial Aid Counseling

by CAROL MACKINTOSH
Director of Financial Aid
Utica College of Syracuse University

Many financial aid offices offer a broad range of services beyond the primary function of providing information concerning aid and aid applications. Most can help you with bureaucratic problems that you may have in processing student-based grants such as the Pell Grant. Generally, a financial aid counselor can help with finding a lender if you wish to process a Guaranteed Student Loan. Many offices provide a job-finder service to help students find part-time jobs in the local community during the school year or during the summer vacation. A counselor may be able to advise students as to how to arrange their academic course load to minimize expenses. The financial aid office can provide you with documentation that you may need for dealing with agencies such as social services or the Food Stamp Administration. Most offices can help you understand your bill from the business office and payment options available to meet that bill. Many financial aid counselors are aware of new legislation or litigation that may apply to your situation and will keep you informed if the laws or cases will affect your aid. Often offices are familiar with public and private health-insurance plans that students may want to take advantage of. Some offices can make provisions for a student to receive an emergency short-term loan.

One of the most complicated problems you may encounter in college is coordinating your academic and financial matters. This is particularly true if you are a student who attends some academic terms part-time and some full-time or if you have a semester of poor academic performance. You will need to get advice from both your academic advising office and your financial aid office.

Consider the case of Alfred, a student who made full use of his college's counseling services. He had decided to go to college after he left the armed forces, and he made normal academic progress for three years, financing his education through a combination of his wife's employment, his own part-time employment, the G.I. Bill, a small Pell Grant, and a Guaranteed Student Loan. At the end of his third year, he and his wife had a child, and his wife did not return to work. Alfred sought the help of an academic adviser and a financial aid counselor. Together they made new arrangements for Alfred to finish school. Alfred would go to school three-fourths time and increase his hours at work. He and his academic counselor arranged that Alfred's graduation would be only three months later than originally planned. And he and the financial aid counselor made arrangements for him to use the college's division of continuing education, which offered a lower tuition rate. They also filed a supplemental Pell Grant application that showed a decrease in income due to the wife's discontinued employment, and this allowed Alfred to receive an increase in his grant. They also notified the Veterans Administration about the new baby so that Alfred could receive additional payments for a third person in his family. Finally, they processed a request for an increase in the Guaranteed Student Loan. Consequently, Alfred did not have to leave college, contrary to his initial fears.

While there are several ways a financial aid officer can help you, there are limitations. The financial aid office is constrained by government regulations and its own budget. You cannot expect the office to change regulations or overspend its budget. You can expect, though, that the office will help you in every way possible.

Personal and Psychological Counseling

by ROBERT E. WOODS
Director of Counseling
Utica College of Syracuse University

No matter what age a student is, college attendance may be accompanied by symptoms of anxiety and stress. Many of the stresses faced by some adults who return to school have been discussed earlier in the book. You should be aware that most colleges provide you with a mental-health service to assist you in coping. This service may range from a staff of psychiatrists and psychologists at a large university to a single counselor at a small college who may deal with financial aid, placement, and student social life in addition to personal counseling. The name given to this service may vary from campus to campus; "counseling center" and "psychological services" are common titles.

Once you have located the source of help, you will want to determine whether the available help is appropriate to your particular concern. Psychiatrists, psychologists, and counselors are different kinds of therapists, trained to do different things. Within each category of therapy are scores of techniques and approaches to practice. The following definitions can serve as a general guide that may enable you to choose a therapist or at least be aware of the type of service you are likely to get.

Psychiatrists are licensed physicians with a specialty in treating mental illness. They are the only mental-health professionals who can prescribe drugs.

Psychologists are trained to assess the emotional and behavioral characteristics of people and to help them overcome difficulties. Not all psychologists engage in counseling; some specialize in research and teaching exclusively. On most campuses, however, you will find at least one psychologist available for counseling.

Counselors are trained to help with problems associated with stress, such as marriage and family difficulties or anxiety arising out of a particular situation. They can help you to talk about your concerns and to reach satisfactory conclusions. Generally, counselors do not engage in long-term therapy or treat severe personality disorders, but they can identify the need for such treatment and make appropriate referrals.

Since the titles of these professionals are often confusing or vague, it's always a good idea to ask a potential therapist or counselor to discuss his or her training and style of practice. Any ethical therapist will be willing to do this.

An ethical issue that may concern you is confidentiality. Except under extraordinary circumstances, mental-health professionals are bound by a code of ethics that requires them to keep counseling information confidential. Thus, you can be assured that your professors and others will not be informed of your personal concerns.

A final word of advice: Don't be timid or hesitant about using this service. Colleges and universities take care to hire only trained professionals for these sensitive positions. Counselors and therapists, after all, can have a strong impact on how students view the institution. We know that happy students are more likely to persist in their studies than unhappy ones. If personal concerns are keeping you from living up to your full potential, visit the counseling center. It may be the key to your success.

We have described, from the top of the administrative structure to the bottom, the college resources that exist to aid you in solving your problems. We suggest, though, that in seeking help you try going from bottom to top. Use the proper channels in order to avoid annoying people who would be bypassed were you to go straight to the top. If the normal channels are not working for you, though, then you will want to use other means. That's what the next chapter is about.

12

Students' Rights
and College Bureaucracy

How can I cut through the red tape that hampers my progress?
What are my rights and avenues of recourse as a student?

How to Deal with Bureaucracy

T he *American Heritage Dictionary of the English Language* provides three definitions of bureaucracy, one of which is: "Any administration in which the need to follow complex procedures impedes effective action." Unfortunately, that definition fits many colleges and universities. You can observe bureaucracy at various places on campus, the bursar's office for example, as depicted by these reflections of an adult college student in a southwestern state:

> The bursar's office has you down for 3 credits even though you are registered for 12. "We wondered why you made such a large tuition payment!" the clerk exclaims. Nevertheless, you are told they have to go by the computer printout; they cannot contradict the computer. You will have to get your counselor to submit a new registration form. Although they have no record of your being granted a state tuition assistance award, they find an award notice in your file. You recall that your checks for payment of tuition are usually not cashed for months on end, and you wonder why. Perhaps, you muse, the college is not concerned about losing interest income or lacking working capital.

Aileen Price, retired registrar of Utica College of Syracuse University, reminds us that " 'An institution is but the shadow of a man . . .' and when shadows thicken bureaucracy develops. Colleges are no different from other public and private organizations students have encountered. But certainly students are entitled to courteous, efficient, and competent services."

College bureaucracy can easily push you to a point approaching paranoia. The battle for your rights as a student could become an obsession. When this happens, your academic goals may become overshadowed and the joy of learning can be seriously diluted. Trivial matters are not worth getting upset over. You should not allow yourself to be sucked into anyone's personal vendetta with the system. The best strategy is usually tolerance and courtesy. Most people respond to being treated with respect, particularly if they are being neglected in this area by their superiors.

Expecting perfection, or even excellence, from everyone you deal with is unrealistic. If an error is made, don't go right to the employee's superiors; first talk to the person in a calm, rational manner and give him or her the opportunity to rectify the situation. In a tactful way, ask for the individual's name and make a note of it. People are more responsive when they are not anonymous. If you've given someone every opportunity to correct a problem and he or she fails to do so, it may be necessary (as a last resort) to complain to the person's superior. But be certain that your complaint is justified and that your victory will be worth the potential cost: being on that person's "list." And if a matter of principle is involved, you may have to take the issue all the way to the top—the president of the college.

Challenging the @!#—*?! Computer

The advent of computerized processing of academic information has added a new dimension to college bureaucracy. In theory, the computer promises to solve the problems of inefficiency and ineptitude by collecting, storing, retrieving, and processing data in a fraction of the time it takes people to perform these functions. In practice, however, the computer often leaves much to be desired. The technological capability is there, but the human element has not been eliminated—as the saying goes, "garbage in, garbage out." Too often the computer printout will contain at least as many errors as the old manual systems. But the computer has a unique feature that is relished by some college staffs—it can't talk back. The computer may have become the latest "cop-out" for the system. When something goes wrong, the computer can be blamed.

The important point to remember is that computers are tools used by people to do a job. A computer malfunction does not release the person from his or her responsibility to get the job done, and it certainly should not transfer the burden to you. Delays of days, weeks, or months are invariably caused by people, not computers. If all else fails, and the situation is urgent, there can be no acceptable reason for not handling your problem manually; after all, isn't this how it was done before the computer? You might have to be insistent, and with the right person, but you are entitled to obtain the proper results from the @!#—*?! computer, and you can.

Students' Rights: First Amendment, Due Process

Landmark court rulings have, in recent years, opened the doors for students to exercise their constitutional right of free expression in schools. The First Amendment to the Constitution, according to a United States Supreme Court decision (*Tinker* v. *Des Moines Independent District*), permits students to air their views on any subject provided they do not "'materially and substantially' disrupt the work and discipline of the school" (Alan H. Levine and Eve Cary, *The Rights of Students*, rev. ed., New York: Avon Books, 1977, p. 24). Levine and Cary point out that students may not be barred from using school facilities, or from gathering, or forming a social club, or distributing literature, or soliciting money to support political and social causes, even if their viewpoint is considered dissident by school officials. Therefore, as long as the *Tinker* test of material and substantial disruption is satisfied, you have the right to use any channel of communication available on campus to express your opinions about any subjects you wish.

Due process is another fundamental right of all Americans. Employees of public colleges and universities are bound by the Fourteenth Amendment to provide any student who is accused of misconduct with a fair and impartial hearing.

Private colleges and universities usually also try to assure students of fair treatment through establishment of procedures similar to those in the following excerpt from a university's student-faculty handbook:

Due Process
Alleged offenders of . . . Rules, Regulations and Procedures shall be guaranteed due process, which is defined as follows:

1. **The student shall be given adequate notice in writing of the specific ground or grounds and the nature of the evidence on which the disciplinary proceedings are based.**
2. **The student shall be given an opportunity for a hearing in which the disciplinary authority provides a fair opportunity for hearing the student's position, explanations, and evidence.**
3. **No disciplinary action shall be taken on grounds which are not supported by substantial evidence.**

Note: Any student may appeal any decision made by a disciplinary authority or hearing board. . . .

Thus you *are* entitled to certain fundamental rights as a student, including freedom of expression and, at most schools, due process. However, you are also required to abide by the rules and regulations of your college. Problems may arise when official policies, procedures, or directives conflict with your basic constitutional rights. You can usually resolve such disputes through the judicial process provided by your school. If you are unable to obtain satisfactory results by appealing to the appropriate hearing board (assuming one exists), you then have the right to take legal action.

Women's Educational Equity

Establishing educational equity for women is generally recognized as the starting point from which the eventual elimination of sex biases, and consequential sex discrimination, in our country might be achieved. With this objective in mind, federal laws and regulations prohibiting sex discrimination in educational institutions have been adopted. The major piece of legislation affecting students is Title IX of the Education Amendments of 1972. The following information was extracted from the "PEER Summary of the Regulation for Title IX Education Amendments of 1972" published by the Project on Equal Education Rights:

> Title IX says: "No person . . . shall, on the basis of sex, be excluded from participation in, be denied the benefits of, or be subjected to discrimination under any education program or activity receiving federal financial assistance. . . ." Letters charging that discrimination has occurred may be sent to the Director, Office for Civil Rights, U.S. Department of Education, 330 Independence Avenue, S.W., Room 3256N, Washington, D.C. 20201, or to the Director of the Regional Office for Civil Rights responsible for enforcement in that state. . . .

Although significant gains have been made since the passage of Title IX, sex discrimination sometimes seems to remain deeply ingrained in our educational system. Extensive literature on sex discrimination against students is available free from the following sources:

Project on the Status and Education of Women
Association of American Colleges
1818 R Street, N.W.
Washington, DC 20009
(202) 387-1300

PEER
1112 13th Street, N.W.
Washington, DC 20005
(202) 332-7337

Women's Educational Equity Act (WEEA)
Distribution Center
39 Chapel Street
Newton, MA 02160
(800) 225-3088; in Massachusetts call (617) 969-7100
(WEEA awards grants to organizations and individuals for activities that promote educational equity for women.)

Age Discrimination Act

The Age Discrimination Act of 1975 prohibits exclusion of any individual from participating in federally funded programs or activities on the basis of age. While factors not directly related to age (such as physical health) might still limit admission of some older people, you cannot legally be denied admission to most colleges because you are too old.

Should you be denied admission because of your age to a college that accepts federal funds, you must first seek recourse through the college administration. If, after you've pursued all available avenues, the college still refuses to reverse its decision, you may then file suit charging violation of the Age Discrimination Act of 1975. Procedures for filing complaints vary from college to college depending upon which federal agencies have provided financial assistance to the institution. Colleges are required to provide students with proper information on how to exercise their rights. Should you not be satisfied with this information, we suggest you contact the nearest office of the U.S. Commission on Civil Rights for advice on how to proceed.

Privacy Act: Access to Your Official Records

The Family Educational Rights and Privacy Act of 1974 guarantees you access to your college records, and provides the means for you to have inaccurate or inappropriate notations in your files changed or deleted. The law also prohibits disclosure of most information about you to outside organizations or individuals without your written consent. College officials may not deny you the right to see any record of your academic or personal progress, even if such record is designated as "confidential" (unless you have signed a waiver of your right to access to a specific piece of information). School officials are entitled to see your records, but only those officials who have a legitimate educational interest and need for access to information about you.

To provide you with an example of the type of information your college might compile about you, we have included this excerpt dealing with the Privacy Act from a university's student-faculty handbook:

> The following educational records are maintained by the University and are considered as subject to this law:
> (a) Student Folders—Dean of Students Office for all undergraduate students, Graduate Dean's Office for all graduate students. Your department or school may also maintain a file . . . for enrolled students.
> (b) Permanent Record Cards—The Dean of Students Office, undergraduates only.
> (c) Academic Transcripts—Office of the Registrar for all students.
> (d) Placement Folders—Office of Counseling and Career Development for all students and alumni.
> (e) Health Records*—Infirmary, Psychological Services Clinic, Social Work Services Clinic.
>
> *Note: These records may not be personally inspected by students or eligible parents, but may be reviewed by an appropriate professional of your choice.

If it is not practical for you to personally inspect your records, you can request copies and the college must furnish them although you will probably have to pay the copying costs. Copies of your academic transcript are always available to you (usually at a nominal fee) from the registrar. If you wish to challenge any entry (other than a properly recorded grade) on your transcript or other school records, you have the right to a hearing within a reasonable time after you request it. Should you have a complaint that is not resolved to your satisfaction by the school, you can write to the Family Educational Rights and Privacy Acts Office, Department of Education, 400 Maryland Avenue, S.W., Washington, DC 20202.

Adult Student Power

Acting individually, adult students have some of the resources necessary to effect changes in the functioning of a college. Acting together, their resources are greatly multiplied.

Change can be accomplished through organized student governments, lobbying, and use of the media. However, strong leadership will be needed to overcome the problem of student apathy. Work and family demands, coupled with the transient nature of college attendance, causes apathy to be particularly acute among adult students. Yet significant progress toward forming adult organizations is being made on college campuses throughout the United States.

Adult students, through organizing, have gotten many things done: proper library staffing in the evening to serve adult students; bursar's and registrar's offices to be open in the evening; the bookstore and cafeteria to remain in service in the evening; a counseling staff for continuing education students where none had existed. The list of improvements brought about through adult students' efforts is a long one. If your college does not have an effective adult student organization, perhaps you should start one, now.

Helen E. Marshall of Plainfield, New Jersey, did just that. Halfway through her first semester at Essex County College, Helen decided to join the traditional Student Government Association. She recalls her early experiences of getting involved:

> Becoming active in the student government gave me the opportunity to get involved, and, with the support of other caring persons, to do something about the problems and concerns of students. Finding viable solutions to problems takes the efforts of all concerned. Getting involved is very time-consuming. It may make you work harder to maintain the standards and grade-point average you want. But you will have the satisfaction of knowing you are a meaningful part of your institution of higher learning, helping yourself and others.

One year later, Helen was officially recognized by Essex County College as president and organizer of the new E.C.C. Evening Students Association.

How can *you* begin to organize adults? You might start by requesting cooperation from the administration and publishing a newsletter. Even token authority can be turned into legitimate power through effective use of mass media. Adult student publications can serve as communication channels to unify nontraditional students.

The influence of a local student association is magnified further if the local organization is a member of a national association. Among the most widely recognized national associations of college students are the following:

- Coalition of Independent College and University Students (COPUS)
- Movimiento Estudiantil Chicano de Atzlan (MECHA)
- National Organization of Black University and College Students
- National Third World Student Coalition
- National Women's Student Coalition
- United Mexican-American Students
- United States Association of Evening Students (USAES)
- United States Student Association (USSA)

Each of these organizations represents a specific segment of the college student population. Some (such as MECHA) obviously serve minorities, while others (such as USSA and COPUS) cater primarily to traditional college students, although they may include provisions for nontraditional students as well.

The only nationwide coalition of college students exclusively serving adults is the United States Association of Evening Students (USAES).

The USAES is a national nonprofit organization of part-time, nontraditional college and university students throughout the United States devoted to the promotion and development of part-time education, and educational opportunity for all. Lorraine Phillips, USAES past president, describes one of the benefits derived by some one-half million adult students represented by the organization:

> The Legislative Program of the USAES provides the constituency with current information regarding legislation for higher education affecting part-time students. Such legislation is researched, reported, and, when approved by the Executive Board, supported for passage in Congress by the membership. USAES has presented testimony supportive of legislation beneficial to nontraditional students on Capitol Hill, as well as in state legislative chambers.

Anthony F. Farma, also a past president of USAES, explained that such services are not the only reasons for getting involved:

There is satisfaction in giving of your time and effort but there is more than satisfaction to be gained from involvement. If all you have to remember after you receive your degree is that you went to class, you will have missed an important part of your education. I urge you to seek participation in evening student government, to serve on a committee, to try to make your college better. I also urge you to *demand* that services that are available to full-time traditional students be made available to evening and part-time students.

If you want to know more about how to organize and operate an evening student government, request *Guidebook for Evening Student Governments* (free) from USAES, c/o Evening College, The University of Akron, 302 East Buchtel Avenue, Akron, OH 44325; telephone (216) 375-7790.

Adult students possess tremendous strength in numbers that can only be realized through organization. Unity of nontraditional college students during our era will surely result in unprecedented adult student power!

STUDENT PROFILE
Anthony F. Farma
(USAES past president)

At the age of 42, with a growing family of five children and plans to embark on self-employment, I decided that a return to college was necessary. Economics dictated that I could take two or three evening courses a semester to avoid straining the family budget and denying my children an opportunity to further their own educational goals. I was fortunate to pick Suffolk University near my home in Boston, Massachusetts.

Anyone who had seen my high school record would have been reluctant to predict I could ever have received A's in anything except recess. However, with maturity came a philosophy that, simply stated, is, "Everything you do is worth 100 percent effort." I received A's in both of my first two courses at Suffolk University.

Naturally the high marks encouraged me to continue. The academic atmosphere was intoxicating, and I was actually enjoying Saturday afternoons in the library doing research papers and reading. The doors of knowledge began opening, with each one more exciting than the last. Soon the routine of work, classes, and weekend study became ingrained into my life as it does with all evening students. However, there was something missing in my college experience.

I noticed that some of my classmates were complaining of problems regarding services that were not being provided, and the attitude of certain administrators toward evening students. I was fortunate not to have run into any of these problems and considered the complaints as natural in an urban university and certainly as having nothing to do with me.

Then it happened!

In an effort to save precious time, I called my adviser to clarify my forthcoming semester courses. His secretary said she was sorry but her boss would not talk to me on the phone. I was told, "If you want to discuss your program you must make an appointment during *daytime* appointment hours."

Needless to say my Italian temper was put to its severest test. Then and there the plight of the much maligned evening student became my personal battle. I began to explore avenues to change the attitudes of the administrators and faculty at this small urban university and to seek ways to help my fellow students.

The way that appeared was the evening student government, which, at that time, was in desperate trouble due to a lack of good public relations and the normal apathy evidenced by most evening and part-time students. Before long I was elected president of the Evening Division Student Association (EDSA).

After taking office I realized that without sufficient funding no organization can ever reach its full potential. With the support of the Evening Division Student Association board, EDSA developed a new constitution that allowed for a collection of $5.00 per year per part-time student. This money, which was under the direct control of the EDSA board, allowed us to properly advertise, develop new programs, and provide scholarship services for officers.

In prior years the Evening Division Student Association had trouble filling its twelve-member board. Now, with a healthy budget and an enthusiastic board, we have more than enough people to run for the positions.

The combined efforts of these dedicated adult students has resulted in significant accomplishments. These include an Oktoberfest, reduced parking rates for evening students in the surrounding garages, and a well-attended and enjoyable Recognition Night dinner dance.

Once the commitment to be totally involved was made, it was just a short step for me to look beyond Suffolk University to the problems and concerns of evening and part-time adult students in other universities. I attended a meeting at Northeastern University of the United States Association of Evening Students (USAES). At the next meeting of the EDSA board I enthusiastically recommended our joining USAES. A vote was taken and we became members.

Within the space of two years, through a series of circumstances, I was elected president of the New England Region of USAES. Liaison was established with my congressman (a former evening student), and he was sympathetic to our cause. Through this contact I was able to keep a close watch on the happenings in Washington and how they would affect our population. At several national meetings, legislation workshops were held in which letter-writing techniques and campaign strategies were discussed. For the first time the organization was having its collective voice heard in Congress.

At the same time I was concentrating on expanding the New England Region, and results were starting to show. By the end of my second elected term, the membership of the region had increased by 100 percent.

Several members of USAES encouraged me to run for president of the National. Following my term as president of the United States Association of Evening Students, I can look back at two appearances before congressional committees, more member universities and colleges than when I took office, and plans for additional expansion which will, I'm sure, bear fruit.

13
Reassessing Goals and Performance

*After having been in college for some time,
I wonder—am I going in the right direction, achieving all I can,
and getting the most satisfaction out of college and life?*

Reviewing Goals, Priorities, Decisions, Activities

Where have I been? Where am I now? Where am I going? What should I be doing now to get there? It is natural for students to have such questions. Unfortunately, too many adults allow these questions to come and go willy-nilly and never purposefully reassess their situation. Consequently, they become confused and discouraged. Many drop out of college. We believe that your chances for success both in college and in your future career are enhanced if, after having been in college for some time, you deliberately review your goals, priorities, decisions, and activities.

Your choices of college and curriculum were based on what you believed some time ago, not what you know and feel now. Ask yourself if those decisions are still valid today, considering your current outlook on life, your newly acquired knowledge, and your personal and professional goals and aspirations. A review of your program to see if it is what you really want should take place before the end of the equivalent of the first year of a two-year program, or of the second year of a four-year program. The longer you wait, if you must change, the more difficult and costly it could become for you.

In the next section we will treat present career relationships. But since so many adults go to college for future career reasons, we would first like to sketch some considerations related to your postcollegiate goals.

To achieve maximum success and satisfaction, you should enjoy your work. You may be good at your job, but if you hate going to work you are probably either in the wrong field or working for the wrong employer. Perhaps you should ask whether self-employment, or maybe a career change, is right for you. If so, does your degree program still meet your needs? If you are not currently employed and are going to college to qualify for a new trade or profession, it should be easier for you to be objective when reconsidering career alternatives. However, it may be more difficult for you to identify and define your particular skills and talents if you haven't been in the job market for some time. In your career reassessment, you may come up with several occupations you think you would enjoy and be good at, but how can you be sure if you've never tried them? Unfortunately, of course, you can't be sure that any job would be right for you. But you can vastly increase the probability of being right by being as introspective as possible.

A valuable tool widely used by career and academic counselors to help others make choices is the computer. For example, National Computer Systems distributes and processes the Career Assessment Inventory (CAI). It is an interest inventory designed for people interested in pursuing additional postsecondary training, such as courses of study offered at technical and vocational schools or at community colleges. The firm also offers the Strong-Campbell Interest Inventory (SCII), which is recommended for those persons interested in careers requiring higher-level technical training or college. For the SCII, the person seeking guidance completes a questionnaire, and the computer prints out a personal assessment in a fifteen-page report, prefaced by the following explanation:

> Choosing your career is an important process which requires that you recognize your abilities, but your interests and personal preferences are also fundamental to choosing a satisfying occupation. Research has indicated that individuals have a better chance of being satisfied in a particular occupation if their interests are similar to those of people already employed in that occupation. The Strong-Campbell Interest Inventory, therefore, points out work areas where your interests do and do not match those of people in different occupations. These results, which are based on your like and dislike responses to the items on the inventory, will help you understand how your preferences fit into the world of work.

More information about CAI, SCII, and other inventories can be obtained from NCS-Interpretive Scoring Systems, P. O. Box 1416, Minneapolis, MN 55440.

Our reference to these inventories demonstrates an important point. Reassessing your future requires objectivity. You should try to "think" like a computer, that is, in a completely unbiased and unemotional way. We are not implying that your feelings should be ignored. Indeed, you must clarify and define your feelings and opinions about many things. Then you must take stock of your assets in terms of talent, abilities, and skills, and realistically evaluate your potential capabilities. If your reassessment indicates that you should change your degree program, good. Better to find out now while there is time to make a change.

Assessing the Present

Your answer to the question, "What should I be doing now in order to get where I want to go?" necessarily involved the three major concerns in your present existence. They are career, college, and family relationships.

Career Relationships

Planning for your future career is important, but you must also pay attention to your present employment. You cannot afford to become so engrossed in your educational and career plans that you lose sight of this basic fact. Martin, a Colorado sales executive, had recently been promoted to territorial vice president with responsibility for directing a team of 20 district sales managers. Soon after his promotion he decided to enroll in a bachelor of business administration degree program at a local university. This would please his employer, he thought. Carrying a 12-credit load throughout the academic year, he was determined to earn straight A's, and he did. Unfortunately, Martin was so preoccupied with his course work that he neglected his duties, and within a year he was demoted to his former position.

College must be kept in proper perspective as it relates to your daily activities. Watch for danger signals: Have you discovered yourself talking often about college during lunch hour or cocktails with the boss? Is your superior making comments (even innocent-sounding ones) about your being enamored of college? Have you found yourself thinking of course work when you should have been concentrating on company work? If so, you might be wiser to cut back on course work and give adequate attention to your present career. Even if your objective is to change careers, finding a new job is considerably easier for an individual who is already employed and who can get a good recommendation from a current employer.

College Relationships

Your assessment of present college relationships should involve not just program and credit review to ensure that you are on the right track to graduation and later a career, as discussed earlier. It should also take into account your total college environment.

After having been in school for some time, you should ask yourself if you are being as effective as possible in your dealings with others. If not, can you find any pattern to your problems? If you can, you are well equipped to discuss the matter with various people—individual professors in whom you place confidence, or academic and personal counselors, or a dean. Out of these discussions might come solutions.

But what if, after having made such an assessment, you believe sincerely that the fault lies not in you but in the college? Have you considered transferring to another institution? It is a routine procedure, and certainly is nothing of which to be ashamed. Even if you have to lose a few credits in the transfer, it might be the right action to take.

When assessing your present college relationships, if you find yourself in an unsatisfactory situation, you have certain choices. You can accept the situation and live with it. Or you can change yourself in order to adapt to it. Or you can effect changes in the other elements of the situation so they are compatible with you. Or you can walk away from it. Consider your alternatives carefully, and then decide.

Family Relationships

by STEPHANIE PHILLIPS
Associate in Science degree with honors from Dutchess Community College, Poughkeepsie, New York

Now that you have experienced a semester or so of college, and probably cleared those initial hurdles of family consternation, nevertheless you should reassess your family relationships. Penny Meek, of Twin Lakes, Colorado, says: "My husband and I have had to reevaluate our expectations and goals as individuals and as a couple. We found at times each of us had to give a little more than we normally might have. As a result, I feel we have developed a nontraditional marriage and family."

For some families, perhaps the smoothness with which everything is proceeding is only a surface condition. Or if the surface is churning, it may not be too late to pour oil on the troubled waters. Sabina Leonard of Trocaire College recognized that serious consequences can result from neglecting to reassess present family relationships: "It seems that in the past few years, more women are going back to college, and once they have their degree, they divorce their husbands. I know that this must bother my husband because he teases me about my divorcing him as soon as I graduate. I usually tell him I have a list of things to do after graduation. First is to buy new shoes; second, divorce Bud. We both chuckle and it's okay for the moment, but he wouldn't tease if it didn't bother him. I make the time to reassure him often that he is more important than my schooling."

Adults in college work and achieve. The achievement may be not only an individual but also a family achievement.

Achievement and Satisfaction

How important is achievement? And what is the relationship between achievement and satisfaction? These questions, to be sure, are important to all of us.

Achievement is a means by which we can demonstrate our worth to society and elicit recognition from our fellow human beings. Does recognition of our achievements, however, provide the satisfaction we seek? Maybe, and maybe not. We can be recognized without being appreciated and respected. What then is the point of achievement if we can't be assured of the appreciation and respect of others?

Here is what some adult students have told us about their college achievements and satisfaction:

Stephanie Phillips dropped out of high school at the age of 16 to get married. Eleven years later, she enrolled in Dutchess Community College with the support of her husband and two children. The going was rough, but achievement made her efforts worthwhile: "Throughout my college education, I experienced many changes and a lot of growth. My final accomplishments are a matter of record. My final grade-point average was a 3.95, my achievements earned me a scholarship to continue my education, and I received a letter of acceptance to Vassar College in Poughkeepsie, New York. In comparison, my growth as an individual can't be measured by a grade-point average."

Virginia B. Mills, at age 45, was widowed after 25 years of marriage. A mother of three children, she was faced with the necessity of becoming self-supporting. Despite considerable difficulty in obtaining financial aid and in coping with family responsibilities and her father's illness, she persevered. As she approached her final semester at Brescia College, Owensboro, Kentucky, looking forward to graduation with honors, she described her feelings: "In just six weeks I will be a degreed and certified special education teacher. Two years ago when I looked at the schedule, I could not believe I could do it all, and now, I just have one semester of student teaching to go. Now I feel comfortable in school, but more importantly, in life. Even if I should never go into teaching, I have a confidence and competence that have made me a fuller, stronger, and more outgoing person. I have discovered my potential and I realize that I am an intelligent person."

Wilma J. Dickey of Mission, Kansas, discovered that her "nesting urge was threadbare" at age 41, and she entered college. She said: "There is no way that I can adequately express what attending Johnson County Community College did for my life. It gave me confidence; it gave me purpose. It gave me friendships; it gave me joy. I relate any good thing in both my professional and personal life today to that year, as the new beginning. Whether I will ever continue and earn a four-year degree, I still do not know. For now, I feel fulfilled."

Now that we've reviewed these descriptions of achievement and satisfaction experienced by this representative sampling of adult college students, perhaps we can draw some conclusions. How important is achievement? We think it is important to everyone. Does achievement lead to satisfaction? Probably, but not necessarily. Achievement without a worthy purpose can be empty. Will lack of recognition minimize the satisfaction you realize through your achievements? Probably not. If the accomplishment is truly significant, lack of recognition should not detract from your sense of self-satisfaction.

But some people might yet ask, "Why bother?" The following excerpts from John W. Gardner's book, *Excellence: Can We Be Equal and Excellent Too?* (New York: Harper & Row Publishers, 1961, pp. 178-9), might help you to clarify your reasons for being an adult college student.

> We fall into the error of thinking that happiness necessarily involves ease, diversion, tranquility—a state in which all of one's wishes are satisfied. For most people happiness is not to be found in this vegetative state but in *striving toward meaningful goals*. The dedicated person has not achieved all of his goals. His life is the endless pursuit of goals, some of them unattainable. He may never have time to surround himself with luxuries. He may often be tense, worried, fatigued. He has little of the leisure one associates with the storybook conception of happiness.
>
> But he has found a more meaningful happiness. The truth is that happiness in the sense of total gratification is not a state to which man can aspire. It is for the cows, possibly for the birds, but not for us.
>
> We want meaning in our lives. When we raise our sights, strive for excellence, dedicate ourselves to the highest goals in our society, we are enrolling in an ancient and meaningful cause—the age-long struggle of man to realize the best that is in him. Man reaching toward the most exalted goals he can conceive, man striving impatiently and restlessly for excellence, has achieved great religious insights, created great works of art, penetrated secrets of the universe and set standards of conduct which give meaning to the phrase "the dignity of man."

14
Life After College

*Is there really a life after college? What about graduate school,
a new career, continued personal growth?*

Gazing into the Crystal Ball

You are nearing completion of your degree. What lies ahead? If you are getting your associate degree, should you go on to take your baccalaureate? If you are getting your baccalaureate, should you plan to go on to graduate school, or go into a new phase of your career, or into a new career entirely? These are questions that undoubtedly you have been pondering. Your academic advising staff, library staff, and career and placement counselors should be able to assist you in planning your future courses of action. With this help, what lies in the crystal ball should become more distinct for you to see. This chapter takes you down the two paths that most students tread in the latter stages of a bachelor's degree program. One leads on to graduate school or postbaccalaureate study, and the other directly to a career.

Weighing Alternatives
for Further Study

If you just want to continue learning, graduate school may not be for you. Undergraduate courses that you were not able to take as part of your degree curriculum might provide your best source of satisfaction. You might even be able to advance your career objectives more effectively by taking selected undergraduate courses. Sharpening your skills in areas that are directly applicable to your work could provide your quickest route to success.

Some colleges, universities, and vocational schools offer certificate programs designed to enhance the potential of college graduates for employment in certain professional fields. These programs usually involve modules of four to eight courses (12–24 credits) in a specific field.

Such programs are well suited for individuals with undergraduate degrees in disciplines affording limited career opportunities. Since certificate programs take less time to complete than most graduate degree programs, they are particularly appealing to many adults.

Some colleges and universities will allow a student to apply credits earned through a postbaccalaureate certificate program toward the requirements for a graduate degree. Thus a professional program might provide quick access to a new career as well as a stepping-stone to a master's or doctoral degree. If graduate credit is important to you, though, be sure to check on credit transferability since many postbaccalaureate certificate programs are composed of undergraduate courses only. Also, the better course of action in many cases might be to get a second bachelor's degree that will allow entry to a particular career field. Often the second degree can be obtained with only somewhat more credit hours than would be accumulated in a certificate program. But an even better approach might be to get a graduate degree, especially if it requires only a few more credit hours than the certificate, and this may be the case.

Sources of information and assistance in making such educational and career decisions can be found in the annual *Directory of Educational and Career Information Services for Adults*. To obtain a copy contact: National Center for Educational Brokering, 1211 Connecticut Avenue, N.W., Suite 310, Washington, DC 20036; (202) 887-6830.

Preparing for Graduate School

When you took that major step forward and entered college, graduate school became a realistic possibility for you. Mary Ellen Schwender of Oceanside, New York, says: "When I started I was only going to try for the associate degree. Now I have that degree and soon will have my B.A. degree. And here I am thinking about graduate school."

Many adult students have decided that higher education need not stop with a bachelor's degree, regardless of one's age. Evelyn M. Greengross, aged 60, of Mamaroneck, New York, says: "From the experiences of earning my B.A. degree I have developed a direction for myself. I have been accepted in a master's degree program in counseling the aging at the University of Bridgeport. This degree will enable me to pursue a professional career based upon the experiences that were developed and nurtured during my four exciting years at the School of New Resources, College of New Rochelle."

Coauthor Charles McCabe, a high school dropout, entered college on a "provisional basis" at age 31. Because of his limited formal education, he was quite concerned about his ability to do college-level work as an adult. Yet within less than two and a half years Chuck earned his high school equivalency diploma, his associate in arts degree, and his bachelor of science degree with a double major (graduating summa cum laude, number one in his class of 141 nontraditional students), and he was admitted to a highly selective executive M.B.A. degree program at Pace University in New York City. Chuck completed his M.B.A. degree within two years, then immediately began pursuing a doctorate in professional studies in management at Pace University.

Success stories such as these are abundant—the list could go on and on. Can such a story be about you? Absolutely! We're convinced that virtually any adult who has demonstrated the motivation and perseverance required to earn a baccalaureate degree can succeed in graduate studies.

Two types of graduate degrees may be attained. They are graduate academic and professional degrees. (See the glossary.) Your college library will contain guides to graduate studies. Some guides will be specialized for such fields as political science, management, psychology, law, and medicine. Others, such as *Peterson's Annual Guides to Graduate Study*, will be comprehensive. Such references will greatly assist you in choosing a graduate program.

Graduate Admission Tests: DAT, GMAT, GRE, LSAT, MAT, MCAT, OCAT, PCAT, VAT

Most colleges and universities require standard admission tests at the graduate level. The following synopses of the most common tests are extracted from the brochure of the Stanley H. Kaplan Education Center (pp. 11-15).

DAT The Dental Admission Test is a comprehensive full-day examination that includes Chemistry (organic and inorganic), Biology, Mathematics, Verbal Skills (reading comprehension, completions, and antonyms), and 2- and 3-dimensional Perceptual Ability. . . . The DAT is administered twice a year, usually in April and October.

GMAT The Graduate Management Admission Test is a half-day examination testing many skills in both math and verbal areas. The content may vary from test to test. Included may be: Reading Recall, Reading Comprehension, Antonyms, Analogies, Sentence Completions, Mathematics (Data Sufficiency, Data Interpretations, and Problem Solving), Practical Judgment (Data Evaluation and Data Application), and Writing Ability. . . . The GMAT is administered four times a year, usually in October, January, March, and July.

GRE APTITUDE AND ADVANCED TESTS The Graduate Record Examination consists of a three-hour morning aptitude examination and a three-hour afternoon advanced test in the candidate's major study area. . . . Question types in the verbal area include: Reading Comprehension, Antonyms, Analogies, and Sentence Completions. The questions in the quantitative area include: Mathematical Problem Solving (sharpening of fundamental concepts in arithmetic, algebra, geometry, and graphs, with practice in applying these concepts in many non-routine situations) and Quantitative Comparisons. The analytical ability section includes Logical Diagrams, Analytical Reasoning, and Analysis of Explanations.... The GRE is administered six times a year, usually in October, December, January, February, April, and June. The GRE Advanced Tests are administered in the afternoon on the same day except in February, when they are not offered.

GRE ADVANCED BIOLOGY The GRE Advanced Biology Test is a three-hour test covering most areas of college-level biology. Subscores are given in three areas: Organismal, Cellular and Subcellular, and Population.

GRE ADVANCED PSYCHOLOGY The GRE Advanced Psychology Test is a three-hour test covering most areas of study in psychology. Subscores are given in two areas: Social and Experimental.

LSAT The Law School Admission Test is a half-day examination. It varies in content from test to test. Any particular test may include four or five of the following: Data Interpretation (graphs and charts), Quantitative Comparisons, Cases and Principles (three of six possible types), Logical Reasoning, Practical Judgment (Data Evaluation and Data Application), Logical Games, and Writing Ability.... The LSAT is administered five times a year, usually in June, October, December, February, and April.

MAT The Miller Analogies Test consists of 100 analogies and is required for admission to many graduate schools. [The MAT, administered by Psychological Corp., is given frequently throughout the year at some 600 test centers at colleges and universities throughout the country.]

MCAT The new Medical College Admission Test is a full-day examination which consists of four parts: Science Knowledge (Biology, Inorganic and Organic, Chemistry, Physics); Science Problems (Biology, Chemistry, and Physics); Skills Analysis: Reading; and Skills Analysis: Quantitative.... It is administered twice a year, usually in April and September.

OCAT The Optometry College Admission Test is a half-day examination which includes Biology, Chemistry, Physics, Quantitative Ability, Verbal Ability, and Non-Referent (study) Reading of Scientific Materials.... The OCAT is given three times a year, usually in November, January, and March.

PCAT The Pharmacy College Admission Test is a half-day exam that covers Verbal Ability, General Non-Scientific Work Knowledge, Quantitative Ability, Biology (basic biology and major human biology), Chemistry (problems and principles in organic and inorganic chemistry), and Reading Comprehension, with an emphasis on scientific topics.... The PCAT is given three times a year, usually in November, February, and May.

VAT The Veterinary Aptitude Test includes Natural Sciences, Quantitative Ability, Study Reading, and Reading Comprehension.... The VAT is usually given several times a year, but dates vary according to the state in which the exam is taken. Some states now require the GRE Aptitude and Advanced Biology tests for admission to veterinary school.

When you have decided which test(s) to take, contact the appropriate testing service and request a copy of their current information bulletin. (Be sure to specify which test(s) you are interested in.) Included in the information you should receive will be application forms and instructions, a complete description of the test, testing dates for the next year, information on arrangements for handicapped individuals, and sample questions.

The tests are administered by the following services:

DAT
American Dental Association
211 East Chicago
Chicago, IL 60611
(312) 440-2500

GMAT, GRE, and **LSAT**
Educational Testing Service
Box 966
Princeton, NJ 08541
(609) 921-9000

MAT, OCAT, PCAT, and **VAT**
Psychological Corporation
757 Third Avenue
New York, NY 10017
(212) 888-3500

MCAT
American College Testing Program
P. O. Box 414
Iowa City, IA 52240
(319) 356-3711

As we indicated earlier in discussing the SAT, questions have been raised about the value of test-coaching programs. But if you think you could be helped by such a program, and you can afford it, we recommend that you seriously consider enrolling.

Caution is advised, though, in choosing the school. Investigate as many schools as possible, including large and small commercial schools and college-sponsored programs. Perhaps your most important criterion for selection will be the opinions of individuals who have taken the course. For this reason you might want to visit the site of a class that is in progress and talk to a few of the students who are taking the course. Fees for commercial test preparation courses may range from $200 to $300 while college programs are usually less expensive. Established commercial coaching schools tend to have more sophisticated teaching techniques and materials as a result of experience, specialization, and greater revenues. Some commercial test preparation schools also offer supplementary aids for independent study. The Stanley H. Kaplan Education Center, for example, provides unlimited use of its extensive "test and tape" library, as well as voluminous home-study materials.

If you can't afford the time or the money required for a course, you can still obtain help with little or no financial investment. Many excellent books (and a few not-so-good books) are available to help you prepare for any of the standardized admission tests. Most large bookstores, particularly those on college campuses, carry a wide variety of guides for graduate school admission tests. Your local library may even have the book you want.

Some students take graduate admission tests with little or no preparation just to see how well they do or to gain experience in taking the test. If necessary, the test may be retaken at a later date. When you retake the test, though, your immediate test score and the most recent previous test result will be reported to all the universities you designate. It is possible, however, to cancel your test score if you think you have done poorly or if you just wanted to take a dry run, but you must do so immediately. The Educational Testing Service bulletin explains: "Notify your test center supervisor before you leave the test center or contact ETS within four days of the test date."

Preparing for That New Career: Career Planning and Placement Services

If you do not plan to pursue further schooling right after graduation, you will probably want to be employed in a place and manner that will be fulfilling to you. Where do you get help?

Three types of career advisement services are generally available: nonprofit public career placement agencies and advisement programs, commercial career counselors, and college career-planning and placement services.

Career counseling services are often made available by school districts, libraries, local governments, and independent community organizations. Many of these free services are listed in the annual *Directory of Educational and Career Information Services for Adults*, mentioned earlier in this chapter. You might also find such programs in your area by consulting your local library, department of education, city hall, colleges, or the yellow pages of your telephone directory under "vocational guidance," or some similar heading.

Commercial career counselors can be found in most major metropolitan areas. Such organizations usually cater primarily to experienced executives and professionals who are either unemployed or wish to change their present jobs or careers. Fees may range from several hundred dollars for appraisal of qualifications and capabilities to several thousand dollars (usually about one month's salary) for handling a complete executive-level, job-finding campaign, from definition of career objectives through acceptance of a position and planning for future career growth. Bernard Haldane Associates (at 598 Madison Avenue, New York, NY 10022, and in other major U.S. cities), like many agencies, offers a choice of a complete package or something less, such as a selection from Haldane's "Checklist of Services," which follows:

- Analysis of career potential
- Determination of long-range career direction
- Planning immediate objective
- Résumé preparation
- Letter-writing
- Portfolio development
- In-company advancement program
- How to make contacts and get interviews
- Interview strategy
- Salary negotiation
- Negotiation of title, benefits, etc.
- Evaluation of offers and job acceptance
- Plan for the future
- Special problems

If you are interested in hiring a commercial career consultant, you would be wise to shop around to compare prices and services. Also, you should ask for references to make sure the firm is reputable.

Your third option, college career-planning and placement services, is provided on most campuses, usually at no cost to students and alumni. To find out what career services your college has to offer, first check the school's bulletin. Typically you will find a policy statement such as the following, which was included in the Northrop University (Inglewood, California) bulletin:

> The Placement Office offers career counseling and guidance to help the graduating student make career decisions and provides information on the employment opportunities and practices of numerous companies and federal agencies. The office maintains a library of career descriptions, complete with company and community information. Materials are furnished for employer contacts; on-campus interviews are arranged and the student is assisted in résumé preparation and the arrangement of off-campus interviews.
>
> There are no fees and all graduates of the University are entitled to free lifetime service which includes job referrals, preparation of a professional résumé, and assistance with correspondence.

Specific information and literature describing the various services that are provided can be obtained from the career center, or its equivalent, at your college. Some college career centers, such as the one at Pepperdine University in Malibu, California, provide psychological testing (vocational and personal) to aid students in self-assessment. Pepperdine also offers a one-credit course on exploring career options. And most colleges vigorously promote on-campus recruiting. Kent State University in Ohio explains in its bulletin that "the on-campus recruiting program attracts representatives who visit the campus to interview candidates for full-time employment in business, industry, government, human services, and education." We recommend that you first determine the degree of assistance your college career center can provide you. To supplement this service, or ensure that all options have been explored, you may then wish to investigate other career services.

Career Opportunities for Women

by JUDITH WEBER WERTHEIM
M.S. in Counseling, C. W. Post College; currently a career counseling consultant for the South Huntington and Harborfields libraries and the Suffolk Cooperative Library System, New York

This decade presents women with opportunities and challenges in the world of work that are greater and more exciting than ever before. But if women expect a greater share of the financial pie, they must rethink and redirect their career choices and goals. The women's movement, various pieces of antidiscrimination legislation, and economic need have spurred women to consider entering the more lucrative, and frequently more stimulating, nontraditional fields. By this we mean fields that have been almost exclusively dominated by men.

Let us consider some of the fields offering the best prospects for employment—the growth fields. Department of Labor projections predict good long-range opportunities in the professional and technical areas. Concern for all types of energy production and conservation, and interest in environmental protection, have created strong demands for scientists and engineers. Prospects for mining and petroleum engineers and for geologists are particularly bright. Science technicians of all types, with specializations partly dictated by local needs, are in short supply. Computer specialists will continue to be marketable, as will economists. All the above are in the nontraditional designation for women. In other areas relatively new to women, financial management, banking, and accounting are exceedingly promising. Women hold about 90 percent of the jobs as tellers in banks, but less than 2 percent of the senior officer positions. There is a great deal of catching up to do!

The "graying" of our population will create expanded opportunities in health care, health-care support, and related fields. Specifically, some of the greatest demands will be for physicians and osteopaths, therapists, hygienists, nurses, laboratory technologists, and health administrators.

A large population of healthy, retired people will stimulate the travel, tourism, and recreation industries.

The importance to women of setting career goals unfettered by centuries of prejudice should be obvious. You must realize that for a woman to be considered a success in positions previously held almost exclusively by men, she most often must use her intelligence to greater effect, and work harder than her male peers. In considering your future employment be sure to understand and evaluate carefully the degree of commitment expected and necessary for your particular choices. Confront honestly your readiness, willingness, and ability to accomplish your goals, or you cannot expect to achieve them.

Graduation! At Last!

During those last several months of college, no doubt you have been busily (frantically?) preparing for graduate school or for that new career. At the same time you have been juggling all of the other important aspects of your life, to include trying to make it successfully to graduation. You have had to order your cap and gown. You have had to ensure that Aunt Mabel gets a commencement invitation and that she has a room reserved on the first floor of the nearby motel because she can't walk up the stairs. And so on, and so on, and so on. And suddenly the day is upon you. **Graduation!**

What is it like? Has it all been worthwhile?

So many adult students have commented on the significance of graduation, there can be no doubt that it stands as one of the few truly important highlights of a lifetime.

"At last the struggle was over," recalls Dorothy June Harris, a 54-year-old mother of six children, of Flat River, Missouri. "The Dean of Instruction introduced me as 'the grandmother who came back to school and proved to all of us that age is no barrier to learning if a deep motivation is present.' "

Lawrence Gaskins, a former prison inmate, and now a respected member of his community, testifies: "The proudest day of my life was when I received that degree."

When you join the ranks of college graduates with Dorothy June Harris and Lawrence Gaskins and all those many other successful adult students, undoubtedly you too will beam with pride. You've made it after all!

Sunset, Sunrise?
Lifelong Learning and You

Will your graduation be a bright new day dawning, or a glorious sunset? Can it be both?

Our world seems to be changing at a rate that is too fast for the average person to keep up. This phenomenon was recognized years ago by Alvin Toffler, author of the classic book *Future Shock* (New York: Bantam Books Inc., 1970):

> The rapid obsolescence of knowledge and the extension of life span make it clear that the skills learned by youth are unlikely to remain relevant by the time old age arrives. Super-industrialized education must therefore make provisions for life-long education [p. 407].

Our federal and state governments and our colleges and universities have begun to undertake the solving of this problem. For example, the American Association of Community and Junior Colleges has set forth a *Bill of Rights* for the lifelong learner:

Bill of Rights
Every adult American has the right to continue to learn throughout life;

Every adult American has the right to equal opportunity for access to relevant learning opportunities at each stage of life;

Diversity and access to educational opportunity are important to democracy in the United States;

Any index of the quality of life in the United States includes opportunities for growth and self-actualization as a right of the learning society;

Neither age, nor sex, nor color, nor creed, nor ethnic background, nor marital status, nor economic status, nor disability should create barriers to the opportunity to continue to grow through participation in organized learning activities;

Coping, living, and working are dimensions which exemplify the range of learning needs of the learning society;

Public investment in the learning society is an investment in human capital and in human condition.

Thus our society has realized that education is not a privilege to be reserved for the young. Adults possess invaluable experiences that, coupled with continuing education, represent intellectual wealth that should be cherished at least as highly as the potential of youth. We must not waste this valuable human resource. And we should not deprive any segment of our society of the right to a satisfying and rewarding life by curtailing education that is an important source of continuing growth and development.

Ronald Gross, author of *The Lifelong Learner* (New York: Simon & Schuster, 1977), summarized significant attitude changes taking place in our society:

> Colleges, which once spurned adult students, are, as we have seen, now bending over backwards to welcome free learners back to the campuses, and, more important, offering them help in learning on their own terms. . . . Most important of all, we Americans as individuals seem to be developing a fresh hunger for experience, for growth, for personal cultivation. Men and women of all ages today feel the urge to seek more in life—to shape a larger self, that quest I call lifelong learning [pp. 168-9].

Indeed, a multitude of adults are realizing their aspirations through lifelong education. Douglas E. Buck of Bellingham, Washington, received his bachelor's degree from Evergreen State College. "In all," he recalled, "it was a very rewarding learning experience. My degree is an end to a personal goal. However, education is a never-ending process. We all learn something new every day, and wouldn't life be boring if we didn't?"

Lifelong learning clearly represents our society's educational direction. This trend will continue for several reasons: First, technological and cultural change is accelerating at such a rapid pace that continuing education is necessary if we are to maintain our stations and standards of living. Second, average life spans are continuously being extended due to advances in science and medicine; thus the gap from the traditional end of formal education to death is widening while the rate of obsolescence of knowledge is increasing. Third, the "graying of America" will bring with it greater dependence upon older people to provide impetus for scientific and social advancement. Fourth, if America is to maintain its position of leadership among industrialized nations of the world, we must fully utilize *all* of our valuable human resources. In fact, we must develop a new social ethic in which productivity and commitment to excellence are once again cherished.

Socrates said, "The unexamined life is not worth living." That statement, twenty-four hundred years old, seems invigoratingly fresh as we—adult students, all of us—set about the remainder of our lives of lifelong learning.

Dorothy June Harris

I had always wanted to complete my interrupted education and my nursing career aspirations. But for several years after my youngest child started school, I stifled my dreams of better things because of timidity and fear of failure. My reasons for not going back to school were my six children and my husband's needing me to help him at the store we owned. Then one summer I realized that my reasons were no longer valid. All but two of my children were grown and married, and I had been away from the store for over a year caring for my invalid mother until she died. It was during this time spent with her that my interest in nursing was revived. Therefore, at the age of 45, I decided to take advantage of the nursing program offered at the local college.

I applied for admission to the program in practical nursing at Mineral Area College in Flat River, Missouri, filling out the application form with trembling hands. I was afraid I had waited too long and would not be able to learn. But I found I hadn't, and that I could.

Being back in school after so many years caused some drastic changes in my family life. My husband and the children at home had to help me more with the housework, and meals were either on short order, making use of convenience foods, or cooked and frozen for later use. I no longer had time to baby-sit with the grandchildren or to watch television. Instead, I spent every available hour studying, often until the wee hours of morning. However, I reserved Friday night for the family to keep them from feeling neglected.

The course of study was more difficult than I thought it would be. After the first day in class I was filled with misgivings, and during the first few weeks I was tempted to quit many times. But soon my interest in learning overcame my fear, and I became determined to succeed.

The year's work soon came to a climax, and the class went to Jefferson City to take the state board examination. All the class passed, and we felt rewarded for the long hours of study. I was thankful for my family whose patience had made my success possible.

After graduation I worked for six months at the hospital where I had received my clinical experience, then at another hospital for a number of years, and I count them as the most happy and fulfilling of my life.

I enjoyed going back to school, and there was still so much that I wanted to know about this body of ours that I began to go to night school to get the academic subjects required in the associate degree program of nursing. Then I was accepted for admission to the program. Once again the schedule at home was one of studying all week. It was a long, hard two years, but at last the struggle was over.

Graduation from Mineral Area College came, and it was with a mixture of pride and disbelief that I stood as valedictorian of my class.

I look back on those years of intensive study and work as the most worthwhile of my life, because of the values acquired. I now have a sense of purpose that I never had before, even though I have had a happy life full of love and blessings. The fact that I was able to do well in school was a real boost to my morale, and gave me new confidence. As Pearl Buck said, "I have discovered the delights of learning," even though I discovered them late in life.

As a registered nurse, I continued to take advantage of every opportunity to learn, attending many seminars and training programs offered by the hospital. Gradually, I became interested in the educational aspect of nursing, so it seemed natural for me to enter the teaching profession.

I became aware that the teaching staff at my alma mater, Mineral Area College, was going to be short two instructors. Once more I filled out an application and was accepted as an instructor in the practical nursing program. I left the hospital where I had worked so happily for years to go into a new phase of my beloved profession. I am now actively engaged in both classroom and clinical instruction of students (some of them adults!), and my aim, at this point, is to try to inspire and motivate them so that they will go forth and serve their fellowman in a way we can all be proud of. I don't feel that I left nursing, but rather that I now have the best of two worlds.

In thinking about what adult education means to me, I can say that I'm very glad that I didn't let middle age, and the hesitancy about starting something new, keep me from going back to school. Today, I feel ten years younger than I did when I started the program, and I'm happier because now I feel that I have fulfilled my purpose and that I am doing work that gives me a chance to really express myself.

Glossary of
College Terms

academic year   The traditional school year, usually September through May, typically divided into two (semester or trimester) terms of equal length. However, many different schedules are being offered by colleges to accommodate such things as accelerated and weekend courses. Additionally, most colleges offer one or more summer sessions during June, July, and August.

accreditation   The official recognition granted to a college by one of the regional, state, or specialized accrediting associations for having satisfied the standards established by the association. Criteria usually include extent and suitability of educational programs and curriculums; caliber of faculty and administration; and quality of library, classroom, and other facilities.

add   To increase one's course load for a particular term by one or more courses.

add date   The deadline by which a student may choose to increase his or her course load for a particular term.

admissions tests, standardized   The nationally recognized tests used as part of the selective admission procedure or, by some colleges, as a device for validating work of doubtful quality. The two major college entrance tests are the American College Testing Program examination (ACT) and the College Board Scholastic Aptitude Test (SAT).

administrative rank   The institutionally designated status of a college official. The titles most typically used (in order of hierarchical rank and formal authority) are:

1. President, Chancellor
2. Vice President, Vice Chancellor*
3. Dean, Provost*
4. Director, Chairperson*
5. Coordinator

admission   Formal notification to an applicant of acceptance by a

---

*Note: Sometimes the added designation of associate or assistant (or occasionally deputy) is applied to these levels.

postsecondary educational institution, program, or activity.

Application for Federal Student Aid   The form designed by the federal government to apply for the Pell Grant. (Formerly called the Pell Grant Application or the Basic Grant Application.) May be used for the same purpose as the FAF or FFS as well as to process college-administered aid.

associate degree   A degree granted for completing a two-year, full-time course of college study or the equivalent (generally at least 60 credits).

audit   To attend a credit course on a noncredit basis (often at a reduced tuition) without being graded.

Auxiliary Loans to Assist Students (ALAS)   A loan program that is available to independent students and parents of dependent students. Interest is 12-14%, and repayment begins within 60 days after the loan is granted.

baccalaureate or bachelor's degree   A degree granted for completing a four-year, full-time course of college study or the equivalent (usually 120-130 credits).

Basic Educational Opportunity Grant (BEOG)   See *Pell Grant.*

blue book   A small ruled booklet used by college students to take written examinations.

branch campus   A unit of a college located at a place other than its main campus and offering courses for credit and programs leading to degrees or certificates.

bulletin   The periodic publication containing compact descriptions of the educational programs offered by a college during a forthcoming semester or other period. (Also see *catalog.*)

bursar   The college administrator responsible for billings and collections of tuitions and fees payable by students.

calendar, college   The divisions of the full college year. The three common types are the semester system, the quarter system, and the trimester system (see separate definitions). College bulletins often include calendars listing the beginning and ending dates of classes, recognized holidays, registration, preregistration, add/drop dates, and dates of final examinations.

catalog (sometimes called *bulletin*)   The annual publication containing compact descriptions of the educational programs, resources, and services provided by a college, as well as details of the school's official regulations and policies. The catalog is an important source of information that the student should carefully review and retain for future reference.

certificate   A credential issued by an institution in recognition of completion of a curriculum other than one leading to a degree or diploma.

class types   Five traditional types of classes found at most colleges are: classroom, lecture hall, seminar, laboratory, and studio (see chapter 8). Nontraditional classes, such as televised lectures followed by telephone communication between individual students and the professor, are being employed by an increasing number of colleges.

closed (closed section) A section or course that has been filled to capacity; no further registrations will be accepted.

college A degree-granting institution of higher education offering instruction above the level of the secondary school.

community college An institution of higher education offering certificate and two-year associate degree programs. Generally publicly owned and serving the needs of the community in which it is located. Credits earned are often transferable toward a bachelor's degree at a four-year college or university. However, credits earned for a terminal certificate or degree program are usually not transferable.

concentration An area of specialization chosen by the student. (See *major* and *minor.*)

consortium A group of educational institutions associated to serve their common interests. Attending a college that belongs to a consortium affords certain benefits such as intercollege library privileges, an opportunity to take courses not offered by the college in which the student is enrolled, and more varied social, cultural, and educational opportunities.

continuing education Extension of education for persons who have completed or withdrawn from full-time school or college programs.

continuing education unit (CEU) A nationally recognized measure used to document the type, quality, and duration of noncredit course work that one has satisfactorily completed. One CEU is equal to ten class hours completed in a continuing education course. CEUs may be accepted by some colleges to satisfy certain requirements for degree or certificate programs.

cooperative education or program The integration of classroom work and practical experience through alternate class attendance and employment in business, industry, or government through contractual agreement between the student's college and the outside agency.

core curriculum Established by the college, a group of fundamental courses that are required for all candidates for a given degree.

course An organized series of instructional and learning activities dealing with a subject.

course outline See *syllabus.*

credit A unit of academic award applicable toward a degree, certificate, or diploma offered by an institution of higher education.

credit hour See *semester hour.*

curriculum (program) The formal educational requirements necessary to qualify for a degree or certificate. May include general education or specialized study in depth, or both.

dean An official presiding over the faculty of a college, an area of college study, or a particular group of college students.

dean's list Common designation for the published list of full-time undergraduate students who have achieved an honor average grade for the term.

degree Title bestowed as official recognition for the completion of a curriculum, or, in the case of an honorary degree, for a certain attainment. (See also associate, baccalaureate, master's, and doctoral degrees.)

degrees (some common types and abbreviations):

undergraduate degrees

A.A.	Associate in Arts
A.A.S.	Associate in Applied Science
A.S.	Associate in Science
B.A.	Bachelor of Arts
B.S.	Bachelor of Science
B.B.A.	Bachelor of Business Administration
B.E.	Bachelor of Engineering
B.Ed.	Bachelor of Education
B.F.A.	Bachelor of Fine Arts
B.P.S.	Bachelor of Professional Studies
B.Tech.	Bachelor of Technology

graduate academic degrees

M.A.	Master of Arts
M.S.	Master of Science
M.Phil.	Master of Philosophy
Ph.D.	Doctor of Philosophy

graduate professional degrees

M.Arch.	Master of Architecture
M.A.T.	Master of Arts in Teaching
M.B.A.	Master of Business Administration
M.Ed.	Master of Education
M.F.A.	Master of Fine Arts
M.L.S.	Master of Library Science
M.P.A.	Master of Public Administration
M.S.	Master of Science
M.S.W.	Master of Social Work
D.D.S.	Doctor of Dental Surgery
Ed.D.	Doctor of Education
J.D.	Doctor of Law
M.D.	Doctor of Medicine
D.V.M.	Doctor of Veterinary Medicine

For a complete listing of academic degrees and abbreviations, see *American Universities and Colleges* (Appendix III, pp. 1760-70), published by the American Council on Education, Washington, DC, available in the reference section of most libraries.

department A unit of the college faculty organized to provide courses of study in a specific discipline such as English, mathematics, or history.

diploma An academic award granted for completion of a curriculum other than one leading to a degree or certificate. In Canada, a diploma often represents the equivalent of an associate degree in the United States.

division One of the groups of related academic disciplines (such as the social sciences, the arts, the humanities, and the natural sciences). Sometimes also an administrative unit of a college.

doctoral degree or doctorate Any academic degree carrying the title of "doctor." The doctorate is the highest academic degree in a given discipline or profession, generally requiring three or more years of graduate work and completion of a special course of study culminating in the preparation of a dissertation approved by a faculty committee.

double major or dual major Official recognition that a student is pursuing or has satisfied the minimum requirements for majors in two disciplines of study.

drop To decrease one's course load for a particular term by one or more courses.

drop date The deadline by which a student may choose, without incurring academic penalty, to decrease his or her course load for a particular term.

elective A course chosen at the discretion of the student to fulfill part of the requirements for a degree.

experiential learning Conceptual knowledge acquired through life experience for which academic credit may be granted.

extension center A site other than the principal center of an institution or any of its branch campuses at which curriculums leading to degrees or certificates are not offered, but at which courses for credit are offered on a limited and temporary basis for the convenience of students.

external degree An academic award earned through one or more of the following means: extrainstitutional learning, credit by examination, special experiential-learning programs, self-directed study, and satisfactory completion of campus or off-campus courses. In some programs the learning is attained in circumstances outside of the sponsorship or supervision of the awarding institution. Generally credit may be granted for documented learning from such sources as work and life experience, and noncollegiate courses previously completed.

faculty rank title The institutionally designated title or grade of a faculty member. The categories most typically used (in descending order of professional achievement) are:

1. Professor ("full professor")
2. Associate Professor
3. Assistant Professor

4. Instructor

5. Other (might include lecturer or undesignated ranks)

The modifiers *adjunct* and *clinical* are sometimes used in conjunction with faculty titles to mean visiting or part-time classroom or laboratory instructors respectively.

Family Financial Statement (FFS) A form designed by the American College Testing Program to provide information to a college to determine a student's eligibility for financial aid. Completing the FFS (or FAF or Application for Federal Student Aid) is usually the first step in applying for financial aid.

fees Charges assessed in addition to tuition to cover costs of administration, required course materials and equipment, or student services and programs (such as application fees, lab fees, and student activity fees).

fellowship A gift of money to a student, ordinarily for support of graduate study. The recipient is rarely required to demonstrate financial need. The award is designed to support free inquiry on the part of the student in his field of interest, and to provide for his educational and living expenses as a full-time student.

final exam A test given at the end of a course that may count for a large percentage of a student's grade. The final exam may be cumulative (including the entire course content) or noncumulative (including only material covered since the midterm or last exam given).

financial aid Any programs sponsored by the federal, state, or local government, the college or university, business institutions, or private agencies or individuals that provide students with ways of meeting the costs of attending college. Includes all categories such as loans, grants, fellowships, and work-study programs.

Financial Aid Form (FAF) This form is designed by the College Board and is used for the same purpose as the Family Financial Statement (FFS).

financial need The difference between your cost of going to a particular college and the money you (and your spouse, if you have one) can provide for your college costs. (See chapter 6.)

full-time Status of an undergraduate student who takes at least 12 credits during a conventional academic semester. For financial aid purposes, 6 credits might be considered as full-time status during the summer if at least 12 credits are taken during the preceding spring and following fall terms.

General Educational Development (GED) tests See *high school equivalency examinations.*

graduate degree Any academic degree conferred by a graduate division or graduate school of an institution of higher education (such as M.A., M.S., Ph.D., Ed.D.). Also includes first professional degrees (such as the M.D., D.D.S., or J.D.), which are conferred by professional rather than graduate schools.

grade-point average (GPA) or quality-point index (QPI) A system of measuring students' average grades for academic rating purposes. Points are given for each credit hour of college course work undertaken based on the grade earned.

graduation requirements A specified group of minimum achievements or other qualifications needed for a student to qualify for a degree. For a bachelor's degree, for example, a college might require the following: (1) successful completion of 120 college credits, at least 30 of which must be earned in residence; (2) a cumulative grade-point average of 2.0 or better; (3) completion of all specified courses in the core curriculum and major area of concentration selected for the degree; (4) payment of all tuition and fees incurred.

graduate study A program of study beyond the bachelor's degree and usually toward a master's or doctoral degree.

grant A gift of money to a student with no expectation of repayment or of services to be rendered. Special kinds of grants are scholarships and fellowships.

Guaranteed Student Loan (GSL) A program of the federal government that provides for low-interest deferred-payment loans for students attending eligible institutions of higher education in the United States and abroad, as well as thousands of vocational, technical, business, and trade schools.

gut course (slang) A college course with a light work load requiring relatively little effort to complete successfully, often with a high grade.

high school equivalency examinations Examinations approved by a state department of education or other authorized agency that are intended to provide an appraisal of a student's achievement or performance in the broad subject matter areas usually required for high school graduation. The tests of General Educational Development (GED) are the most widely recognized high school equivalency examinations, and are administered by each state department of education in the 56 states, commonwealths, and territories of the United States and in five Canadian provinces. The tests are prepared by the General Educational Development Testing Service, One Dupont Circle, Washington, DC 20036.

honors Recognition of academic excellence achieved by a student. At the undergraduate level, one of the following Latin terms traditionally designates graduation with honors: *cum laude* (with honors), *magna cum laude* (with high honors), and *summa cum laude* (with highest honors). At the graduate level, one term only, graduation with distinction, is generally used.

honors program A more challenging than usual program extended to students who have demonstrated superior academic ability in their fields of specialization. Students who succeed in satisfying the stringent requirements of an honors program are generally graduated with honors.

incomplete A temporary designation assigned to a student's record of a course in which the student was unable for a valid reason to take the final exam or complete a required course assignment. The student must make arrangements with the course professor to make up the exam or submit the missing assignment within a certain time period (determined by college policy) to have the incomplete changed to a regular grade.

independent study A course of study undertaken by a student to earn credit outside of the classroom under the sponsorship and guidance of a faculty member of the college.

institutional aid form The college's own form of application for financial aid. Students usually must complete both the institutional aid form and the FFS, FAF, or Application for Federal Student Aid to receive financial aid.

interdisciplinary A curriculum or course of study that includes two or more academic disciplines.

intersession The period between semesters during which short, intensive courses might be scheduled to satisfy the special interests of groups of students, or to provide an additional opportunity for acceleration of progress toward a degree. Many colleges use the "4-1-4" plan; that is, a four-month term in the fall (September to December), one month of school during what normally is the intersession break (January), and a four-month term in the spring (February to May).

junior college (two-year college) A higher educational institution that is authorized to offer undergraduate curriculums below the baccalaureate level that normally lead to the associate degree.

liberal arts The broad scope of academic disciplines encompassed by the humanities, the social sciences, and the natural sciences (generally exclusive of professional fields of study).

load (credit, course) The credit hours or courses required for graduation divided by the number of semesters or terms normally required for graduation determines the normal full-time load. A heavier than normal load is usually permitted when a student demonstrates exceptional academic ability. A lighter than normal course load for a full-time student may require special permission.

loan, student See *Auxiliary Loans to Assist Students, Guaranteed Student Loan,* and *National Direct Student Loan.*

lower-division courses Introductory-level courses usually taken during the first two years of college study.

major A student's primary area of concentration. Can be in a specific discipline or some combination of disciplines (a combined major). Usually one-quarter to one-half of the student's degree program must be taken in the established major.

master's degree A degree granted for completing a one- to two-year, full-time course of study usually encompassing 30 to 60 credits beyond the baccalaureate degree.

matriculation   Official registration of a student as a degree candidate following admission to a college.

minor   A secondary concentration in a specific discipline or field of study, usually comprising about half the number of credits required in the student's major.

National Direct Student Loan (NDSL)   A low-interest loan available through joint sponsorship of the federal government and the individual postsecondary institution.

nonmatriculated   Status of a student who has been admitted to a college and allowed to take courses on either a credit or noncredit basis but not as an official degree candidate. Nonmatriculated students are often referred to as special students. Students may be able to take courses and accumulate credits toward a degree while matriculation is pending due to some unfulfilled admissions requirement.

nontraditional   A term used to define a college or college program that does not conform to the conventional tenets of American higher education. (Increasing use of formerly nontraditional programs has made them almost traditional.)

open admissions   A liberal admissions policy under which all applicants are accepted by a college (space permitting) as long as they meet minimum requirements mandated by the state education department.

part-time   Status of a student who takes fewer than 12 credits during a conventional academic semester.

pass-fail option   A provision enabling a student to take a course without receiving a grade, just an annotation of having passed or failed. Pass-fail is excluded in computing the student's grade-point average (GPA).

Pell Grant (formerly Basic Educational Opportunity Grant)   A federal grant for the support of undergraduate study. Eligibility requires attendance at an approved institution on at least a half-time basis and demonstrated financial need. (See chapter 6.)

Pell Grant Application   See *Application for Federal Student Aid.*

percentile   A measure of the relative standing of a student among all students in the same category. An individual percentile of 70 in the verbal portion of a standard graduate school admission exam, for example, means that only 30 percent of all students who took the same exam in the current testing group scored higher in verbal skills than did the individual.

postgraduate study   Another term for graduate study. Also can mean study beyond the master's degree but below the doctorate. For the completion of a postgraduate program, a certificate of advanced graduate study, an advanced professional certificate, or a diploma of advanced graduate study may be awarded.

preregistration   The plan by which students select and are assigned courses for a succeeding term well in advance of the official opening date of registration for the term.

prerequisite A course that must be taken, or a requirement that must be satisfied, before a student will be permitted to take a more advanced course in the same field of study.

probation, academic A warning (as opposed to a penalty) resulting from unsatisfactory scholarship, and an opportunity to improve. Academic probation usually involves the compulsory reduction of academic load, interviews for diagnosis of difficulties, and academic counseling.

professional degree The first degree satisfying completion of the minimum academic requirements for practice of a profession. Includes certain bachelor's, master's, and doctoral degrees.

proficiency examination A test taken by a student to demonstrate competence in the subject matter of a particular college course in order to receive equivalent college credit for that course.

program (curriculum) The formal educational requirements necessary to qualify for a degree or certificate. May include general education or specialized study in a particular field, or both.

provisional registration Permission to attend classes pending the adjustment of standing.

quarter A period of about 10 weeks representing one-fourth of a school year (as compared to a semester or trimester, which is usually about 16 weeks in length).

registrar The college administrator responsible for supervising course and program admissions and enrollments, academic recording, and certification.

registration Official enrollment in a course or program, or approval of a student's curriculum in a college.

rank, class The position of a student in relation to others being graduated in that class as determined by a comparison of academic records.

residence Pursuit of full- or part-time study in classes on campus.

residence requirement A minimum period of required attendance at a college to qualify for a degree awarded by that college; often stated in terms of credits. For example, 30 credits of course work might be required to be completed "in residence" at a particular college in order to qualify for a degree.

rolling admissions A system by which college admission applications are evaluated upon receipt throughout the year and applicants are notified as soon as a decision can be made, as compared to notification of all applicants soon after a specified deadline for admission applications.

satellite center See *branch campus.*

schedule, class The list of courses and sections offered, together with the names of the instructors, the days, hours, and places of meeting.

scholarship A gift of money to a student, ordinarily for the support of undergraduate study. It is granted in recognition of academic or other distinction and may require that the recipient be in need of financial assistance. The donor may specify particular conditions or restrictions in addition to demonstrated financial need.

school   A division of a university organized to provide training in a professional field (such as school of business, school of nursing).

section   A division of a course into two or more classes, each having the same subject matter, but not necessarily taught by the same instructor, or at the same hour.

semester   Traditionally half an academic year, usually about 16 weeks, beginning in August/September or January/February.

semester hour   A unit representing one hour of classroom instruction per week for a semester of not less than 15 weeks. One credit, point, or other academic unit is traditionally granted for the successful completion of each semester hour. This basic measure must be adjusted proportionately to translate the value of academic calendars and formats of study other than that of the traditional two-semester academic year (this includes summer sessions and independent study).

summer session   A session not a part of the academic year (September through May).

Supplemental Educational Opportunity Grant (SEOG)   A federally funded grant administered by the college for undergraduate students who have exceptional financial need not entirely satisfied by the Pell Grant. (See chapter 6.)

survey course   A course designed to provide a general overview of an area of study. Completed by a student either prior to undertaking specialized work in a given field, or to provide broad, general concepts about an area in which one does not plan to specialize.

syllabus   A sequential outline of topics to be covered by the professor, and assignments to be completed by the students during a college course.

tenure   The institutional designation that serves to identify the status of the employee with respect to permanence of position. A faculty member on tenure cannot be discharged except for extreme reasons such as moral turpitude of the individual or financial exigency of the institution.

term   The period of time that a course runs with specific beginning and ending dates. Usually a semester, trimester, or quarter.

transcript   A student's official record of courses taken, credits earned, and grades received, which is maintained by the college registrar. Students are entitled to unofficial copies of their transcripts upon request (usually upon payment of a nominal fee). Official transcripts imprinted with the college's seal will be sent at the student's request to admissions offices of other colleges or graduate schools and prospective employers.

transfer   Admission to a new college with acceptance of previously earned college credits toward the degree or program requirements of the new college.

trimester A period of about 16 weeks representing one-third of a school year. A college using the trimester system is on a normal academic schedule during the summer months when colleges operating on a traditional semester system would be closed except for summer session courses. Two trimesters constitute an academic year.

tuition The amount of money charged to students for instructional services. Tuition may be charged on a per-term, per-course, or per-credit basis. Fees (see definition) may also be charged to students.

undergraduate study College study at the associate or baccalaureate level.

university A higher-education institution that confers graduate as well as undergraduate degrees in various fields of study. A university has at least two degree-granting colleges or professional schools.

upper-division courses Advanced courses usually taken as part of a student's major during the last years of college study.

Veterans Administration (VA) Educational Benefits Benefits paid for student financial assistance at approved postsecondary educational institutions for three types of beneficiaries: (1) surviving spouse and children, (2) discharged veterans, and (3) active armed-service employees in special programs.

withdrawal A release from enrollment. A student may usually withdraw from a course officially within a specified period without being graded. Withdrawal without permission will probably result in a failing grade.

work-study A plan of part-time work for which a student receives pay. May be on- or off-campus, and often has no relationship to the student's degree program.

Appendix A

The Accrediting
Process and Agencies

The following is reprinted, with permission, from Accredited Institutions of Postsecondary Education, *published by the American Council on Education. (The 1981-82 edition is available from the ACE.)*

The Accrediting Process

Accreditation is a system for recognizing educational institutions and professional programs affiliated with those institutions for a level of performance, integrity, and quality which entitles them to the confidence of the educational community and the public they serve. In the United States this recognition is extended primarily through nongovernmental, voluntary institutional or professional associations. These groups establish criteria for recognition; arrange site visits and evaluate those institutions and professional programs which desire recognition status; and approve for recognition those which meet their criteria.

Institutional accreditation is granted by the accrediting commissions of associations of schools and colleges which collectively serve most of the institutions chartered or licensed in the United States and its possessions. These commissions and associations accredit total operating units only.

Specialized accreditation of professional schools and programs is granted by commissions on accreditation set up by national professional organizations in such areas as business, dentistry, engineering, or law. Each of these groups has its distinctive definitions of eligibility, criteria for accreditation, and operating procedures, but all have undertaken accreditation activities, primarily to provide quality assurances concerning the educational preparation of members of the profession. Many of the specialized accrediting bodies will consider requests for accreditation reviews only from programs affiliated with accredited institutions. Some specialized agencies, however, accredit professional programs at institutions not otherwise accredited, these generally being independent institutions which offer only the specified discipline or course of study.

Procedures in Accreditation

The accrediting process is continuously evolving. The trend has been from quantitative to qualitative criteria, from the early days of simple checklists to an increasing interest and emphasis on measuring the outcomes of educational experiences.

The process begins with the institutional or programmatic self-study, a comprehensive effort to measure progress according to previously accepted objectives. The self-study considers the interests of a broad cross-section of constituencies—students, faculty, administrators, alumni, trustees, and in some circumstances the local community. The resulting report is reviewed by the appropriate accrediting commission and serves as the basis for evaluation by a site-visit team from the accrediting group. The site-visit team normally consists of professional educators (faculty and administration), specialists selected according to the nature of the institution, and members representing specific public interests. The visiting team considers the institution or program according to the dimensions of the self-study and adds judgments based on its own expertise and its external perspective. The evaluation team completes a report, which is reviewed by the institution or program for factual accuracy. The original self-study, the team report, and any response the institution or program may wish to make are forwarded to an accreditation review committee. The review body uses these materials as the basis for action regarding the accreditation status of the institution or program. Negative actions may be appealed according to established procedures of the accrediting body.

Accrediting bodies reserve the right to review member institutions or programs at any time for cause. They also reserve the right to review any substantive change, such as an expansion from undergraduate to graduate offerings, and will consider such changes within two years after the change becomes effective. In this way accrediting bodies hold their member institutions and programs continually accountable to their educational peers, to the constituencies they serve, and to the public interest.

Historically and currently accreditation at the postsecondary level may be said to:

- foster excellence in postsecondary education through the development of criteria and guidelines for assessing educational effectiveness;
- encourage improvement through continuous self-study and planning;
- assure the educational community, the general public, and other agencies or organizations that an institution or program has clearly defined and appropriate objectives, maintains conditions under which their achievement can reasonably be expected, appears in fact to be accomplishing them substantially, and can be expected to continue to do so;

- provide counsel and assistance to established and developing institutions and programs; and endeavor to protect institutions against encroachments which might jeopardize their educational effectiveness or academic freedom.

COPA's Role in Accreditation

Postsecondary education in the United States derives its strength and excellence from the unique and diverse character of its many individual institutions. Such qualities are best sustained and extended by the freedom of these institutions to determine their own objectives and to experiment in the ways and means of education within the framework of their respective authority and responsibilities.

Public as well as educational needs must be served simultaneously in determining and fostering standards of quality and integrity in the institutions and such specialized programs as they offer. Accreditation, conducted through nongovernmental institutional and specialized agencies, provides a major means for meeting these needs.

The Council on Postsecondary Accreditation is a nongovernmental organization that works to foster and facilitate the role of accrediting agencies in promoting and ensuring the quality and diversity of American postsecondary education. The accrediting agencies, while established and supported by their membership, are intended to serve the broader interests of society as well. To promote these ends, COPA periodically reviews the work of recognized accrediting agencies, determines the appropriateness of existing or proposed accrediting agencies and their activities, and performs other related functions.

Accrediting Groups Recognized by COPA

COPA periodically evaluates the accrediting activities of institutional and professional associations. Upon determining that those activities meet or exceed COPA provisions, the accrediting organizations are publicly recognized through this listing. Groups that are regional in nature are identified with their geographical areas; all others are national in their activities.

AMERICAN ASSOCIATION OF BIBLE COLLEGES (AABC)
John Mostert, Executive Director
Box 1523
130-F North College Street
Fayetteville, Arkansas 72701
Tel. (501) 521-8164

ASSOCIATION OF INDEPENDENT COLLEGES AND SCHOOLS
(AICS)
> James M. Phillips, Executive Director
> Accrediting Commission, AICS
> 1730 M Street, N.W.
> Washington, D.C. 20036
> Tel. (202) 659-2460

MIDDLE STATES ASSOCIATION OF COLLEGES AND SCHOOLS
Delaware, District of Columbia, Maryland, New Jersey, New York,
Pennsylvania, Puerto Rico, Virgin Islands
> Robert Kirkwood, Executive Director
> Commission on Higher Education
> 3624 Market Street
> Philadelphia, Pennsylvania 19104
> Tel. (215) 662-5606

NATIONAL ASSOCIATION OF TRADE AND TECHNICAL SCHOOLS
(NATTS)
> William A. Goddard, Executive Director
> 2021 K Street, N.W., Room 305
> Washington, D.C. 20006
> Tel. (202) 296-8892

NATIONAL HOME STUDY COUNCIL (NHSC)
> William A. Fowler, Executive Secretary
> Accrediting Commission, NHSC
> 1601 Eighteenth Street, N.W.
> Washington, D.C. 20009
> Tel. (202) 234-5100

NEW ENGLAND ASSOCIATION OF SCHOOLS AND COLLEGES
Connecticut, Maine, Massachusetts, New Hampshire, Rhode Island,
Vermont
> 131 Middlesex Turnpike
> Burlington, Massachusetts 01803
> Tel. (617) 272-6450
>
> Charles M. Cook, Director of Evaluation
> Commission on Institutions of Higher Education
>
> Daniel S. Maloney, Director of Evaluation
> Commission on Vocational, Technical, Career Institutions

NORTH CENTRAL ASSOCIATION OF COLLEGES AND SCHOOLS
Arizona, Arkansas, Colorado, Illinois, Indiana, Iowa, Kansas, Michigan,
Minnesota, Missouri, Nebraska, New Mexico, North Dakota, Ohio,
Oklahoma, South Dakota, West Virginia, Wisconsin, Wyoming
> Thurston E. Manning, Director
> Commission on Institutions of Higher Education
> 159 North Dearborn Street

Chicago, Illinois 60601
Tel. (312) 263-0456

NORTHWEST ASSOCIATION OF SCHOOLS AND COLLEGES

Alaska, Idaho, Montana, Nevada, Oregon, Utah, Washington

James F. Bemis, Executive Director
Commission on Colleges
3700-B University Way, N.E.
Seattle, Washington 98105
Tel. (206) 543-0195

SOUTHERN ASSOCIATION OF COLLEGES AND SCHOOLS

Alabama, Florida, Georgia, Kentucky, Louisiana, Mississippi, North Carolina, South Carolina, Tennessee, Texas, Virginia

795 Peachtree Street, N.E.
Atlanta, Georgia 30365
Tel. (404) 897-6126

Gordon W. Sweet, Executive Director
Commission on Colleges

Executive Director
Commission on Occupational Education Institutions
Tel. (404) 897-6164

WESTERN ASSOCIATION OF SCHOOLS AND COLLEGES

American Samoa, California, Guam, Hawaii, Trust Territory of the Pacific

Kay J. Andersen, Executive Director
Accrediting Commission for Senior Colleges and Universities
c/o Mills College, Box 9990
Oakland, California 94613
Tel. (415) 632-5000

Robert E. Swenson, Executive Director
Accrediting Commission for Community and Junior Colleges
P. O. Box 70
Aptos, California 95003
Tel. (408) 688-7575

ALLIED HEALTH (Through the American Medical Association) COPA recognizes the AMA and its Committee on Allied Health Education and Accreditation (CAHEA) as an umbrella agency for 26 review committees representing 47 collaborating professional organizations in the accreditation of programs in the following areas of allied health. All questions concerning accreditation of these programs should be directed to CAHEA at the address given. The programs are Assistant to the Primary Care Physician, Cytotechnologist, Diagnostic Medical Sonographer, EEG Technologist, EMT-Paramedic, Histologic Technician, Medical Assistant, Medical Assistant in Pediatrics, Medical Laboratory Technician, Medical Record

Administrator, Medical Record Technician, Medical Technologist,
Nuclear Medicine Technologist, Occupational Therapist, Ophthalmic
Medical Assistant, Perfusionist, Physical Therapist, Radiation Therapy
Technologist, Radiographer, Respiratory Therapist, Respiratory
Therapy Technician, Specialist in Blood Bank Technology, Surgeon's
Assistant, and Surgical Technologist.

> American Medical Association Committee on Allied Health
> Education and Accreditation
> John G. Fauser, Director
> Department of Allied Health Education and Accreditation, AMA
> 535 North Dearborn Street
> Chicago, Illinois 60610
> Tel. (312) 751-6272

ARCHITECTURE
First professional degree programs

> National Architectural Accrediting Board
> Karen S. Bradbury, Acting Executive Director
> 1735 New York Avenue, N.W.
> Washington, D.C. 20006
> Tel. (202) 783-2007

ART
Institutions offering professional preparation

> National Association of Schools of Art and Design (NASAD)
> Samuel Hope, Executive Director
> Commission on Accreditation
> 11250 Roger Bacon Drive, Suite 5
> Reston, Virginia 22090
> Tel. (703) 437-0700

BUSINESS
Bachelor's and master's degree programs

> American Assembly of Collegiate Schools of Business (AACSB)
> William K. Laidlaw Jr., Executive Vice President
> 11500 Olive Street Road, Suite 142
> St. Louis, Missouri 63141
> Tel. (314) 872-8481

CHEMISTRY
Undergraduate professional programs

> American Chemical Society
> Bonnie R. Blazer, Secretary
> Committee on Professional Training, ACS
> 1155 Sixteenth Street, N.W.
> Washington, D.C. 20036
> Tel. (202) 872-4589

CHIROPRACTIC EDUCATION
Institutions offering professional degrees

Council on Chiropractic Education
Ralph G. Miller, Executive Secretary
3209 Ingersoll Avenue
Des Moines, Iowa 50312
Tel. (515) 255-2184

CLINICAL PASTORAL EDUCATION
Professional training centers
Association for Clinical Pastoral Education, Inc.
Charles E. Hall Jr., Executive Director
Interchurch Center, Suite 450
475 Riverside Drive
New York, New York 10027
Tel. (212) 870-2558

Clinical Pastoral Education is offered and accredited in health-care facilities. Many theological seminaries recognize the accreditation of these programs and allow students credit toward theological degrees. A list of these institutions may be obtained from the ACPE headquarters.

CONSTRUCTION EDUCATION
Baccalaureate programs
American Council for Construction Education
I. Eugene Thorson, Executive Vice President
P. O. Box 1266
103 South Fourth Street, Suite 6
Manhattan, Kansas 66502
Tel. (913) 776-1544 or (913) 532-5964

DENTISTRY AND DENTAL AUXILIARY PROGRAMS
First professional programs in dental education; degree and certificate programs in dental auxiliary education
American Dental Association
Robert J. Pollock Jr., Secretary
Commission on Dental Accreditation
211 East Chicago Avenue
Chicago, Illinois 60611
Tel. (312) 440-2721

DIETETICS
Coordinated baccalaureate programs
American Dietetic Association
Gloria Archer, Coordinator
Commission on Accreditation
430 North Michigan Avenue
Chicago, Illinois 60611
Tel. (312) 280-5040

ENGINEERING
Professional engineering programs at the basic (baccalaureate) and

advanced (master's) levels; baccalaureate programs in engineering technology; and two-year (associate degree) programs in engineering technology

> Accreditation Board for Engineering and Technology (ABET)
> David R. Reyes-Guerra, Executive Director
> 345 East 47th Street
> New York, New York 10017
> Tel. (212) 644-7685

FORESTRY

Professional schools

> Society of American Foresters
> Ronald R. Christensen, Director of Professional Programs, SAF
> 5400 Grosvenor Lane
> Washington, D.C. 20014
> Tel. (301) 897-8720

HEALTH SERVICES ADMINISTRATION

Graduate programs

> Accrediting Commission on Education for Health Services Administration
> Gary L. Filerman, Executive Secretary
> One Dupont Circle, N.W., Suite 420
> Washington, D.C. 20036
> Tel. (202) 659-4354

HOME ECONOMICS

Undergraduate programs

> American Home Economics Association
> Katherine B. Hall, Director
> Office of Professional Education, AHEA
> 2010 Massachusetts Avenue, N.W.
> Washington, D.C. 20036
> Tel. (202) 862-8355

INDUSTRIAL TECHNOLOGY

Baccalaureate programs

> National Association for Industrial Technology
> Harvey A. Pearson, Director/Secretary
> University of North Florida
> Division of Technologies
> P. O. Box 17074
> Jacksonville, Florida 32216
> Tel. (904) 646-2684 or (904) 646-2573

INTERIOR DESIGN

Programs at the two-year, three-year, baccalaureate, and master's levels

> Foundation for Interior Design Education Research
> Edna Kane, Director of Administration

242 West 27th Street, Suite 6B
New York, New York 10001
Tel. (212) 929-8366

JOURNALISM
Program (sequences) leading to the first professional degree
American Council on Education in Journalism and Mass
Communication
Baskett Mosse, Executive Secretary
Accrediting Committee, ACEJMC
563 Essex Court
Deerfield, Illinois 60015
Tel. (312) 948-5840

LANDSCAPE ARCHITECTURE
Professional programs
American Society of Landscape Architects
Samuel C. Miller, Director of Education and Research
Landscape Architectural Accreditation Board
1900 M Street, N.W., Suite 320
Washington, D.C. 20036
Tel. (202) 466-7730

LAW
Professional schools
American Bar Association
James P. White, Consultant on Legal Education, ABA
Indianapolis Law School
Indiana University-Purdue University at Indianapolis
735 West New York Street
Indianapolis, Indiana 46202
Tel. (317) 264-8071

Association of American Law Schools
John A. Bauman, Executive Director
One Dupont Circle, N.W., Suite 370
Washington, D.C. 20036
Tel. (202) 296-8851

LIBRARIANSHIP
First professional degree programs
American Library Association
Elinor Yungmeyer, Accreditation Officer
Committee on Accreditation, ALA
50 East Huron Street
Chicago, Illinois 60611
Tel. (312) 944-6780

MEDICAL ASSISTANT AND MEDICAL LABORATORY
TECHNICIAN
Diploma, certificate, and associate degree programs

Accrediting Bureau of Health Education Schools
Hugh A. Woosley, Administrator
Oak Manor Offices
29089 U.S. 20 West
Elkhart, Indiana 46514
Tel. (219) 293-0124

MEDICINE

Programs leading to first professional degree and programs in the basic medical sciences

Liaison Committee on Medical Education
(in odd-numbered years beginning each July 1, contact)
Edward S. Petersen, Secretary
Council on Medical Education, AMA
535 North Dearborn Street
Chicago, Illinois 60610
Tel. (312) 751-6310

or

(in even-numbered years beginning each July 1, contact)
J. R. Schofield, Secretary
Association of American Medical Colleges
One Dupont Circle, N.W., Suite 200
Washington, D.C. 20036
Tel. (202) 828-0670

MUSIC

Baccalaureate and graduate degree programs, also non-degree-granting institutions

National Association of Schools of Music (NASM)
Samuel Hope, Executive Director
11250 Roger Bacon Drive, Suite 5
Reston, Virginia 22090
Tel. (703) 437-0700

NURSING

Associate, baccalaureate, and higher degree programs; also diploma and practical nurse programs

COPA recognizes 293 diploma programs accredited by the NLN at hospital schools of nursing; in addition, 109 practical nursing programs are accredited by the NLN, approximately 45 percent in academic settings. For information on the above programs not listed in this directory, contact Mary F. Liston, Deputy Director for Program Affairs, NLN.

National League for Nursing (NLN)
Margaret E. Walsh, General Director and Secretary
10 Columbus Circle
New York, New York 10019
Tel. (212) 582-1022

Practical nursing programs only
>National Association for Practical Nurse Education and Service
>Lucille L. Ethridge, Executive Director
>254 West 31st Street
>New York, New York 10001
>Tel. (212) 736-4540

OPTOMETRY
Professional programs in optometry and optometric technology
>American Optometric Association (AOA)
>Sally A. Bowers, Executive Secretary
>Council on Optometric Education, AOA
>243 North Lindbergh Boulevard
>St. Louis, Missouri 63141
>Tel. (314) 991-4100

OSTEOPATHIC MEDICINE
First professional degree programs
>American Osteopathic Association
>Douglas Ward, Director
>Bureau of Professional Education
>212 East Ohio Street
>Chicago, Illinois 60611
>Tel. (312) 280-5800

PHARMACY
First professional degree programs
>American Council on Pharmaceutical Education (ACPE)
>Daniel A. Nona, Executive Director
>One East Wacker Drive
>Chicago, Illinois 60601
>Tel. (312) 467-6222

PHYSICAL THERAPY
First professional degree programs
>American Physical Therapy Association
>Patricia Yarbrough, Director
>Department of Educational Affairs, APTA
>1156 Fifteenth Street, N.W.
>Washington, D.C. 20005
>Tel. (202) 466-2070

PODIATRY
Professional schools
>American Podiatry Association
>Warren G. Ball, Director
>Council on Podiatry Education, APA
>20 Chevy Chase Circle, N.W.
>Washington, D.C. 20015
>Tel. (202) 537-4970

PSYCHOLOGY
Doctoral programs leading to professional practice of psychology
American Psychological Association
Meredith P. Crawford, Administrative Officer for Accreditation
1200 Seventeenth Street, N.W.
Washington, D.C. 20036
Tel. (202) 833-7600

PUBLIC HEALTH
Graduate schools of public health and master's degree programs in
community health education
Council on Education for Public Health
Patricia Evans, Executive Director
1015 Fifteenth Street, N.W., Suite 403
Washington, D.C. 20005
Tel. (202) 789-1050

REHABILITATION COUNSELING
Master's degree programs
Council on Rehabilitation Education
Ivan M. Lappin, Executive Director
162 North State Street, Room 601C
Chicago, Illinois 60601
Tel. (312) 346-6027
or
Peers, Ltd. (Consultant to CORE)
8 South Michigan Avenue
Chicago, Illinois 60603
Tel. (312) 332-7111

SOCIAL WORK
Baccalaureate and master's degree programs
Council on Social Work Education
Sidney Berengarten, Director, Division of Education
Standards and Accreditation, CSWE
111 Eighth Avenue, Suite 501
New York, New York 10011
Tel. (212) 242-3800

SPEECH PATHOLOGY AND AUDIOLOGY
Master's degree programs
American Speech, Language, and Hearing Association
Billie Ackerman, Assistant Director, Education and Scientific
Programs
10801 Rockville Pike
Rockville, Maryland 20852
Tel. (301) 897-5700

TEACHER EDUCATION

Bachelor's and higher degree programs

> National Council for Accreditation of Teacher Education (NCATE)
> Lyn Gubser, Director
> 1919 Pennsylvania Avenue, N.W., Suite 202
> Washington, D.C. 20006
> Tel. (202) 466-7496

THEOLOGY

Graduate professional schools and programs

> Association of Theological Schools in the United States and Canada
> Leon Pacala, Executive Director
> 42 East National Road
> P. O. Box 130
> Vandalia, Ohio 45377
> Tel. (513) 898-4654

VETERINARY MEDICINE

First professional degree programs

> American Veterinary Medical Association
> R. Leland West, Director
> Scientific Activities, AVMA
> 930 North Meacham Road
> Schaumburg, Illinois 60196
> Tel. (312) 885-8070

Appendix B

State Sources of Grant and Loan Information

The information below is from Sections One and Four of the Federal Student Financial Aid Handbook '81-'82, *published by the U.S. Department of Education/Office of Student Financial Assistance.*

State Programs of Undergraduate Financial Aid	Sources of Information on the Guaranteed Student Loan Program
Alabama Alabama Commission on Higher Education Suite 221, One Court Square Montgomery, AL 36197 (205) 832-6555	Same address (205) 832-3790
Alaska Alaska Commission on Postsecondary Education Pouch F, State Office Building Juneau, AK 99811 (907) 465-2854	Same address (907) 465-2962
Arizona Arizona Commission for Postsecondary Education 1937 West Jefferson Phoenix, AZ 85009 (602) 255-3109	Arizona Educational Loan Program 301 East Virginia Avenue, Suite 3900 Phoenix, AZ 85004 (602) 252-5793

State Programs of Undergraduate Financial Aid	Sources of Information on the Guaranteed Student Loan Program

Arkansas
Department of Higher Education
1301 West Seventh Street
Little Rock, AR 72201
(501) 371-1441 Ext. 23
	Student Loan Guarantee
	  Foundation of Arkansas
	1515 West Seventh Street,
	  Suite 515
	Little Rock, AR 72202
	(501) 371-2634

California California Student Aid Commission 1410 Fifth Street Sacramento, CA 95814 (916) 445-0880	Same address and phone

Colorado
Colorado Commission on Higher
  Education
1550 Lincoln Street, Room 210
Denver, CO 80203
(303) 866-2748
	Colorado Guaranteed Student
	  Loan Program
	ABS Building
	7000 North Broadway, Suite 100
	Denver, CO 80221
	(303) 427-0259

Connecticut
Connecticut Board of Higher
  Education
61 Woodland Street
Hartford, CT 06105
(203) 566-3913
	Connecticut Student Loan
	  Foundation
	25 Pratt Street
	Hartford, CT 06103
	(203) 547-1510

Delaware
Delaware Postsecondary
  Education Commission
1228 North Scott Street, Suite 1
Wilmington, DE 19806
(302) 571-3240
	Delaware Higher Education
	  Loan Program
	% Brandywine College
	P. O. Box 7139
	Wilmington, DE 19803
	(302) 478-3000 Ext. 34

District of Columbia
Department of Human Services
801 North Capitol Street, N.E.,
  Room 700
Washington, DC 20002
(202) 727-0310
	Higher Education Assistance
	  Foundation
	Higher Education Loan Program
	  (HELP) of D.C., Inc.
	1001 Connecticut Avenue, N.W.,
	  Suite 825
	Washington, DC 20036
	(202) 861-0701

State Programs of Undergraduate Financial Aid

Sources of Information on the Guaranteed Student Loan Program

Florida
Florida Student Financial
  Assistance Commission
Department of Education
Knott Building,
  Room 563
Tallahassee, FL 32301
(904) 487-1800

Same address and phone

Georgia
Georgia Student Finance
  Authority
9 LaVista Perimeter Park,
  Suite 110
2187 Northlake Parkway
Tucker, GA 30084
(404) 393-7253

Georgia Higher Education
  Assistance Corporation
Same address
(404) 393-7108

Hawaii
State Postsecondary Education
  Commission
124F Bachman Hall,
  University of Hawaii
2444 Dole Street
Honolulu, HI 96822
(808) 948-6862

Hawaii Education Loan Program
1314 South King Street,
  Suite 613
Honolulu, HI 96814
(808) 536-3731

Idaho
Office of State Board
  of Education
650 West State Street,
  Room 307
Boise, ID 83720
(208) 334-2270

Student Loan Fund of Idaho,
  Inc.
Route 5
Caldwell, ID 83605
(208) 459-8963

Illinois
Illinois State Scholarship
  Commission
102 Wilmot Road
Deerfield, IL 60015
(312) 948-8500

Illinois Guaranteed Loan
  Program
Same address
(312) 945-7040

Indiana
State Student Assistance
  Commission of Indiana
219 North Senate Avenue
Indianapolis, IN 46202
(317) 232-2353

Same address
(317) 232-2366

State Programs of Undergraduate Financial Aid

Sources of Information on the Guaranteed Student Loan Program

Iowa
Iowa College Aid Commission
201 Jewett Building
9th and Grand Avenue
Des Moines, IA 50309
(515) 281-3501

Same address
(515) 281-8537

Kansas
Board of Regents–State of
   Kansas
1416 Merchants National Bank
Topeka, KS 66612
(913) 296-3421

Higher Education Assistance
   Foundation
34 Corporate Woods
10950 Grand View Drive
Overland Park, KS 66210
(913) 648-4255

Kentucky
Kentucky Higher Education
   Assistance Authority
691 Teton Trail
Frankfort, KY 40601
(502) 564-7990

Same address and phone

Louisiana
Governor's Special Commission
   on Educational Services
4637 Jamestown Avenue
P. O. Box 44127, Capitol Station
Baton Rouge, LA 70804
(504) 925-3630

Same address and phone

Maine
Department of Educational and
   Cultural Services
State House, Station 23
Augusta, ME 04333
(207) 289-2183, 2184

Same address and phone

Maryland
Maryland State Scholarship
   Board
2100 Guilford Avenue,
   Room 206
Baltimore, MD 21218
(301) 659-6420

Maryland Higher Education Loan
   Corporation
Same address
(301) 659-6555

State Programs of Undergraduate Financial Aid	Sources of Information on the Guaranteed Student Loan Program

Massachusetts

Massachusetts Board of Regents of Higher Education
One Ashburton Place, Room 611
Boston, MA 02108
(617) 727-7785

Massachusetts Higher Education Assistance Corporation
1010 Park Square Building
Boston, MA 02116
(617) 426-9434

Michigan

Michigan Department of Education
P. O. Box 30008
Lansing, MI 48909
(517) 373-3394

Michigan Department of Education
Guaranteed Student Loan Program
P. O. Box 30047
Lansing, MI 48909
(517) 373-0760

Minnesota

Minnesota Higher Education Coordinating Board
400 Capitol Square, 550 Cedar Street
St. Paul, MN 55101
(612) 296-3974

Higher Education Assistance Foundation
1100 Northwestern Bank Building
55 East Fifth Street
St. Paul, MN 55101
(612) 227-7661

Mississippi

Mississippi Postsecondary Education Financial Assistance Board
P. O. Box 2336
Jackson, MS 39205
(601) 982-6578

Student Financial Assistance
Department of Education
101 Marietta Tower, Suite 423
Atlanta, GA 30323
(404) 221-5658

Missouri

Department of Higher Education
Missouri Student Grant Program
600 Monroe Street
P. O. Box 1437
Jefferson City, MO 65102
(314) 751-3940

Missouri Department of Higher Education
P. O. Box 1438
Jefferson City, MO 65102
Same phone

Montana

Montana University System
33 South Last Chance Gulch
Helena, MT 59620
(406) 449-3024

Montana Guaranteed Student Loan Program
Same address and phone

State Programs of Undergraduate Financial Aid	Sources of Information on the Guaranteed Student Loan Program

Nebraska

Nebraska Coordinating
  Commission for Postsecondary
  Education
301 Centennial Mall South
P. O. Box 95005
Lincoln, NE 68509
(402) 471-2847

Nebraska Education Assistance
  Foundation
3600 South 48th Street
Lincoln, NE 68506
(402) 488-0989

Nevada

University of Nevada System
405 Marsh Avenue
Reno, NV 89509
(702) 784-4952

Nevada State Department of
  Education
400 West King Street
Carson City, NV 89710
(702) 885-5700

New Hampshire

New Hampshire Postsecondary
  Education Commission
61 South Spring Street
Concord, NH 03301
(603) 271-2555, 2695

New Hampshire Higher
  Education Assistance
  Foundation
143 North Main Street
P. O Box 877
Concord, NH 03301
(603) 225-6612

New Jersey

Department of Higher Education
Office of Student Assistance
225 West State Street
Trenton, NJ 08625
(609) 292-8770

New Jersey Higher Education
  Assistance Authority
C. N. 00538
Trenton, NJ 08638
(609) 292-3906

New Mexico

Board of Educational Finance
1068 Cerrillos Road
Santa Fe, NM 87503
(505) 827-2115

New Mexico Student Loan
  Program
Bandelier West
University of New Mexico
Albuquerque, NM 87131
(505) 277-6304

New York

New York State Higher Education
  Services Corporation
99 Washington Avenue
Albany, NY 12255
(518) 474-5592

Same address
(518) 473-1574

State Programs of Undergraduate Financial Aid	Sources of Information on the Guaranteed Student Loan Program

North Carolina
North Carolina State Education
   Assistance Authority
P. O. Box 2688
Chapel Hill, NC 27514
(919) 549-8614

Same address and phone

North Dakota
North Dakota Student Financial
   Assistance Program
10th Floor, State Capitol
Bismarck, ND 58505
(701) 224-4114

Student Financial Assistance
Department of Education
11037 Federal Office Building
Denver, CO 80294
(303) 837-3676

Ohio
Ohio Board of Regents
3600 State Office Tower
30 East Broad Street
Columbus, OH 43215
(614) 466-6000

Ohio Student Loan Commission
P. O. Box 16610
Columbus, OH 43216
(614) 466-3091

Oklahoma
Oklahoma State Regents for
   Higher Education
500 Education Building
State Capitol Complex
Oklahoma City, OK 73105
(405) 521-8262

Same address
(405) 521-2444

Oregon
Oregon State Scholarship
   Commission
1445 Willamette Street
Eugene, OR 97401
(503) 686-4166

Same address
(503) 686-3200

Pennsylvania
Pennsylvania Higher Education
   Assistance Agency
660 Boas Street, Towne House
Harrisburg, PA 17102
(717) 787-1937

Same address
(717) 787-1932

Rhode Island
Rhode Island Higher Education
   Assistance Authority
274 Weybosset Street
Providence, RI 02903
(401) 277-2050

Same address and phone

State Programs of Undergraduate Financial Aid	Sources of Information on the Guaranteed Student Loan Program

South Carolina

Higher Education Tuition Grants
Agency
411 Keenan Building, Box 11638
Columbia, SC 29211
(803) 758-7070

South Carolina Student Loan
Corporation
Interstate Center, Suite 210
P. O. Box 21337
Columbia, SC 29221
(803) 798-0916

South Dakota

Department of Education and
Cultural Affairs
Office of the Secretary
Richard F. Kneip Building
Pierre, SD 57501
(605) 773-3134

South Dakota Education
Assistance Corporation
105 First Avenue, S.W.
Aberdeen, SD 57401
(605) 225-6423

Tennessee

Tennessee Student Assistance
Corporation
B-3 Capitol Towers, Suite 9
Gay Street
Nashville, TN 37219
(615) 741-1346

Same address and phone

Texas

Coordinating Board
Texas College and
University System
P. O. Box 12788, Capitol Station
Austin, TX 78711
(512) 475-8169

Texas Guaranteed Student Loan
Corporation
Champion Tower, Suite 510
Austin, TX 78752
(512) 835-1900

Utah

Utah State Board of Regents
807 East South Temple,
Suite 204
Salt Lake City, UT 84102
(801) 533-5617

Utah Education Loan Service
1800 South West Temple
Salt Lake City, UT 84108
(801) 486-5921

Vermont

Vermont Student Assistance
Corporation
5 Burlington Square
Burlington, VT 05401
(802) 658-4530

Same address and phone

State Programs of Undergraduate Financial Aid

Sources of Information on the Guaranteed Student Loan Program

Virginia
State Council of Higher
Education for Virginia
James Monroe Building
101 North 14th Street
Richmond, VA 23219
(804) 225-2600

Virginia State Education
Assistance Authority
6 North Sixth Street
Richmond, VA 23219
(804) 786-2035

Washington
Council for Postsecondary
Education
908 East Fifth Avenue
Olympia, WA 98504
(206) 753-3241

Washington Student Loan
Guaranty Association
Westland Building, Suite 560
100 South King Street
Seattle, WA 98104
(206) 625-1283

West Virginia
West Virginia Board of Regents
950 Kanawha Boulevard East
Charleston, WV 25301
(304) 348-0112

Higher Education Assistance
Foundation
Higher Education Loan Program
of West Virginia, Inc.
Union Building, Suite 900
723 Kanawha Boulevard East
Charleston, WV 25322
(304) 345-7211

Wisconsin
Wisconsin Higher Educational
Aids Board
137 East Wilson Street
Madison, WI 53703
(608) 266-1095

Wisconsin Higher Education
Corporation
Same address
(608) 266-2074

Wyoming
Wyoming Community College
Commission
1720 Carey Avenue, Boyd
Building
Cheyenne, WY 82002
(307) 777-7763

Higher Education Assistance
Foundation
American National Bank Building
20th Street at Capitol, Suite 320
Cheyenne, WY 82001
(307) 635-3259

American Samoa
Department of Education
Government of American Samoa
Pago Pago, American Samoa
96799
(Overseas) 633-4256

Student Financial Assistance
Department of Education
50 United Nations Plaza
San Francisco, CA 94102
(415) 556-9137

State Programs of Undergraduate Financial Aid

Sources of Information on the Guaranteed Student Loan Program

Guam

University of Guam
P. O. Box EK
Agana, Guam 96910
(734) 2177

Student Financial Assistance
Department of Education
50 United Nations Plaza
San Francisco, CA 94102
(415) 556-9137

Puerto Rico

Council on Higher Education
Box F—UPR Station
Rio Piedras, PR 00931
(809) 751-5082, 1136

Student Financial Assistance
Department of Education
26 Federal Plaza
New York, NY 10007
(212) 264-4022

Trust Territory

Office of the High Commissioner
  Trust Territory of the Pacific
  Islands
Saipan, Mariana Islands 96950
(Saipan) 9870

Student Financial Assistance
Department of Education
50 United Nations Plaza
San Francisco, CA 94102
(415) 556-9137

Virgin Islands

U.S. Virgin Islands Department of
  Education
P. O. Box 630
Charlotte Amalie
St. Thomas, Virgin Islands 00801
(809) 774-0100

Pupil Personnel Services
Same address
(809) 774-5191

Have You Seen These Other Publications from Peterson's Guides?

Guide to Independent Study Through Correspondence Instruction 1980-1982
Editor: Joan H. Hunter

Lists more than 12,000 correspondence course titles available in over 1,000 subject areas from data processing to meteorology. Covers elementary, high school, undergraduate, graduate, and noncredit courses.

8½" x 11", 112 pages   Stock no. 1204
ISBN: 0-87866-120-4 $4.50 paperback

Who Offers Part-Time Degree Programs?
Editorial Coordinator: Patricia Consolloy

A national survey of postsecondary institutions offering daytime, evening, weekend, summer, and external degree programs. Institutional profiles give a concise overview of the percentage of students in part-time degree programs, tuition figures, types of part-time options available, and which graduate units permit part-time study.

7" x 9¼", 350 pages   Stock no. 1212
ISBN: 0-87866-121-2 $6.95 paperback

Learning Vacations
Fourth Edition
Gerson G. Eisenberg

An expanded, updated edition of this popular international guide to year-round educational vacations. The vacations are indexed by subject, institution, and geographic location, with a separate index for elderhostels—weeklong educational vacations for those aged 60 and over.

6" x 9", 273 pages   Stock no. 1751
ISBN: 0-87866-175-1 $7.95 paperback

Your Own Financial Aid Factory: The Guide to Locating College Money
Robert Leider

This completely updated edition reflects all of the latest regulations. It contains a section on calculating the difference between what college will cost and what families are expected to contribute; describes some 50,000 available scholarships, cooperative education opportunities, and Pell Grants; and tells how to locate sources of student loans.

6" x 9", 184 pages   Stock no. 0220
ISBN: 0-917760-22-0 $5.95 paperback

After Scholarships, What? Creative Ways to Lower Your College Costs—and the Colleges That Offer Them
Editorial Coordinator: Patricia Consolloy

This campus-by-campus survey of expenses and cost-cutting options at 1,600 four-year colleges and universities gives college applicants and their families new ways to plan their college finances.

7" x 9¼", 385 pages   Stock no. 1298
ISBN: 0-87866-129-8 $8.00 paperback

Dollars for Scholars Student Aid Catalogs
A new series of books that list sources of financial aid for college students on a state-by-state basis. Each catalog covers hundreds of nationwide sources of aid as well.

Dollars for Scholars Student Aid Catalog: Minnesota Edition
Marlys C. Johnson and Linda J. Thompson
8½" x 11", 200 pages (approx.)
Stock no. 1948
ISBN: 0-87866-194-8 $7.95 paperback

Dollars for Scholars Student Aid Catalog: New Hampshire Edition
Linda J. Thompson and Marlys C. Johnson
8½" x 11", 100 pages (approx.)
Stock no. 6193
ISBN: 0-87866-193-X $5.95 paperback

Peterson's Guide to College Admissions: Getting into the College of Your Choice
Second Edition
R. Fred Zuker and Karen C. Hegener

This brand-new edition takes students behind the scenes in the college admissions office and provides practical advice on how they can increase their chances of getting into the college of their choice.

8½" x 11", 310 pages   Stock no. 1220
ISBN: 0-87866-122-0 $8.95 paperback

Peterson's Annual Guide to Undergraduate Study
1982 Edition
Editor: Kim Kaye

This is the only college guide that contains in one volume detailed data profiles of over 3,000 two-year and four-year colleges, a directory that cross-indexes 400 majors with the colleges that offer them at the two-year and four-year levels, test score and college data in tabular form, plus special announcements and two-page narrative descriptions of nearly 1,000 colleges written for this book by admissions directors and deans. All information in this Guide is completely updated every year.

8½" x 11", 1,998 pages   Stock no. 1301
ISBN: 0-87866-130-1 $13.00 paperback

National College Databank
Second Edition
Editor: Karen C. Hegener

This is the updated and expanded second edition of the innovative reference book that helps college-bound students zero in on the colleges that have special features and characteristics. It groups more than 2,700 colleges by hundreds of characteristics, from size to price range to special programs.

7" x 9¼", 950 pages   Stock no. 1654
ISBN: 0-87866-165-4 $8.95 paperback

Peterson's Guide to Undergraduate Engineering Study

David R. Reyes-Guerra and Alan M. Fischer

This comprehensive publication presents in-depth guidance plus all the detailed information necessary for students, parents, teachers, and counselors to compare the 244 U.S. colleges that offer accredited bachelor's-level engineering programs (including computer science).

8½" x 11", 561 pages   Stock no. 1638
ISBN: 0-87866-163-8 $14.00 paperback

The Competitive Colleges: Who Are They? Where Are They? What Are They Like?

Editorial Coordinator: Patricia Consolloy
Research Assistant: Mary Jane Legere

A look at the colleges with the most competitive admissions pictures in the country today. For each school, this book provides a full page of comparative information, including enrollment and faculty statistics; resources and special programs; student backgrounds, attrition patterns, and test levels; majors and sports; costs and financial aid available; the application timetable; and more.

7" x 9¼", 245 pages   Stock no. 1271
ISBN: 0-87866-127-1 $6.95 paperback

Peterson's Annual Guides to Graduate Study: Graduate and Professional Programs: An Overview

1982 Edition
Series Editor: Karen C Hegener
Manuscript Editor: Margaret G. Dutt
Data Editor: James Laity

Covers the whole spectrum of American and Canadian graduate programs in a single reliable volume. While it includes such basics as financial aid, degrees offered, and research opportunities, it also gives institutions an opportunity to express what makes their graduate programs distinctive.

8½" x 11", 695 pages   Stock no. 1328
ISBN: 0-87866-132-8 $13.00 paperback

Jobs for English Majors and Other Smart People

John L. Munschauer

This book recognizes the realities of the job market for the generalist, the inexperienced, the career changer. The author offers down-to-earth advice about such concerns as when to send and when not to send a résumé, how to identify alternative careers, and how to create a job when there is no advertised opening.

5½" x 8½", 180 pages   Stock no. 1441
ISBN: 0-87866-144-1 $6.95 paperback

Where to Start: An Annotated Career-planning Bibliography

Third Edition
Madeline T. Rockcastle

Resources for career exploration, graduate study, and immediate employment in academic and professional areas. This book is published by Cornell University's Career Center and is updated yearly.

8½" x 11", 150 pages (approx.)
Stock no. 1468
ISBN: 0-87866-146-8 $10.00 paperback

Peterson's Guide to Engineering, Science, and Computer Jobs 1982

Editor: Sandra Grundfest, Ed.D.

This updated and revised edition includes information from over 1,000 manufacturing, research, consulting, and government organizations currently hiring technical graduates. Gives employer profiles, salaries, benefits, locations, who to contact.

8½" x 11", 787 pages   Stock no. 1794
ISBN: 0-87866-179-4 $12.00 paperback

These publications are available at all good booksellers, or you may order direct from Peterson's Guides, Dept. 2601, P.O. Box 2123, Princeton, New Jersey 08540. Please note that prices are necessarily subject to change without notice.

- Enclose full payment for each book, plus postage and handling charges as follows:

Amount of order	4th-Class Postage and Handling Charges
$1-$10	$1.25
$10.01-$20	$2.00
$20.01 +	$3.00

- For faster shipment via United Parcel Service (UPS), add $2.00 over and above the appropriate fourth-class book rate charges listed.
- Bookstores and tax-exempt organizations should contact us for appropriate discounts.
- You may charge your order to VISA, MasterCard, or American Express. Please include the name and account number on your charge card, the expiration date, and, for MasterCard, the four-digit Interbank Number.
- New Jersey residents should add 5% sales tax to the cost of the books, excluding the postage and handling charge.
- Write for a free catalog describing all of our latest publications.